DATE DUE

JAN 12 '98			
AP 23 '98			
RENEW			
DE 8 '99			
FE - 1 '10			

HAYDN'S SYMPHONIC FORMS

HAYDN'S SYMPHONIC FORMS

Essays in Compositional Logic

ETHAN HAIMO

CLARENDON PRESS · OXFORD

1995

Oxford University Press, Walton Street, Oxford OX2 6DP

Oxford New York

Athens Auckland Bangkok Bombay
Calcutta Cape Town Dar es Salaam Delhi
Florence Hong Kong Istanbul Karachi
Kuala Lumpur Madras Madrid Melbourne
Mexico City Nairobi Paris Singapore
Taipei Tokyo Toronto
and associated companies in
Berlin Ibadan

Oxford is a trade mark of Oxford University Press

Published in the United States
by Oxford University Press Inc., New York

British Library Cataloguing in Publication Data
Data available

Library of Congress Cataloging in Publication Data
Haimo Ethan, 1950–
Haydn's symphonic forms: essays in compositional logic/
Ethan Haimo.
p.   cm. —(Oxford monographs on music)
Includes bibliographical references and index.
1. Haydn, Joseph, 1732–1809. Symphonies. 2. Symphonies–
Analysis, appreciation. I. Title II. Series.
MT130.H4H35 1995 784.2′ 184′ 092–dc20 94-49097
ISBN 0–19–816392–4

1 3 5 7 9 10 8 6 4 2

Typeset by Pure Tech India Ltd, Pondicherry
Printed in Great Britain
on acid-free paper by
Bookcraft Ltd.
Midsomer Norton, Avon

Dedicated to the memory of

HOWARD MAYER BROWN

Preface

HAYDN wrote more than a hundred symphonies over a period of approximately forty years, beginning some time before 1760 and ending in 1795. By itself, the sheer number of his symphonies demonstrates an important characteristic of artistic life in the late eighteenth century: stylistic change was so rapid that compositions quickly fell out of fashion and had to be replaced with newer, up-to-date works. It is discomfiting, but revealing, to recognize that Haydn would scarcely have impressed London audiences had he brought an 'old' work like Symphony No. 49 for performance on either of his two trips in the 1790s.

The impermanence of compositions in the late eighteenth century stands in stark contrast with the reigning ideology of art in the late twentieth century. We have become accustomed, without a hint of embarrassment, to speak of the 'immortality' of art, of the 'timelessness' of great works of genius, and of the transcendent 'universality' of musical language and thought. We have come to think that it is normal to grow up with a virtually immutable canon of commonly acknowledged 'masterpieces' that were in the repertoire long before we were born and will still be a part of that repertoire long after we die. Yet it is clear that this past century represents a radical departure from prior norms of artistic life. In earlier ages of music, it was expected that works would have a relatively short lifespan and would be not only succeeded but totally displaced by their successors. Although the first steps toward what Carl Dahlhaus has termed the 'historicization of the repertoire' can be traced to the pioneering work of Johann Forkel and Gottfried van Swieten from Haydn's time, the process was not so far advanced as to have given Haydn the illusion that his works had a chance for any real permanence.

Haydn would, most likely, have been quite surprised to see his works a central part of the repertoire two centuries after their composition. Paradoxically, Haydn's works (or at least his later compositions) are far more firmly established as a feature of today's musical scene than are the works of most of the composers who have come to artistic prominence since the end of the Second World War.

The apparent permanence of works from the past in our contemporary life might make it difficult for us to recognize just how far removed these artistic creations are from our own day. Although we may study, perform, or hear Haydn's works today and although we have literally grown up with them, they are not contemporary works, but are the product of the artistic, social, economic, religious, philosophical, and political climate of a period that is now more than two centuries in the past. We must not assume that we really understand these works simply because we have 'known' them all of our lives.

In recent years, the historical performance movement has helped clarify just how much music has changed, at least in some dimensions. Even beyond the supremely practical issue of what eighteenth-century notation meant, we have come to realize how different this music must have sounded from how we used to think it did. To compare a recent CD of Haydn's symphonies recorded by a group such as the Hanover Band with an LP of the same works by the Cleveland Orchestra with George Szell from the 1960s, or a keyboard sonata in a performance on a fortepiano by Malcolm Bilson with the same work as recorded on a Steinway three or four decades ago is to be struck with the aural equivalent of culture shock.

Although the historical performance movement has been tremendously successful in showing us just how different the music of the eighteenth century might have sounded, we must not forget that this is only part of the story—and the most external part at that. If we perform on authentic instruments with authentic pitch (whatever that was), authentic tempos, and just the right amount (if any) of *messa di voce*, we still may make a complete hash of it if we do not free ourselves from the aesthetic attitudes of the intervening two centuries, or if we do not understand the artistic, social, and compositional background for this music, bringing that understanding to bear on the music.

The present book is an attempt to address some of those questions. Using Haydn's compositions, and in particular the symphonies, I have endeavored to reconstruct Haydn's formal thought, trying to account for and explain specific details of the music. It has been my goal to see whether it might be possible to determine what Haydn's basic principles of form might have been, and to use those principles as a means of analyzing (i.e. understanding) the music on its own terms. I analyze the form in Haydn's symphonies not by means of procedures or aesthetic notions that are universally valid, but by attempting to recreate Haydn's specific ideas of form. As such, this book represents a fusion of theory and analysis with history.

For some time, it has been the norm in academe to separate theory and musicology from one another, treating them as distinct disciplines. Analysis is allegedly the province of 'theorists' who concern themselves with the inner workings of music, while 'musicologists' are supposed to busy themselves with archival work, source studies, issues of authenticity, patterns of influence, and the like.

One towering figure in our field, however, argued forcefully and passionately that theory and musicology should not be separate enterprises. At the time of the establishment of the Society for Music Theory, the then president of the American Musicological Society, Howard Mayer Brown, wished the new society well, but also expressed the wish that its establishment as an independent body would not mean the end of interaction and dialogue between theorists and musicologists.

One of the central premises of this book is the belief that analysis cannot be divorced from historical context. In that spirit, therefore, the book is dedicated fondly to the memory of that towering figure, a wonderful teacher and friend. As is clear from virtually everything he ever wrote, Brown's work was an exemplification of the belief that we understand music best when we place it in context. Whether that context involved the study of ornamentation, or iconography, or liturgy, or poetry, or dramaturgy, Howard Mayer Brown was entirely undeterred by the distinctions others might wish to draw between disciplines. We are much the richer for his work and for his inimitable presence.

It is also both my duty and my distinct pleasure to take this opportunity to thank my colleagues at the University of Notre Dame for their help in preparing this book. Professors Alexander Blachly, Paul Johnson, Peter Smith, and Susan Youens are ideal colleagues in every sense—ready and willing to read my work with a properly skeptical eye and to provide the most trenchant, sober, and constructive criticisms. I have also been fortunate to have two talented graduate assistants, Lewis Coleman and Aaron Gauthier (candidates for the MA at the University of Notre Dame), who have with great efficiency helped me verify the accuracy of innumerable factual statements made in the course of the book. I would like to thank Dr Horst Walter of the Haydn Institute in Cologne for his prompt answer to my questions about Symphony No. 81, and Professors Elaine Sisman of Columbia University and Edward Cone of Princeton University for their helpful criticisms of an earlier draft of this book. Ultimately, of course, all errors that remain are entirely my responsibility.

Many thanks are also due to the indefatigable editor of music books at Oxford University Press, Mr Bruce Phillips. His support and advice have been invaluable, and I am acutely aware of how much time and effort he has devoted to this project. I would also like to thank the highly professional staff at Oxford University Press for all of the care and attention they have given this book throughout the production process.

Finally, it is with the abashed realization that authors in general (and the present author in particular) can be the most moody and preoccupied of creatures that I thank my wife, Martha, for her infinite patience and good humor. Few have been tried more for so few pages.

Notes on the Examples

Although the optimum way to read the analyses in Chapters 2 through 9 would be with the complete scores of the relevant symphonies, obvious practical realities make it impossible to provide complete scores of the works discussed within the confines of a single book. Therefore, the author has made short scores of selected passages from the symphonies under discussion. Wherever possible, different instruments have been combined on the same staff. Many doublings, both unison and octave, have been omitted without comment. The most common instruments omitted are the viola, bassoon, timpani, and horns. Without exception, the bass-line appears on the bottom staff, though other lines may be added to that staff (frequently the viola), usually with stems pointing up to differentiate them from the bass. If an internal line (frequently the second violin or the viola) does not double another part, it will be assigned to any appropriate staff (sometimes its own) and thus may migrate during the course of an example. To the extent that it is convenient, the individual parts are identified, although no attempt has been made to keep the voices distinct if that is not necessary for the sense of the example. The abbreviations used (hn., fl., cl., ob., and so forth) may refer to a single instrument or a group of instruments depending on the context. If there is more than a single brace in an example, the bottom brace is always reserved for the strings, which are not usually further specified. Horns and other transposing instruments appear at concert pitch if they share a staff with another part. Otherwise, they appear in their original transposed form. It should go without saying that short scores are only a compromise, born of practical necessity, and the reader is encouraged to consult the complete scores as they appear in reliable critical editions.

Identifying Haydn's Compositions

In this book, Haydn's symphonies are identified according to the numbers assigned them by Edward Mandyczewski nearly a century ago, and since adopted as Category I by Anthony van Hoboken in his catalogue of Haydn's works. String quartets are identified according the commonly used (though inauthentic) opus numbers by which they are now popularly known (Opp. 9, 17, 20, 33, etc.). All other genres (keyboard sonatas, string trios, baryton trios, etc.) are identified using the appropriate category and number from the Hoboken catalogue. Movements are identified by lower-case roman numerals following a slash. Thus, Symphony No. 49/iii denotes the third movement of Symphony No. 49.

The dates assigned in this book to Haydn's compositions are from Georg Feder's list of works in *The New Grove Dictionary of Music and Musicians* (London, 1980). Feder provides the following explanations for the symbols he uses: 1766 = composed 1766; [1766] = year of composition 1766 not documented; −1766 = composed by 1766; −?1766 = possibly composed by 1766.

Contents

I

Introduction: Principles of Form

FOR well over a century the question of how best to define or describe the forms of late eighteenth-century instrumental music (sonata form, rondo, sonata-rondo, and so forth) has been the focus of an often bitter scholarly debate. One reason for the durability of the controversy has been the very imprecision of the questions. When we ask what a particular form is ('What is sonata form?'), do we mean in general, or at a specific time, or for a certain composer, or even for an individual composition? Are we trying to create a typology of forms in an attempt to account for the wide variety of formal types in the late eighteenth-century repertoire?[1] Do we wish to know how eighteenth-century theorists defined various forms,[2] or are we trying to reconstruct how the composers themselves conceived of the idea? Are we attempting to determine the contemporaneous listeners' expectations?[3] Are we using the terms in an effort to categorize compositions (to include some and

---

[1] A number of different studies have been devoted to identifying formal types in late 18th-cent. music. For an early, and very ambitious attempt see Rudolf von Tobel, *Die Formenwelt der klassischen Instrumentalmusik* (Berne, 1935). More recent studies include Michelle Fillion, 'The Accompanied Keyboard Divertimenti of Haydn and his Viennese Contemporaries (*c*.1750–1780)', Ph.D. diss. (Cornell Univ., 1982), 160–223; Charles Rosen, *Sonata Forms*, rev. edn. (New York, 1988); Mark Evan Bonds, 'Haydn's False Recapitulations and the Perception of Sonata Form in the Eighteenth Century', Ph.D. diss. (Harvard Univ., 1988), 204–33.

[2] William S. Newman, 'The Recognition of Sonata Form by Theorists of the 18th and 19th Centuries', *Papers of the American Musicological Society* (1941), 21–9; Leonard Ratner, 'Harmonic Aspects of Classic Form', *Journal of the American Musicological Society*, 2 (1949), 159–68, repr. in Ellen Rosand (ed.), *The Garland Library of the History of Western Music*, vii: *Classic Music* (New York, 1985), 101–10. A number of recent studies have analyzed or discussed Haydn's compositions in terms of the contemporary theorists, particularly Koch, Galeazzi, Kollmann, and Reicha: Elaine Sisman, 'Small and Expanded Forms: Koch's Model and Haydn's Music', *Musical Quarterly*, 68 (1982), 444–75; Hermann Forschner, *Instrumentalmusik Joseph Haydns aus der Sicht Heinrich Christoph Kochs* (Munich, 1984); Richard Gwilt, 'Sonata-Allegro Revisited', *In Theory Only*, 7/5–6 (1984), 3–33; Uwe Höll, *Studien zum Sonatensatz in den Klaviersonaten Joseph Haydns* (Tutzing, 1984); Günther Wagner, 'Anmerkungen zur Formtheorie Heinrich Christoph Kochs', *Archiv für Musikwissenschaft*, 41 (1984), 86–112; Siegfried Schmalzriedt, 'Charakter und Drama: Zur historischen Analyse von Haydnschen und Beethovenschen Sonatensätzen', *Archiv für Musikwissenschaft*, 42 (1985), 37–66; Wilhelm Seidel, 'Haydns Streichquartett in B-dur op. 71 Nr. 1 (Hob. III: 69)—Analytische Bemerkungen aus der Sicht Heinrich Christoph Kochs', in Georg Feder, Heinrich Hüschen, and Ulrich Tank (eds.), *Joseph Haydn: Tradition und Rezeption* (Regensburg, 1985), 3–13.

[3] Bonds, 'Haydn's False Recapitulations'; David P. Schroeder, *Haydn and the Enlightenment: The Late Symphonies and their Audience* (Oxford, 1990), 91 ff.

exclude others) or as a means of comparing a specific composition with a well-understood model?[4] Can form be independent of any one particular composition?[5] Do we wish to think of form as prescriptive (a set of rules dictating compositional choices) or, rather, as a general notion of procedure?[6]

Whichever of these (or other, equally valid) questions we choose to address will, necessarily, circumscribe the range of our answers. Indeed, much of the disagreement over this topic may have been a consequence, not so much of disputes over answers, as of differences over questions. If we take seriously the observation that the understanding of a text implies the reconstruction of the question to which it represents an answer, then we should recognize that Adolph Bernhard Marx's definition of sonata form is different from Heinrich Schenker's, which is, in turn, different from Leonard Ratner's, at least in part because the questions they have asked are so different.[7] Therefore, before we proceed any further we ought to identify the issues we want to confront and the questions we wish to address.

In this book I would like to come to a more thorough understanding of how form works in Haydn's symphonies (and, by analogy, in his other instrumental compositions).[8] I propose to do so by approaching the problem from the composer's viewpoint, attempting to reconstruct Haydn's formal logic. I intend to explicate, in detail, the rationale for his decisions, demonstrating how and why particular choices were made and

---

[4] The pitfalls of this approach have been oft-noted. Charles Rosen has remarked: 'The most dangerous aspect of the traditional theory of "sonata form" is the normative one. Basically the account is most comfortable with the works that Beethoven wrote when he was closely following Mozart's lead. The assumption that divergences from the pattern are irregularities is made as often as the inference that earlier eighteenth-century versions of the form represent an inferior stage from which a higher type evolved.' *The Classical Style* (New York, 1971), 32.

[5] As von Tobel argued: 'Jedes Werk hat seine Form, ist eine Form, und jede Form ist ein konkretes Werk; abstrakt sind nur Typen: sie fassen Formen mit Gemeinsamkeiten zu Gruppen zusammen.' *Die Formenwelt*, 2.

[6] Leonard Ratner has suggested understanding 18th-cent. forms as a process, not as a plan. See his 'Theories of Form: Some Changing Perspectives', in Jens Peter Larsen, Howard Serwer, and James Webster (eds.), *Haydn Studies: Proceedings of the International Haydn Conference, Washington D.C., 1975* (New York, 1981), 347–51.

[7] Adolph Bernhard Marx's theories of form were expounded in his influential treatise, *Die Lehre von der musikalischen Komposition, praktisch-theoretisch*, 4 vols. (Leipzig, 1837–47). Beginning approximately in the 1920s, this view of sonata form came under bitter attack—undoubtedly as a reflection of the new questions that were being asked. Heinrich Schenker argued that the 'concept of sonata-form as it has been taught up to now lacks precisely the essential characteristic—that of organic structure', and presented a view of sonata form in which the surface melodies were subsidiary in formal importance to the underlying voice-leading connections. See 'Organic Structure in Sonata Form', trans. Orin Grossman, *Journal of Music Theory*, 12 (1968), 164–83; repr. in Maury Yeston (ed.), *Readings in Schenker Analysis and Other Approaches* (New Haven, Conn., 1977), 38–53; also repr. in Rosand (ed.), *History of Western Music*, vii. 112–31. For a re-evaluation of A. B. Marx and his theories, see Scott Burnham, 'The Role of Sonata Form in A. B. Marx's Theory of Form', *Journal of Music Theory*, 33 (1989), 247–71.

[8] And, to the extent it is possible, with the compositions of Haydn's contemporaries. This will be discussed in Ch. 11 below.

what their implications are for the formal structure. I want to do this with as much precision as possible in order to account for the shape and content both of the specific compositions discussed below, and, by inference and deduction, the far greater number of compositions that could not possibly be analyzed in a single book. In short, I am posing the following question: What are the governing principles of Haydn's formal thought and how are they employed?

What follows, therefore, is a brief outline of Haydn's formal thought, a description of five fundamental compositional principles that constitute the foundation of his approach to form (and which have been inferred from his music). This outline will then be fleshed out and illustrated by means of the detailed analyses of specific compositions in the chapters that follow.

I take as my cue, my starting-point, a remark made by Edward Cone in his much-admired book *Musical Form and Musical Performance*. Cone argued that a fundamental principle of form in the Classical style[9]—what he termed the 'sonata principle'—'requires that important statements made in a key other than the tonic must either be re-stated in the tonic, or brought into a closer relation with the tonic, before the movement ends.'[10]

The sonata principle constitutes an essential component of Haydn's thought. It is no compositional prescriptive, admitting of one and only one response to the premises of a given work, nor does it suggest a fixed form, a framework to be filled in with details. But it is a remarkably suggestive idea, describing a basic principle of Haydn's approach to form: highly etched statements outside of the tonic, toward the beginning of a movement, create a formal imbalance that needs to be corrected by the

---

[9] The terms 'Classical style' and 'Classic era', though commonly used, have been the subject of much disagreement. See: Hans Engel, 'Haydn, Mozart und die Klassik', *Mozart-Jahrbuch* (1959), 46–79; the symposium discussion 'Sources of the Classical Idiom', in Jan LaRue (ed.), *International Musicological Society: Report of Eighth Congress* (New York and Kassel, 1961), ii. 135–9; Ludwig Finscher, 'Zum Begriff der Klassik in der Musik', *Deutsches Jahrbuch der Musikwissenschaft für 1966*, 11 (1967), 9–34, repr. in Rosand (ed.), *History of Western Music*, vii. 21–46; Warren Kirkendale, *Fugue and Fugato in Rococo and Classical Chamber Music*, rev. edn. (Durham, NC, 1979), pp. xxvi–xxvii; Leonard Ratner, *Classic Music: Expression, Form, and Style* (New York, 1980), p. xv; William S. Newman, *The Sonata in the Classic Era*, 3rd edn. (New York, 1983), 3–7; James Webster, *Haydn's 'Farewell' Symphony and the Idea of Classical Style: Through-Composition and Cyclic Integration in his Instrumental Music* (Cambridge, 1991), 335–57. Even for those who accept (or are resigned to) the term 'Classic era' or its common subdivisions ('pre-Classic', 'high-Classic', and 'late-Classic' eras), little consensus exists about the dates. Cf. e.g. Newman, *The Sonata in the Classic Era*, 3–7; Peter Rummenhöller, *Die musikalische Vorklassik* (Kassel, 1983), 8–9; Wagner, 'Anmerkungen zur Formtheorie Heinrich Christoph Kochs', 86.

[10] *Musical Form and Musical Performance* (New York, 1968), 76–7. The sonata principle has also been described as a large-scale dissonance relationship: 'all the material played in the dominant is consequently conceived as dissonant, i.e., requiring resolution by a later transposition to the tonic.' Rosen, *Sonata Forms*, 25 (see also p. 287). For a more extended discussion of Cone's principle, see Rosen, *The Classical Style*, 72–6. Cone's sonata principle must not be confused with the like-named concept described in Philip T. Barford, 'The Sonata-Principle: A Study of Musical Thought in the Eighteenth Century', *Music Review*, 13 (1952), 255–63.

restatement of that material in the tonic toward the end of the move-ment.[11]

To understand how important this principle is for Haydn's thought, it is necessary to recognize that from a purely harmonic point of view, the return of the tonic after the development section could be conceived as sufficient in and of itself to resolve the large-scale harmonic instabilities created by the tonicization of keys other than the tonic. Or, to put it negatively, from a purely harmonic point of view most of the recapitula-tion might be thought to be unnecessary.

The very fact that Haydn did not regard the return of the tonic by itself as sufficient to complete the formal structure gives us an indication of how central the sonata principle was to his sense of form. By the very content of his recapitulations he consistently demonstrated that he felt it was necessary not only to return to the tonic key, but also to restate previous non-tonic passages in the tonic.

It is also important to emphasize that the sonata principle is applicable to a broad array of formal types that are not usually declared to be in 'sonata form'. Depending on the structure of the individual movement, the sonata principle can operate in works that might otherwise be described as binary (and rounded binary), aria,[12] concerto,[13] fugue,[14] and rondo.[15] However, as we shall see in more detail in the following chapters, the sonata principle does not normally function in formal types (like strophic variations) that result from the concatenation of tonally complete formal units.

The second basic compositional principle might be termed the 'unity principle'. Haydn constructs his compositions so that later events within a movement are related by repetition, transposition, derivation, or variation to earlier events. The prescriptive force of the unity principle increases exponentially along the time-line of a movement. Toward the beginning of a work, it is not essential for a given passage to be derived

[11] For a description of the evolving recognition of this principle by 18th-cent. theorists see Fred Ritzel, *Die Entwicklung der 'Sonatenform' im musiktheoretischen Schrifttum des 18. und 19. Jahrhunderts*, 2nd edn. (Wiesbaden, 1969), 53 ff.

[12] Rosen discusses, at length, the relationship of aria forms to sonata: *Sonata Forms*, 28–70. For a discussion of sonata form in Haydn's arias see Mary K. Hunter, 'Haydn's Sonata-Form Arias', *Current Musicology*, 37–8 (1984), 19–32. Much more detailed information is found in her Ph.D. diss.: 'Haydn's Aria Forms' (Cornell Univ., 1982). For an 18th-cent. theorist's description of the sonata principle in the aria see Heinrich Christoph Koch, *Introductory Essay on Composition*, trans. Nancy Kovaleff Baker (New Haven, Conn., and London, 1983), 171.

[13] For a discussion of late 18th- and early 19th-cent. treatises that show features of both sonata and concerto see Jane R. Stevens, 'Theme, Harmony, and Texture in Classic-Romantic Descriptions of Concerto First-Movement Form', *Journal of the American Musicological Society*, 27 (1974), 25–60; repr. in Rosand (ed.), *History of Western Music*, vii. 133–68. See also Shelley Davis, 'H. C. Koch, the Classic Concerto, and the Sonata-Form Retransition', *Journal of Musicology*, 2 (1983), 45–61.

[14] Kirkendale, *Fugue and Fugato*, 78–88.

[15] Malcolm S. Cole, 'The Development of the Instrumental Rondo Finale from 1750 to 1800', Ph.D. diss. (Princeton Univ., 1964), *passim*.

from a preceding passage. The further the movement progresses, the more necessary it is that events not be formed *ex nihilo*, but be derived in a clearly recognizable way from at least one antecedent passage.[16] By the end of the movement, it becomes a virtual necessity that passages be repetitions, transpositions, variations, or transformations of earlier events.

There is an important corollary to the unity principle. The unity principle also implies that most of the ideas stated at the beginning of a composition will have to return later at least once. A distinctive event that appeared only at the beginning of the composition would be anomalous, having no relationship to the remainder of the movement.

The unity principle should not be mistaken for the idea of 'organic unity', a concept that has dominated so much of the analytical thought of this century.[17] Haydn's unity principle certainly does not preclude the possibility of organic unity, but it functions in a different manner and has far different consequences. An important goal of analyses based on the principle of organic unity is to demonstrate that seemingly unrelated events spring from a common motive (or, to use the common organicist metaphors, 'seed' or 'cell'). Haydn's unity principle, on the other hand, is entirely dependent on clearly apprehended *surface* relationships. An event late in the movement that has no clearly recognizable surface motivic or thematic connection to earlier events would violate this principle, even if it could be demonstrated that it was organically related to some prior passage.

Haydn's unity principle is operative most clearly within formal types which are an expansion of a single harmonic progression. In formal types that are composed of the juxtaposition of complete, or nearly complete, harmonic units (like menuet–trio–menuet), the unity principle normally functions only within each of the discrete components.

The third fundamental principle will be termed the 'redundancy principle': Haydn regarded multiple statements of identical, or nearly identical, events as potentially redundant. Unlike that of the unity principle, the force of the redundancy principle increases exponentially,

---

[16] Some articulation of this principle can be found in the 18th-cent. theoretical literature. For example, Johann Joachim Quantz (referring to the form of the solo concerto) says: 'The piece must not conclude with entirely new ideas; in the last solo section the most pleasing of the ideas previously heard must be repeated.' See *On Playing the Flute*, trans. Edward R. Reilly (London, 1966), 312; Originally pub. as *Versuch einer Anweisung die Flöte zu spielen* (Berlin, 1752). A half-century later, Koch admonishes the beginning student, remarking: 'Four different melodic sections joined into a period can indeed contain a complete plan for a larger composition; never, however, can they make up a complete whole by themselves without fragmentation and manipulation of ideas. For what would preserve the unity of such a composition when no section of it would be repeated in another connection or given a new turn? And if this does not happen, the sections are connected without any purpose and make up no self-sufficient whole.' *Introductory Essay*, 84.

[17] For a critique of the assumptions behind organicism and the metaphors commonly used, see Ruth Solie, 'The Living Work: Organicism and Musical Analysis', *19th Century Music*, 4 (1980–1), 147–56.

not along the time-line of the composition, but in direct proportion to the number of times a particular event is stated. One should not be dogmatic and attempt to define the precise number of repetitions that would be regarded as unacceptable. The exact point where an additional repetition would be considered redundant is dependent upon a number of variables, including—but not limited to—the size of the movement, the length of the phrase or theme that was to be repeated, the immediacy of the potential repetition, and the position of the movement in a multimovement cycle (evidently, a higher degree of repetition was acceptable in a finale than in a first movement). Generally speaking, the verdict of redundancy would be made more easily when the repetitions were in the same key; multiple statements in different keys did not seem to pose a problem—indeed, quite the opposite.

The redundancy principle is not limited in its applicability to thematic or motivic repetitions; it applies to harmonic and cadential issues as well. A succession of phrases concluding with perfect authentic cadences in the same key could be considered redundant even if the phrases employed contrasting motivic material. Cadential redundancy, like thematic redundancy, cannot be reduced to a numerical formula. Furthermore, the impression of cadential redundancy is at least partly dependent upon the style of the composition—that is, whether it is in sonata or symphonic style. It has been demonstrated that there is a distinction between the sonata and symphonic styles, and this distinction rests on differences in their phrase and cadence structures. Movements in sonata style contain more frequent and more clearly articulated cadences, while movements in symphonic style tend to elide or suppress cadences, creating a more continuous flow. As a result, a higher level of cadential frequency would be acceptable in a sonata-style movement than in a work in a symphonic style, and the threshold for the verdict of redundancy would have to be adjusted accordingly. Although the distinction between the two styles was not absolute (sonatas could be in symphonic style and symphonies could be in sonata style), some evidence exists that Haydn adhered fairly clearly to the sonata and symphonic styles within their respective genres, at least for much of his career.[18]

Like the sonata and unity principles, the redundancy principle has different implications for different formal types. In movements formed by the juxtaposition of harmonically complete units, the redundancy principle is effectively operative within each of the discrete units. Consequently, strophic variations, by their very nature, lie outside the purview of this principle.

---

[18] Michael Broyles, 'The Two Instrumental Styles of Classicism', *Journal of the American Musicological Society*, 36 (1983), 210–42. See also his *Beethoven: The Emergence and Evolution of Beethoven's Heroic Style* (New York, 1987), 9–36.

Although the redundancy principle is generally invoked to reduce repetitions, there are many situations in which repetition is not only possible, but demanded. When a movement begins with a tonally closed form (such as a rounded binary), and is followed by another tonally closed form, then the opening formal unit will return, either immediately, as in a strophic variation, or following a contrasting section or couplet, as in a rondo, or menuet and trio, or hybrid variation. And, of course, on the more local level, some degree of repetition is an essential aspect of the unity principle.

The fourth component of Haydn's formal thought will be termed the 'variation principle'.[19] This principle suggests that the longer, more immediate, and more explicit a potential repetition, the more likely it is to be subjected to variation. The most obvious application of this principle would be in sets of variations and related formal types, but Haydn's employment of the variation principle is in no sense limited to those kinds of forms. Rather, it is a fundamental aspect of his compositional thought, regardless of the formal type involved.[20]

The force of the variation principle is strongest when potential repetitions are adjacent to one another, as in strophic variations. But if something sizable is inserted between two identical statements, there is no necessity for the second statement to be varied, particularly if the insertion is itself a tonally complete formal unit (as, for example, the trio between the two statements of the menuet in a menuet and trio).

The variation principle functions as one of the principal means of mediation between the unity and redundancy principles. The unity principle implies that a composition will be structured so that later events are understood to be related to or derived from earlier events. However, if all later events are identical to earlier events, then the redundancy principle needs to be invoked. The application of variation technique thus permits the composer to achieve unity without redundancy.

Variation procedures were also frequently used by Haydn to effect a teleological dynamic in his compositions. Often, the specific content and character of a variation resulted from the incorporation of elements from disparate locations earlier in the piece. The later, varied passage might thereby be viewed as a synthesis or combination of prior events.

The fifth and final principle will be termed the 'normative principle'. This principle suggests that a normative sequence of events requires no special response, no further answer. By corollary, a significant

[19] As with the sonata principle, it could be argued that the unity and variation principles have a counterpart in 18th-century aesthetics—Jean Pierre de Crousaz's familiar doctrine of 'unity in variety'. For a comprehensive account of the manifold appearances of this aesthetic principle in late 18th-cent. music-theoretical treatises, see Ritzel, *Die Entwicklung*, 76 ff.

[20] For a discussion of general applications of the variation principle, see Sisman, 'Small and Expanded Forms'. See also her *Haydn and the Classical Variation* (Cambridge, Mass., 1993), 79–108.

infringement of norms will require some kind of compensatory response, something that will resolve the instabilities occasioned by the violation of norms.[21]

There are two basic kinds of norms: inter-opus and intra-opus.[22] Inter-opus norms are the commonly recognized stylistic norms from the time when the composition was written. Intra-opus norms, by contrast, are determined by the internal details of the composition. An infringement of intra-opus norms results when there is a recognizable deviation from a pattern previously established within the composition itself. Normally speaking, the infringement of intra-opus norms could not be recognized outside the context of the composition.

Irrespective of their origin (inter- or intra-opus), Haydn's treatment of the violation of norms is essentially the same. Significant deviations from normative patterns create a formal instability that has to be resolved. This is accomplished not merely by recalling the anomalous event at a later point in the composition, but by recalling and restating the problematic idea in a normative context, thereby resolving the instability.

Violations and subsequent resolutions of inter- and intra-opus norms are a central aspect of Haydn's multimovement strategies. In some of his symphonies, significant violations of norms are not resolved in the movements in which they occur, but rather are addressed only in subsequent movements. This means that the later movements can be understood to be responses to the earlier movements, with all this implies for multimovement unity.

The normative principle, and its assumption that there are identifiable norms whose infringement would be recognized, implies an active and informed interaction between the composer and his intended audience. For the normative principle to function, the composer must know what kinds of expectations will be raised by his material, and must know what must be done to gratify (or frustrate) those assumptions. By corollary, the audience must be familiar enough with the style of the time and the syntax of its harmonic and formal language for the composer's stratagems to work. In the analyses that follow, much attention will be given to the likely expectations of the listener, and throughout it will be assumed that a knowledge of those expectations was a motivating factor behind Haydn's specific compositional decisions.

---

[21] Like the sonata principle, the normative principle is adapted from an idea of Edward Cone's. See his 'Schubert's Promissory Note, *19th Century Music*, 5 (1981–2), 233–41, and 'Schubert's Unfinished Business', *19th Century Music*, 7 (1983–4), 222–32. For a discussion of norms and the listener's expectations, see Bonds, 'Haydn's False Recapitulations', 21–79, and id., *Wordless Rhetoric: Musical Form and the Metaphor of the Oration* (Cambridge, Mass., 1991), 13–52.

[22] For a related discussion see Leonard B. Meyer, *Style and Music: Theory, History, and Ideology* (Philadelphia, 1989), 23–30.

Interestingly enough—and this will be a central issue in the analyses to follow—the five principles are often incompatible. For example, the sonata principle dictates that passages outside the tonic in the exposition should be transposed back to the tonic in the recapitulation. However, in many cases, if everything that had occurred in the dominant were to be transposed, there might be cadential or even thematic redundancy. Similarly, it is easy to imagine a situation where the unity and redundancy principles might come into conflict.

These last points indicate that although the principles outlined above may be simple in theory, they are anything but simple in application. Therefore, we have come to the limit of what we can accomplish with this description of Haydn's principles of form in the absence of concrete musical examples. But before we can begin our analyses, we must touch upon some issues of methodology.

In recent years scholars have employed many different techniques in an attempt to reconstruct a composer's thought. For some composers, their autographs have survived and have yielded important clues about compositional process. In the case of other composers, their sketches have been invaluable sources of information about their thought. Still other composers were the authors of theoretical treatises or essays, providing us with the opportunity to use the ideas expressed in their writings to aid in the reconstruction of their compositional approach.

For a study of Haydn's formal thought, none of these methods would be particularly effective. Although many of his autographs are extant, it is not clear that they can reveal much that is applicable to the present problem. Some sketches have survived (perhaps only a minuscule proportion of what may once have existed), and although their study has revealed interesting facets of his compositional technique, the very paucity of the sources means that the sketches are of limited use to the present study.[23] And, as is well known, Haydn wrote no work of music theory, nor do his letters or diaries discuss compositional process or substance.

---

[23] But suffice it to say, nothing in the surviving sketches contradicts the theory of formal thought presented in this book. Indeed, it is possible to interpret aspects of the sketches as supporting my conclusions, as I will indicate in Ch. 10 below. For discussions of Haydn's sketches see Leopold Nowak, 'Die Skizzen zum Finale der Es-dur-Symphonie GA 99 von Joseph Haydn', *Haydn-Studien*, 2 (1969–70), 137–66; László Somfai, ' "Ich war nie ein Geschwindschreiber...": Joseph Haydns Skizzen zum langsamen Satz des Streichquartetts Hoboken III: 33', in Nils Schiørring, Henrik Glahn, and Carsten Hatting (eds.), *Festskrift Jens Peter Larsen* (Copenhagen, 1972), 275–84; Georg Feder, 'Bemerkungen zu Haydns Skizzen', *Beethoven Jahrbuch*, 9 (1973–7), 69–86; id. 'Joseph Haydns Skizzen und Entwürfe', *Fontes artis musicae*, 26 (1979), 172–88; Somfai, 'An Introduction to the Study of Haydn's String Quartet Autographs (with Special Attention to Opus 77/G)', in Christoph Wolff (ed.), *The String Quartets of Haydn, Mozart, and Beethoven: Studies of the Autograph Manuscripts* (Cambridge, Mass., 1980), 5–51; Hollace Ann Schafer, ' "A Wisely Ordered *Phantasie*": Joseph Haydn's Creative Process from the Sketches and Drafts for Instrumental Music', Ph.D. diss. (Brandeis Univ., 1987).

What we do have, and have in abundance, are compositions, more than enough raw material from which principles of Haydn's formal thought can be induced. And of the various types of compositions he cultivated, it seems particularly appropriate to devote our attention to his symphonies. Not only are they representatives of a serious and important genre, but also, they were composed over nearly forty years—from the late 1750s until 1795. Moreover, there are a plethora of examples from which to choose—more than one hundred complete compositions, with no extended gaps in the chronology. These are advantages enjoyed by no other single genre. To be sure, it would be a plausible option to discuss not just symphonies, but string quartets, keyboard sonatas, and trios as well. But several disadvantages outweigh the possible advantages. In the first place, it is scarcely necessary to broaden the database beyond the symphonies. I can think of no problem pertinent to the theory I have outlined that cannot be exemplified by at least one of the symphonies. Secondly, as indicated above, some evidence exists that Haydn differentiated between symphonic and sonata styles. This manifests itself most clearly in the more frequent cadences of the sonata style—but there are some other important differences as well.[24] As a result, it seems sensible to avoid the complications that would result from mixing analyses of symphonic and chamber works.

In any event, I shall not ignore Haydn's other instrumental compositions. Frequent reference will be made (primarily in the footnotes) to formal features of works in the other genres. And it would be a relatively simple matter to apply the results derived from the symphonies to other kinds of compositions, making appropriate modifications to account for peculiarities of the individual genres and styles.

Finally, I must say a word about the choice of works to be analyzed. In order to flesh out my outline of Haydn's formal thought, it is necessary to look at compositions in extensive detail. If so, then it should be self-evident that I cannot analyze all 107 symphonies. Unfortunately, this means that since Haydn composed so many interesting symphonies, it is impossible to choose a few works for discussion without leaving out several times that number of equally marvelous examples.

My selection of works is based on several factors. First and foremost, I wanted to make sure that my theory of Haydn's compositional thought was adequately illustrated, while at the same time I did not want to try the patience of the reader with too many analyses. I also felt it would be most useful if analyses were presented of compositions from all stages of

---

[24] Some of these differences will be cited during the course of the analyses to come. William Rothstein has suggested that, at least in his earlier compositions (and perhaps again in the 1790s), 'there are obvious differences in phrase rhythm between Haydn's keyboard sonatas and his divertimenti for string quartet, and between both of these genres and the symphony.' *Phrase Rhythm in Tonal Music* (New York, 1989), 131.

his symphonic career.[25] As a result, the symphonies chosen (until the last few) are spaced at intervals of approximately five years. This will help place the individual compositions into a meaningful historical and chronological context. Furthermore, I felt it necessary to select both some works that were unique in some important dimension (e.g. Symphony No. 99) as well as some symphonies that were more ordinary (e.g. Symphony No. 75)—to the extent that is ever the case with Haydn. There were also a number of specific issues that I wanted to address and formal types I wished to illustrate (binary variants, false recapitulations, hybrid variations, rondos, sonata-rondos, and so on), and this helped determine which works were to be chosen. Finally, I thought it would be best to discuss some symphonies that have received comparatively little analytical attention (e.g. Symphonies Nos. 1, 21, 55, 75, 81, 96), and not to concentrate solely on works that have been more thoroughly scrutinized—although some of the more frequently discussed symphonies (Nos. 49, 85, 99) are included as well.

---

[25] The division of Haydn's career into periods has been the topic of substantial debate. Carl Geiringer sees five periods (youth 1750–60, preparatory period 1761–70, middle period 1771–80, full maturity 1781–90, and period of supreme mastery 1791–1803): see *Haydn: A Creative Life in Music*, 3rd edn. (Berkeley, Calif., 1982), 204. H. C. Robbins Landon has suggested seven periods for the symphonies (to *c*.1761/2, 1761–5, 1766–70, 1771–4, 1774–84, 1785–8, 1791–5): see *The Symphonies of Joseph Haydn* (London, 1955; New York, 1956), 172–3. Larsen proposes eight periods—see 'Zu Haydns künstlerischer Entwicklung', in Hans Zingerle (ed.), *Festschrift Wilhelm Fischer zum 70. Geburtstag überreicht im Mozartjahr 1956* (Innsbruck, 1956), 123–9; trans. Ulrich Krämer as 'On Haydn's Artistic Development', in Jens Peter Larsen, *Handel, Haydn, and the Viennese Classical Style* (Ann Arbor, Mich., 1988), 109–15. James Webster suggests five periods between 1761 and 1790 (1761–1765/6; 1765/6–1772; 1773–*c*.1779; *c*.1779–*c*.1784; *c*.1785–1790): see *Haydn's 'Farewell'*, 359–61, 362.

2

Symphony No. 1

(–25 November 1759)

ALTHOUGH some evidence indicates that the Symphony in D major
Hob. I: 1, might be Haydn's first symphony,[1] much uncertainty remains
about the dating of this and many other early works.[2] In any event, it is
undoubtedly one of Haydn's earliest symphonies and as such is a good
example of his compositional technique at the initial stages of his career.
Cast in three movements (Presto–Andante–Presto) for the small orchestra
characteristic of the period (strings, continuo, two oboes, two horns), it
exemplifies, both through the formal organization of the individual
movements and through its overall multimovement plan, some of the
enormous variety of formal approaches possible in Haydn's early symphonies.[3]

[1] Throughout this book, I will use the dates from Georg Feder's worklist for the Haydn entry in
Stanley Sadie (ed.), *The New Grove Dictionary of Music and Musicians* (London, 1980), repr. in *The New
Grove Haydn* (New York, 1983). For another, somewhat more speculative, set of dates for the
symphonies, see: H. C. Robbins Landon (ed.), *Joseph Haydn, Kritische Ausgabe sämtlicher Symphonien/ Criti-
cal Edition of the Complete Symphonies*, 2nd rev. edn. (12 vols., Vienna, 1981). Problems of chronology are
discussed in Jens Peter Larsen, 'Probleme der chronologischen Ordnung von Haydns Sinfonien', in
Walter Gerstenberg, Jan LaRue, and Wolfgang Rehm (eds.), *Festschrift Otto Erich Deutsch zum 80.
Geburtstag* (Kassel, 1963), 90–104; id., 'Haydn's Early Symphonies: The Problem of Dating', in Alan
Atlas (ed.), *Music in the Classic Period: Essays in Honor of Barry S. Brook* (Stuyvesant, NJ, 1985), 117–31,
repr. in Larsen, *Handel, Haydn*, 159–70; Sonja Gerlach, 'Die chronologische Ordnung von Haydns
Sinfonien zwischen 1774 und 1782', *Haydn-Studien*, 2 (1969–70), 34–66. The commonly used numbering
for Haydn's symphonies was established by E. Mandyczewski in 1907 and has since been adopted as
category I by Anthony van Hoboken in his catalogue: *Thematisch-bibliographisches Werkverzeichnis* (Mainz,
1957–78), i.

[2] According to Griesinger (the most reliable of his early biographers), Haydn reported that this
work was his first symphony and had been composed in 1759. Landon suggests that it may have been
written somewhat earlier. His chronology for Haydn's early symphonies is based on the Festetics
Collection of the Fürnberg–Morzin MSS in Keszthely Castle: see *Haydn: Chronicle and Works*
(Bloomington, Ind., and London, 1976–80), i. 239–42 and 280–3. Doubts about the reliability of the
Festetics Collection are raised in James Webster, 'Prospects for Haydn Biography after Landon',
Musical Quarterly, 68 (1982), 484–6. More recently, Sonja Gerlach has argued that a date of 1757 for
Symphony No. 1 may be deduced from information drawn from several sources. See her 'Haydns
"chronologische" Sinfonienliste für Breitkopf & Härtel', *Haydn-Studien*, 6 (1986–92), 125–6.

[3] An account of the range of possibilities for the number and type of movements appears in Jens
Peter Larsen, 'Zur Entstehung der österreichischen Symphonietradition (ca. 1750–1775)', *Haydn
Yearbook*, 10 (1978), 72–80; trans. as 'Concerning the Development of the Austrian Symphonic
Tradition (*circa* 1750–1775)', in Larsen, *Handel, Haydn*, 315–25. Ludwig Finscher compares the stylistic

We will begin our analysis of the first movement with an examination of the thematic, cadential, and harmonic premises of the first part of the work, up to the internal double bar after m. 39—the exposition. In this work, as in most of Haydn's compositions, essential aspects of the second half of the movement are, to a large degree, determined by what transpires in the first half.

As is often the case in Haydn's sonata forms, it is useful to see the exposition as divided into three distinct sections, corresponding to their harmonic functions: a tonic definition section (mm. 1–9), a transition to the secondary key (mm. 10–28), and a confirmation of the secondary key (mm. 29–39).[4] The boundaries of the three sections are marked off by clear cadences (mm. 9, 28, and 39),[5] that are—with one crucial exception (and more on that shortly)—the only sharply articulated pauses in the exposition (see Ex. 2.1).[6]

A prominent characteristic of the exposition is the striking variety of its thematic material. Although the transition section begins (m. 10) with a variant of the opening theme,[7] that is—again, with one important

---

diversity of Haydn's symphonies of the 1760s with the relative stylistic unity of his string quartets from the same period (Opp. 1 and 2) and suggests that the lack of models and a specific tradition for the quartets accounted for their uniformity, while the very existence of a number of powerful symphonic traditions (Italian, Mannheim, Viennese) made it difficult, initially, for Haydn to find his own symphonic style. See *Studien zur Geschichte des Streichquartetts*, i: *Die Entstehung des klassischen Streichquartetts* (Kassel, 1974), 161.

[4] This is an adaptation of ideas presented in Jens Peter Larsen, 'Sonatenform-Probleme', in Anna Amalie Abert and Wilhelm Pfannkuch (eds.), *Festschrift Friedrich Blume zum 70. Geburtstag* (Kassel, 1963), 221–30; trans. as 'Sonata Form Problems', in Larsen, *Handel, Haydn*, 269–79. Larsen points out that in Haydn's expositions the dominant section is normally longer than the tonic section. How Haydn and other composers expanded the dominant region is described in William Caplin, 'The "Expanded Cadential Progression": A Category for the Analysis of Classical Form', *Journal of Musicological Research*, 7 (1987), 215–57. Although three-part expositions are common in Haydn's works, other subdivisions occur. Some examples of two-part expositions in the keyboard sonatas are cited in Michelle Fillion, 'Sonata-Exposition Procedures in Haydn's Keyboard Sonatas', in Larsen, Serwer, and Webster (eds.), *Haydn Studies*, 475–81.

[5] Cadences play an essential role in determining the large-scale structural divisions of a movement. See Lester S. Steinberg, 'Sonata Form in the Keyboard Trios of Joseph Haydn', Ph.D. diss. (New York Univ., 1976), 94–9. A. Peter Brown has suggested a useful scale for determining the strength of cadences in 'The Structure of the Exposition in Haydn's Keyboard Sonatas', *Music Review*, 36 (1975), 104. Other studies have adapted Koch's categories of the comparative strength of closes. See Forschner, *Instrumentalmusik Joseph Haydns*, 109 ff, and Höll, *Studien zum Sonatensatz*, 8–9.

[6] The same subdivision of this exposition has been proposed in Niels Krabbe, 'A Critical Review of Fritz Tutenberg's Theory of First-Movement Form in the Early Classical Symphony', in Larsen, Serwer, and Webster (eds.), *Haydn Studies*, 491. Krabbe notes that Tutenberg's analysis of this movement was 'somewhat inadequate', as it was based on thematic, not harmonic criteria. This led Tutenberg to place the beginning of the *Nebensatz* at m. 10, and to invest the GP in m. 22 with formal significance. See Fritz Tutenberg, *Die Sinfonik Johann Christian Bachs* (Wolfenbüttel and Berlin, 1928), 179–80.

[7] The opening theme has been called, probably mistakenly, a Mannheim crescendo. The source for Haydn's crescendo may not have been Mannheim, but Italy, and in particular Niccolò Jommelli (who may well have been the real innovator of this orchestral device). Jommelli's overture to *Artaserse*—which contains a clear 'Mannheim' crescendo on a D major chord (as in Haydn's

exception—the only obvious repetition in the exposition. Instead of thematic repetition, Haydn proceeds with an exuberant, seemingly ingenuous loquacity, continually introducing new and contrasting thematic ideas all the way up until the internal double bar.[8]

In Haydn's sonata forms, the internal double bar normally marks the end of the introduction of new material—as we would expect, given the increase in force of the unity principle along the time-line of the composition.[9] That certainly is the case here, for the development section is no compilation of stock clichés and empty passage-work, but the artful reformulation and combination of some of the ideas that Haydn had introduced in the exposition (in particular, the rhythmic motive first heard in m. 23).[10]

Having made this survey of the principal thematic, cadential, and harmonic events, from the beginning of the exposition to the end of the development section, we should now be able to make some guesses about what will occur in the remainder of the work. If the principles outlined in the first chapter accurately describe Haydn's basic compositional approach, we should be able to predict, with some degree of precision, Haydn's responses to the premises he had posed in the opening sections of the composition.[11]

---

symphony)—was performed in Vienna in 1749. See Eugene K. Wolf, 'On the Origins of the Mannheim Symphonic Style', in John Walter Hill (ed.), *Studies in Musicology in Honor of Otto E. Albrecht: A Collection of Essays by his Colleagues and Former Students at the University of Pennsylvania* (Kassel, 1980), 210; repr. in Rosand (ed.), *History of Western Music*, vii. 244. See also his *The Symphonies of Johann Stamitz: A Study in the Formation of the Classic Style* (Utrecht and Antwerp, 1981), 235. For yet another suggestion concerning the origins of Haydn's theme (the overture to Florian Gassmann's opera *L'Issipile*—also in D major), see Landon, *Chronicle and Works*, i. 88, 112, and 283.

[8] It was a common stylistic device in Haydn's early symphonies to heighten the contrast with the primary key-area by touching on the dominant minor in the secondary key-area, as in mm. 29 ff. See Bathia Churgin, 'The Italian Symphonic Background to Haydn's Early Symphonies and Opera Overtures', in Larsen, Serwer, and Webster (eds.), *Haydn Studies*, 332. See also Rosen, *Sonata Forms*, 153–5. Landon points out that examples of this procedure can be found in Symphonies Nos. 1/i, 37/i, 2/i, 15/i, 4/i, 32/i, 32/iv, 27/i, 20/i, and 36/i: see *Chronicle and Works*, i. 283–96 and 561–2. This procedure occurs in other genres as well. See the String Quartet Op. 9 No. 1/i, mm. 19–24.

[9] In both Haydn's music and that of his contemporaries, it was not particularly unusual for the development section to begin with new material. Galeazzi even preferred such a technique to the transposition of the opening material to the dominant. See Bathia Churgin, 'Francesco Galeazzi's Description (1796) of Sonata Form', *Journal of the American Musicological Society*, 21 (1968), 194–5. Rosen suggests that development sections which are composed entirely of new thematic material reflect the influence of the concerto on the sonata. See *Sonata Forms*, 89. The introduction of new material in the development section may also reflect the influence of the aria. See Hunter, 'Haydn's Sonata-Form Arias', 28.

[10] John Vinton, 'The Development Section in Early Viennese Symphonies: A Re-valuation', *Music Review*, 24 (1963), 13–22.

[11] I describe Haydn's writing of the recapitulation as a 'response' to the premises of the exposition. However, this should not be taken to imply that Haydn wrote the exposition without any idea of what should come later. Rather, I suspect that as he composed the exposition, he was simultaneously calculating what the response of the recapitulation would have to be. There is evidence from the surviving sketches to support this hypothesis. See Ch. 10 n. 20.

Ex. 2.1

(continued)

Ex. 2.1 continued

First and foremost, we should anticipate that although the tonic definition section could return without change, the material in the dominant area needs to be transposed back to the tonic, particularly given the variety of contrasting thematic ideas presented in the latter half of the exposition (sonata principle).[12] As the dominant key was first suggested in m. 14, was solidified by the overreach in m. 17, and was not left again in the exposition,[13] it seems inescapable that everything from around m. 19 or so has to be brought back to the tonic. There must also be a rewriting of the transition before coming to the passage corresponding to m. 14, in order to avoid the modulation to the dominant. We should not anticipate that the redundancy principle would present any problems, either with respect to cadences or themes. In the thirty-nine measures of the exposition, there were only three prominent cadences. Even if the half-cadence in the tonic were to be retained and both authentic cadences formerly in the dominant were to be restated in the tonic, there would hardly be a surfeit of cadences in the recapitulation. Indeed, there would be just two authentic cadences in the tonic in the entire movement. Similarly, the very thematic diversity of the exposition makes it highly unlikely that the activation of the sonata principle could cause any problems in thematic redundancy. As the material in the dominant region was a succession of contrasting thematic ideas, a transposition of the entire dominant region back to the tonic could not possibly cause redundancy; it would simply result in a succession of contrasting ideas, now in the tonic. We certainly would expect the unity principle to dictate that no new material should be introduced in the recapitulation, as was the case in the development section. We might expect to find some activation of the variation principle, as Haydn could take the opportunity to elaborate upon some of the material heard in the exposition or development section. But the thematic diversity of the exposition and the correspondingly few number of repetitions could mean that there would not be much opportunity or motivation to apply the variation principle.

When we compare the exposition with the recapitulation, we find that, to a large measure, our theory has been a most accurate predictor of specific details of Haydn's actual compositional choices (see Table 2.1). After repeating the opening nine measures (the tonic definition section)

---

[12] Leonard Meyer makes a useful distinction between 'repetition' and 'return'. See *Explaining Music: Essays and Explorations* (Berkeley, Calif., 1973), 49–52. In those terms, the statement of the opening thematic material at the beginning of the recapitulation might be thought of as a 'return', not a 'repetition'.

[13] Haydn often solidifies the move to the dominant by a kind of tonal overreach. Although, strictly speaking, one need only raise the fourth degree to tonicize the dominant, he often raises the first degree as well, at least for a moment. This latter inflection has the effect of erasing the tonic. Then, by cancelling that inflection, he makes the modulation to the dominant seem more secure. See mm. 17–18 in this movement, mm. 12–14 in the second movement, and mm. 11–19 in the final movement.

TABLE 2.1 *Symphony No. 1/i: Correspondences between Exposition and Recapitulation*

Exposition (mm.)	Recapitulation (mm.)
1–11	59–69
12–22	—
—	70–1
23–4	72–3 (transposed)
25–6	—
27–39	74–86 (transposed)

note for note, Haydn makes a small change in the orchestration at the repetition of what had been mm. 10–11, and then, in order to remain in the tonic, diverges from the model of the exposition before reaching the passage corresponding to m. 14.[14] We then arrive in mm. 72–3 at a version of mm. 23–4, now in the tonic, followed (mm. 74–5) by a transposition of mm. 27–8. From this point to the end of the movement (mm. 76–86), everything is a restatement, in the tonic, of the corresponding passage from the exposition (mm. 29–39). In keeping with the unity principle, nothing new is introduced in the recapitulation, but the transposed repetitions are not completely literal, as Haydn takes the opportunity to make slight variations (cf. mm. 35–6 and 82–3). All three cadences of the exposition are retained (appropriately transposed when necessary) in the recapitulation.

However, if our goal is a precise understanding of Haydn's formal logic, then we must admit that we have not yet completely succeeded on several important counts. Although most of the material in the dominant area is transposed back to the tonic, the specific point where the transposition begins was not exactly where we guessed it would be (shortly after m. 19), but considerably later. When the dominant material first returns in the tonic, something is not quite right: the passage corresponding to mm. 23–4 is not followed by a transposed version of mm. 25 ff, but rather, Haydn splices directly to a transposition of mm. 27 ff, omitting mm. 25–6. Whereas it is quite true that he takes the opportunity to make some variations in the transposition of the dominant confirmation section back to the tonic, to state simply that there are variations is inadequate, for we have in no sense accounted for the specific features of those variations. Therefore, we need to look more carefully at the exposition

---

[14] In m. 71, Haydn does touch on G♯, thus suggesting he will tonicize the dominant. But the G♯ is immediately cancelled in the next measure. This is a common device in Haydn's compositions: it also occurs in Symphony No. 1/iii (see mm. 61–3). It is similar to the idea of overreach (described in n. 13 above).

and the development section, to see if there are rational explanations for the apparent anomalies of the recapitulation and sources for the variations.

The crux of the problem is that we have glossed over a striking event in the exposition, an event so striking that Tutenberg 'accorded it formal significance'.[15] Shortly after moving into the dominant key, Haydn began the preparations for what we would expect to be a solid cadence in the dominant (see Ex. 2.1, above). A plethora of familiar signs is in place in m. 21: the slowing of the harmonic rhythm, the harmonic progression (V^{6-5}_{4-3}), the octave drop in the bass, and the trill on the supertonic (of the new key) in the topmost voice.

What follows is an almost violent frustration of the expectations that have been so carefully nurtured. Instead of a cadence confirming the new key, Haydn lunges past the newly tonicized dominant to its V^6_5 —on the second beat of the measure—and abruptly stops, leaving a skewed and unstable rhythm, one without precedent to this point in the movement.[16] The following GP lasts a full two beats, leaving the unresolved V^6_5 hanging.

The next two measures are, if anything, even more disruptive. Rather than resolve the hanging V^6_5 to its tonic, Haydn leaps in the other direction, up the circle of fifths, directly to a II^6. The dynamics drop suddenly to piano. Even the voice-leading is—to put it mildly—unconventional, as the bass makes a jagged leap across the GP, up a tritone to a D, leaving the leading-tone unresolved, while the violin leaps up a third from the seventh of the dominant chord.

All of this instability and disruption (violations of inter-opus voice-leading and harmonic norms) is smoothed over in m. 25. Haydn returns to the forte dynamic level, returns to the dominant chord, left hanging since m. 22, and most important of all, returns to motives and textures unmistakably related to mm. 18–19 (a particularly striking connection in light of the surrounding thematic diversity). Immediately following this, Haydn goes through the familiar routine of cadential preparation. This time there is no denial of expectations and the dominant is finally confirmed with a clear and unequivocal cadence in m. 28. In some essential respects, mm. 25–8 are a varied (but far more stable) restatement of mm. 18–22, resolving, at least partially, the instability of those measures by restating the disruptive material in a normative context.

We are now in a far better position to understand why Hadyn omitted, or drastically altered, mm. 18–26 in the recapitulation. It hinges around

---

[15] See n. 6 above.

[16] There may be no precedent for this rhythmic pattern, but there is a consequent. A reminiscence of the offbeat accent of m. 22 resurfaces in the closing cadence at the end of the exposition (and correspondingly, the recapitulation). See mm. 38 and 85. By restating this rhythm in a more normative context, Haydn has resolved the instabilities of m. 22.

the redundancy principle. Compared with the multiple harmonic functions of the exposition (tonic definition, transition, confirmation of the
secondary key), the harmonic role of the recapitulation is simple—merely
the reconfirmation of the tonic. Therefore, the abortive cadence of m. 22
and the jagged abruption of m. 23 have no proper place in the
recapitulation. In the exposition, that frustrated cadence and its improbable continuation functioned to defer and deflect the confirmation of the
new key, prolonging and renewing the energy of the harmonic motion,
just at the point where the listener's expectations were prepared for a
point of relative repose on the newly tonicized dominant. In the
recapitulation, a slavish transposition of this passage would be an event
without purpose. The recapitulation is already in the tonic, has already
come to a half-cadence in the tonic key (with two further cadences in
store—not to mention the half-cadence at the end of the development
section), and there are no expectations for the confirmation of a new key
to defer or deflect. Clearly these measures, and indeed the entire passage
leading up to them, are redundant and must be excised.

This, in turn, presents Haydn with an additional problem. The sonata
principle suggests that prominent events outside the tonic need to be
restated in the tonic before the movement is over. If so, then the excision
of mm. 23–4, while necessary to avoid the disruptive cadence, poses
something of a problem. Surely the new and contrasting theme with its
highly etched rhythmic motive in mm. 23–4 (which, significantly, is the
focus of the development section) is a prominent event and should be
restated in the tonic in the recapitulation.

In mm. 72–3, immediately before he begins the transposition of the
dominant region, Haydn does respond to the dictates of the sonata
principle by restating (and recasting) mm. 23–4 in the tonic. But unlike
all of the other non-tonic events from the exposition, this repetition is not
down a fifth (or up a fourth). Instead of expanding a ii^6 chord, as in m.
23, the passage in the recapitulation prolongs V (see Ex. 2.2, and compare
with Ex. 2.1). Moreover, the canonic texture is absent in mm. 72–3, the
motive in the first violin in these measures is not a literal transposition of
mm. 23–4, and Haydn splices directly from the restatement of mm. 23–4
to a passage corresponding to mm. 27, omitting mm. 25–6 entirely.

It would be tempting to dismiss the differences between the passage in
Ex. 2.2 and the corresponding passage in the exposition as insignificant
changes: minor variety added by the composer to break up the stark
symmetry of the exposition and recapitulation. It might seem supererogatory to devote—as I am about to do—anything more than a sentence
or two to identifying the differences between the passages. However, we
cannot dismiss differences of this sort so lightly. To the contrary, passages
that are almost, but not quite, parallel are, in fact, crucial for understanding Haydn's formal logic and must be subjected to careful scrutiny.

Ex. 2.2

When Haydn does not take the most obvious path, but instead, purposely and with obvious premeditation, recomposes a later passage so that it diverges markedly from an earlier model, the changes are never arbitrary, casual, or happenstance. Rather, significant deviations from previously established norms are usually designed to refer to (and perhaps to resolve or complete) at least one other event (though perhaps more).[17] Measures 72 ff are a primer in the application of this principle to Haydn's music.

The most immediate and obvious consequence of the changes in the topmost voice is the establishment of motivic connections with the theme that follows the cadence (see Ex. 2.3). Haydn has transformed what had been two sharply contrasting ideas in the exposition (mm. 23–4 and 29–30) into two closely related variants in the recapitulation (mm. 72–3, Ex. 2.3*a*, and mm. 76–7, Ex. 2.3*b*)—an interesting metamorphosis.

---

[17] The normative principle will be considered to imply that, unless there is good reason to the contrary, the recapitulation should restate the material of the exposition in order: the thematic order of the exposition constitutes an intra-opus norm. See Meyer, *Style and Music*, 24. A violation of that order—as here—should invoke the corollary of the normative principle.

Ex. 2.3

(a)

(b)

At the same time, the abandonment of the canonic texture in mm. 72–3 has the function of connecting these measures with the development section. The central focus of that section had been an intensive working-out of the motive from mm. 23–4. At first, the emphasis had been on its rhythm. But in mm. 51–2, shortly before the retransition, the two uppermost voices (the first and second violins), come back, not only to the rhythm, but to a similar intervallic succession, moving in parallel thirds up to a high point on C/A, the seventh and fifth degrees of a diminished seventh chord, which then resolve down by step to B/G (see Ex. 2.4).

Ex. 2.4

These very features return in mm. 72–3. Instead of the canonic texture of mm. 23–4,[18] Haydn borrows from mm. 51–2, in the development section, with the top two voices now moving in parallel thirds. Like the comparable place in the development section, here too the top two voices move in parallel thirds up to C/A, the fifth and seventh degrees of a

---

[18] The canonic texture is absent from mm. 72–3. But mm. 76–8, like their counterparts from the exposition (mm. 29–31), have canonic imitation between the upper and lower voices. Thus, although the canonic texture is omitted from mm. 72–3, it is preserved in mm. 76–8—which Haydn has now made into a related passage by the metamorphosis of mm. 72–3.

seventh chord—this time a dominant seventh chord—and resolve directly down by step to B/G (see Exx. 2.2 and 2.4).

On the most immediate level the specific alterations to mm. 23–4 that are made in mm. 72–3 serve to connect these latter measures with at least two other events in the composition. Yet the importance of these changes is not limited merely to motivic relationships and surface connections.

It is essential to remember that in the exposition mm. 23–4 were a dramatically disruptive and unstable event, a significant infringement of inter-opus norms. The alterations made in this passage when it is 'repeated' in the recapitulation serve not only to forge motivic connections with other passages in the movement; they also serve to resolve that instability. Unlike mm. 23–4, the passage in mm. 72–3 is fully integrated into the fabric. Its motive is not new and contrasting, but intimately related to the next prominent theme. It is not harmonically disjunct, but follows smoothly from the preceding applied dominant and proceeds directly to the tonic. Its voice-leading is not unorthodox, but completely unremarkable. In short, Haydn has woven an initially anomalous event back into the fabric of the movement, resolving its instabilities. This process works in tandem with and complements the harmonic function of the recapitulation, in which the large-scale instabilities occasioned by the tonicization of the secondary key in the exposition are finally resolved.

Tutenberg was right after all—the GP at m. 22 does have 'formal significance'. Understanding its role in the exposition is the key to the formal plan of the movement as a whole. Essential details of the development and recapitulation represent logical responses that Haydn devised to the extraordinary, formally significant, deflected cadence and improbable continuation from the exposition.

In Haydn's symphonies, a fast opening movement could be followed by one of only two possible types: a slow movement or a menuet. In a three-movement symphony—like the present work—the only possible choice was a slow movement. Contrast seems to be one of the basic principles that govern compositional choices for adjacent movements— and not only contrast in tempo.[19] In his early symphonies Haydn normally dropped the winds and horns from interior slow movements.[20] He also heightened contrast by employing new thematic ideas, by choosing a new meter, and frequently by casting slow movements (and often the trios from menuets) in closely related keys—in compositions in major the possible choices (in his early symphonies) were IV, V, i, and vi.

[19] See Webster, *Haydn's 'Farewell'*, 176–8.
[20] For a discussion of trends in instrumentation for slow movements during this period, see Dennis C. Monk, 'Style Change in the Slow Movement of the Viennese Symphony: 1740–1770', Ph.D. diss. (UCLA, 1971), i. 38–46.

For symphonies in D major before 1771, there does appear to be a pattern to Haydn's choices. Of the ten pre-1771 D major symphonies (Nos. 1, 4, 6, 10, 13, 15, 19, 24, 31, 72), none casts the slow movement in the dominant or the relative minor, and only two slow movements (Nos. 4 and 19) are in the parallel minor, both in symphonies with three movements. The slow movements in the remaining eight symphonies are all in G major, the subdominant. But after 1771 this consistency breaks down for the D major symphonies (until the final five, all of whose slow movements are in the subdominant). In any event, none of the other keys for symphonies appears to dictate the key of the slow movement at any point in Haydn's career. For example, there are ten symphonies in C major with interior slow movements dating from before 1771 (Nos. 2, 7, 9, 20, 30, 32, 33, 37, 38, 48). Of these, four are in the dominant, three in the subdominant, and three in the parallel minor.

Beyond the contrasts in tempo, theme, orchestration, meter, and key, it was well recognized that the formal plan of a slow movement might differ from that of the opening movement, and that the differences would often be apparent after the internal double bar. Here is how Heinrich Christoph Koch described the possible formal layout of the second half of a slow movement:

With the second section, the question is whether or not the andante is to be greatly extended. If the movement is to be very long, then it tends to have two main periods, which in their external structure are very similar to both those periods of the second section of the allegro described above . . . The most important external difference is that in the andante the melodic ideas are less extended and not so often compounded; thus more formal phrase-endings are used than in the the the allegro. . . .

On the other hand, if the andante is not to be very long, then these two periods are contracted into a single one. This happens if the working-out of the melodic ideas in the minor key of the sixth or second and the cadence in this key are omitted. After the theme has been presented in the fifth and there has been a modulation back to the main key, the minor key of the sixth, second, or third is touched either not at all or only in passing. Then the theme is repeated again or, without that repetition, those phrases which followed the V-phrase in the first period are presented again in the main key.[21]

It seems clear that the second movement of Symphony No. 1 exemplifies some of Koch's suggestions. It is readily apparent that, by comparison with the first movement, the 'melodic ideas are less extended and not so often compounded' in the Andante. There are also frequent cadences (in the exposition: mm. 4, 10, 20, 22–4, 28). Although it is less

---

[21] *Introductory Essay*, 201–2. Koch also remarks that formal types other than sonata form may also be employed in a slow movement (he mentions rondos and variations). But in Haydn's early symphonies, sonata forms are—by far—the most common formal type.

TABLE 2.2. *Symphony No. 1/ii: Correspondences between Exposition and Recapitulation; Two Viewpoints*

Scenario I: recapitulation begins in minor mode

Exposition, 28 mm.	(Development, mm. 29–49)	Recapitulation, 29 mm.
1–4		
5–10		— (but m. 50 ff similar to 5 ff—in parallel minor)
—		50–60
11–28		61–78 (transposed)

Scenario II: binary variant

Exposition, 28 mm.	(Development, mm. 29–60)	Recapitulation, 18 mm.
1–10		—
11–28		61–78 (transposed)

clear that Haydn was interested in abbreviating the movement, as per the other possibility suggested by Koch (the exposition is twenty-eight measures; the remainder of the work is almost twice as long: see Table 2.2), there is some doubt (as will be discussed in detail below) as to whether the opening theme is repeated at the beginning of the reprise, and where the reprise actually begins.

In contrast with the first movement, whose second half divides neatly into clearly demarcated sections (development section and recapitulation), the formal divisions in the second part of the second movement are far from unequivocal. By one scenario, the recapitulation might be said to begin in m. 50 with a minor-mode restatement of mm. 5 ff (see Ex. 2.5*a*, the first fourteen measures of the exposition, and Ex. 2.5*b*, the end of the development section and the beginning of the recapitulation), or, by another scenario, in mm. 61 ff with a transposition of mm. 11 ff to the tonic. In the latter case, this movement might be said to belong to a class of forms which has been given a wide variety of names in the musicological literature: 'binary sonata form', 'expanded binary form', 'binary variant', 'incomplete recapitulation', and 'polythematic binary form'.[22]

---

[22] Rey M. Longyear, 'Binary Variants of Early Classic Sonata Form', *Journal of Music Theory*, 13 (1969), 162–85; Jan LaRue, *Guidelines for Style Analysis* (New York, 1970), 188–9; James Webster, 'Binary Variants of Sonata Form in Early Haydn Instrumental Music', in Eva Badura-Skoda (ed.), *Joseph Haydn: Proceedings of the International Joseph Haydn Congress, Wien, 1982* (Munich, 1986), 127–35; Bathia Churgin, 'The Recapitulation in Sonata-Form Movements of Sammartini and Early Haydn Symphonies', ibid. 135–40; Rosen, *Sonata Forms*, 152–3; Bonds, 'Haydn's False Recapitulations', *passim*.

The second movement of this symphony offers a particularly useful opportunity to study Haydn's formal logic. We should like to be able to explain why by either scenario—and unlike the procedure in the first movement—the opening measures of the Andante do not return in the recapitulation.

In addition to the contrast in the number of cadences, a prominent difference between the first and second movements is in how concise they are in their use of motivic material. The first movement was rather prolix, jumping from one thematic idea to the next, none of them—at least initially—seeming particularly closely related. By contrast, in the second movement, even though there are a number of different thematic ideas, virtually every passage in the exposition (both in the tonic and dominant regions) contains some version of the opening motive of the composition (a descending, arpeggiated sixteenth-note triplet, followed by a succession of eighth-notes) or is derived by a smooth process of motivic transformation from that motive.

These two factors—the number of cadences and the motivic concision of the exposition—are essential determinants of the form in this movement. The premises are such that if the beginning of the exposition were repeated *in toto*, followed by a complete, transposed repetition of the dominant region, there would be clear redundancy, both cadential and thematic.

Even taking into consideration the more frequent number of cadences typical of slow movements (as compared with quick first movements), it should be at least intuitively clear that too many cadences would have resulted unless Haydn made some cut. If all the cadences from the exposition were preserved (appropriately transposed to the tonic when necessary), there would be at least three rather powerful authentic cadences as well as several strong half-cadences, all in the tonic key. So too, the frequent appearances of versions of the opening motive in both the tonic and dominant areas of the exposition would guarantee a degree of redundancy in the recapitulation were there not some cuts, for all of these statements would be in the tonic.

Yet another motivation for the excision of the opening measures of the exposition from the recapitulation can be traced to the development section. It has long been recognized that development sections in Haydn's early symphonic sonata forms often begin with a statement of the principal theme in the dominant which is followed immediately by a restatement of the theme in the tonic, after which the development

Webster does not include the present movement in his table 1 (p. 130), but lists it among a number of works in which the double return may arguably be present (p. 128). Bonds includes the movement in his list of recapitulations in the parallel mode (p. 241).

Ex. 2.5

(a)

(b)

'proper' begins.[23] But in the development sections of Haydn's early works, there are often areas in the tonic (sometimes quite extensive) not associated with the restatement of the principal theme.[24] The present movement is a case in point.

After the virtually obligatory restatement of the theme in the dominant after the double bar, Haydn returns to the tonic key in mm. 35–8, and leaves it for a moment in mm. 39–41, but is back again in mm. 42 ff, even confirming G major in mm. 44–5 with a V–I progression, highlighted by a dramatic change in texture. With the exception of the F♮ in m. 47 (immediately canceled in m. 48), the remainder of the development section (if we take it to end in m. 49) remains solidly in the tonic key.[25]

Even if the potential cadential and motivic redundancy was not enough to motivate the excision of the opening measures of the exposition from the recapitulation, the structure of the development section ensures that the recapitulation cannot mechanically follow the patterns of the exposition. The long emphasis on the tonic throughout the development section and, in particular, the prominent, almost cadential arrival on a root-position tonic triad in m. 45 add to the potential for redundancy already present in the material of the exposition. All of these factors combine to guide Haydn's decision to excise the opening measures of the exposition from the recapitulation. Beginning the recapitulation with a passage corresponding to m. 5 (or 11) can be ascribed, not merely to a vague compositional whim, but to the specific requirements of the material used in this composition.[26]

---

[23] Webster calls this restatement in the tonic an 'immediate reprise'. See 'Binary Variants', 128. Bonds divides binary variants into several subtypes. If the principal theme is stated in the tonic shortly after the beginning of the development section, but does not return at the beginning of the recapitulation, he classifies this as a 'disjunct recapitulation'. If the principal theme occurs both after the beginning of the development section and at the beginning of the recapitulation, he classifies this as a 'precursory recapitulation'. See 'Haydn's False Recapitulations', 220 ff.

[24] In many of Haydn's sonata forms, the restatement (in the tonic) in the development section of material first heard in the exposition makes unnecessary the restatement of that material in the recapitulation. See e.g. the Keyboard Sonata Hob. XVI: 2/i. The passage corresponding to mm. 6–21 is omitted from the recapitulation. But versions of almost all of the omitted measures occurred in the tonic key in the development section.

[25] For a survey of harmony in Haydn's development sections, see Harold L. Andrews, 'The Submediant in Haydn's Development Sections', in Larsen, Serwer, and Webster (eds.), *Haydn Studies*, 465–71.

[26] In Haydn's works, the procedure of beginning the recapitulation by excising the opening measures of the exposition can often—though not always—be explained as a response to the dictates of the redundancy principle. I will cite a few but, I believe, representative examples from other genres. In the String Trio Hob. V: 19/i, the recapitulation begins with a transposed version of m. 11. Since a variant of the opening material is present (in the tonic key) in the retransition (mm. 24 ff), just a few measures before the recapitulation (m. 32), a repetition of the opening theme in the tonic would be redundant. In the Keyboard Sonata Hob. XVI: 14/iii, the first ten measures of the exposition are excised from the beginning of the recapitulation. In the exposition, the opening theme appears, not only in the tonic (mm. 1–2 and 6–7), but also in sequence on inversions of V and vi (mm. 11–14), and, most importantly, initiates the dominant confirmation section (mm. 32–7). In the recapitulation, the

Normally speaking, in Haydn's symphonic sonata forms, unless there is a reason to the contrary, the definitive, functional return to the tonic in the latter third or so of the movement begins with a restatement of the opening measures of the composition. If we take m. 50 to be the point of return, then, at a minimum, Haydn has excised mm. 1–4 from the exposition, and we may quite reasonably ascribe this excision to the similarities between mm. 1 ff and mm. 5 ff (cf. Exx. 2.5*a* and *b*).

But it is by no means clear that the recapitulation begins in m. 50. Indeed, a strong case could be made that it does not begin until m. 61 (second scenario). Since mm. 50 ff are in the parallel minor, the sense of return is at least partially compromised and the sense of arrival is not totally satisfactory. Not until m. 61, when mm. 11 ff return, transposed to the tonic major, is the sense of return secure. In other words, the return of the minor tonic in m. 50 might be thought to be a kind of false reprise.[27]

The second movement of this symphony should serve as an instructive illustration of some of the dangers one can encounter when one assumes that there must be an unambiguous dividing line between the development section and recapitulation, or indeed that the two terms are always apt. In a considerable number of Haydn's sonata forms, the point of arrival of the return of the tonic and opening thematic material is purposefully ambiguous.

In many such cases, as in the present movement, an interplay with the listener's expectations is implied by the formal structure of the latter half of the movement.[28] When we arrive at m. 49 with its strongly articulated half-cadence, we might reasonably assume that the reprise will follow. But

equivalent of mm. 32–7, when transposed back to the tonic, would be virtually the same as the equivalent of mm. 1 ff. In the String Quartet Op. 1 No. 2/i, the recapitulation begins in m. 85 with the equivalent of the tenth measure of the exposition. Since mm. 1 ff are repeated in varied form in mm. 10 ff, the redundancy principle would motivate their excision from the recapitulation.

[27] For a similar example, see Symphony No. 24/i, m. 61. Bonds includes the minor reprise as one of his categories of false recapitulations: see 'Haydn's False Recapitulations', 241–4. Other cases in which the return of the opening theme in the parallel minor compromises the authority of the beginning of the reprise (or can be thought to be part of the development section): Nos. 19/iii, mm. 65 ff, 31/i, mm. 111 ff., and 47/i, mm. 114 ff. For an example in another genre, see the Keyboard Sonata Hob. XVI: 39/iii, mm. 69 ff. From these cases we might conclude that Haydn did not treat the tonic minor as a stable replacement for the tonic major. Other examples support this hypothesis: in Symphony No. 27/ii and iv, the tonic minor is used as the principal key of the development section; in No. 34/ii, the sudden turn to the tonic minor a few measures before the reprise helps make clear that the preceding passage in the tonic major did not initiate a definitive return to the tonic (see mm. 66–73). In No. 72/iii (Menuet), the restatement of the opening theme in the tonic minor marks the beginning of the A' section (m. 17). But Haydn 'corrects' this with a mini-coda (see mm. 29–32), restating the theme in major. For the past century or so, we have become accustomed to describing the parallel minor as a more-or-less stable substitute for the major ('mixture') and not as a destabilizing factor. Haydn's treatment suggests that it is a highly disruptive and destabilizing force, particularly when it occurs in a place where we had expected the major. See the analyses of Symphonies Nos. 81 and 85 in Chs. 7 and 8 below.

[28] See Bonds, 'Haydn's False Recapitulations', *passim*.

when m. 50 begins, we ought to be puzzled by the modal switch, which confounds the expectations for the return of the tonic in its original mode (an inter-opus norm). Have we really returned? Our sense of unease should be compounded by the continuation: with the virtually immediate tonicization of B flat major (mm. 51–4), Haydn makes us wonder whether the tonic has been reaffirmed after all—the tonic area in the development section was more solid than here. This view should be strengthened by the continuation, for with the arrival and then comparatively extended agogic emphasis on the dominant (mm. 57–60), the indications are that—finally—the definitive return to the tonic is at hand. However, after the strong half-cadence in m. 60, we hear not a return to the tonic with a restatement of the opening theme, but a transposed repetition of mm. 11 ff. Therefore, we may wish to amend our conclusions about what we have heard thus far. Perhaps m. 50 did mark the definitive return of the tonic.

In trying to understand the formal structure of this movement, much—too much—would be lost if we were to give a definitive answer to the question: 'Where does the recapitulation begin?' The (purposeful) ambiguities in the form of the second movement should encourage us to recognize that there is not always a single point which can be identified as the point of return. Haydn employs many different techniques to throw the definitive return to the tonic into doubt. The substitution of the parallel mode at the point of expected arrival is but one of these.[29]

In the first movement, we found that—following Jens Peter Larsen—a tripartite division of the exposition was a useful analytical tool, and that the specific responses of the recapitulation were predicated on the harmonic structure of the exposition. But the exposition of the second movement cannot be divided into three sections, and this, in turn, has a profound impact on the recapitulation (wherever it is that we feel it begins).

In the exposition of the second movement, the tonic definition section concludes in m. 10 with a half-cadence. Immediately following, in m. 11, we find that we have leapt, without transition, directly into the dominant key (see Ex. 2.5a above).[30] This kind of structure, with the dominant key established immediately after a half-cadence in the tonic, has been called a 'bifocal close'.[31]

---

[29] Other techniques include the use of a non-dominant chord (e.g. V/vi) at the end of the development section, the lack of any clear rhythmic articulation separating the development section and recapitulation, the departure from the tonic key, and the thematic parallels to the exposition immediately after the point of return. All of these techniques will be examined in subsequent chapters.

[30] Sonata forms with this type of harmonic structure in the exposition, though relatively rare in the symphonies, are more common in the keyboard sonatas: see Höll, *Studien zur Sonatensatz*, 14. They also occur in early string quartets, e.g. Op. 1 No. 6/i.

[31] Robert S. Winter, 'The Bifocal Close and the Evolution of the Viennese Classical Style', *Journal of the American Musicological Society*, 42 (1989), 275–337. When this close is found only in the exposition,

Ex. 2.6

When—as in m. 11—the dominant is established, not in the middle of
a transition section, but immediately after the tonic definition section, the
response of the recapitulation must be substantially different from that
which we found in the first movement. Instead of having to recompose
the transition section to remain in the tonic, Haydn could simply
transpose the entire dominant section down a fifth (or up a fourth). That
is precisely what he does in this movement. After coming to the literal
equivalent of the half-cadence of m. 10 (m. 60), Haydn continues, not in

Winter terms it 'expositional'. When it occurs in both the exposition and recapitulation, he calls it
'complementary'. Winter stresses that there are four conditions for the harmonic structure to be
classified as 'bifocal': '(1) a diatonic first group that reaches a half cadence on the dominant, (2) the
articulation of this half cadence by a prominent rest immediately after, (3) the continuation and
immediate tonicization in the second group of the local dominant harmony of the half cadence, and,
when an expositional bifocal close is carried into the recapitulation to create a complementary bifocal
close, (4) a parallel structure in the recapitulation in which the half cadence now functions as a local
dominant to the second group in the tonic.' See Winter's letter in 'Communications', *Journal of the
American Musicological Society*, 43 (1990), 160–1. The present movement is not included in Winter's list
of Haydn's symphonies that include bifocal closes: 'The Bifocal Close', 313. Although it may be
arguable whether the close in question meets all of Winter's four conditions (perhaps the rest is not
prominent enough; perhaps the tonicization of the dominant is not immediate and unequivocal
because of the overreach to G♯ and the octave texture), the structure seems so similar to that of the
bifocal close as defined and described by Winter, and has an identical formal function (complementary close and all), that I believe it warrants being added to his list.

the dominant key, but in the tonic (see Ex. 2.6). From m. 61 to the end of the recapitulation, he restates, in transposition and in its entirety, what was the dominant region of the exposition.

In forms with bifocal closes in the exposition, the recapitulation could be constructed so that it would be a virtually note-for-note, tonally modified, repetition of the exposition. That is, the recapitulation could repeat *in toto* the opening tonic definition section, up to the bifocal half-cadence, and then proceed by a complete restatement of what had been the dominant section, transposed to the tonic. No other changes would be necessary. But Haydn virtually never avails himself of this formal option in ambitious genres like the symphonies.[32] It is much more common in works like the early small-scale keyboard sonatas.[33] Rather, even when he employs the 'complementary' as well as the 'expositional' close, he makes other changes to prevent a strictly parallel correspondence between the exposition and recapitulation.[34] Perhaps his desire to avoid the literal parallelism of the exposition and recapitulation is another motivation for his decision to excise the beginning measures of the exposition and begin the (false?) reprise in the parallel minor.

Motivic concision, a bifocal cadence in the exposition, and extensive tonic emphasis in the development section are prominent features of this movement. They are not, however, external properties, separable from the formal structure. Rather, they are the very features that determine

---

[32] See e.g. Symphony No. 9/i. In the exposition, the half-cadence that ends in m. 23 is followed immediately in mm. 24 ff by the dominant region. In the recapitulation, the half-cadence ending in mm. 111 (= m. 23) is followed in m. 112 by a transposition back to the tonic of the equivalent of mm. 24 ff. Haydn could have continued from m. 112 to the end of the movement with a precise transposition of mm. 24–48, but instead made a number of changes in the recapitulation. Cf. mm. 32–3 with 120–2; mm. 41 with 130. This movement was not included in Winter's list, undoubtedly because there is no prominent rest after the half-cadence. However, by standing on the dominant chord for five measures (mm. 19–23), the effect is similar to that of a rest (the harmonic motion has ceased). Therefore, in the recapitulation, the complementary close can occur, followed by a transposition of the dominant material to the tonic. For another work with a complementary bifocal close (without a prominent rest) yet with an altered repetition, see Symphony No. 40/i. In another symphony (No. 27/i) where a half-cadence (m. 16) separates the tonic and dominant regions in the exposition, the recapitulation is almost an exact, tonally modified repetition of the exposition (they are both 41 measures long). The one significant alteration Haydn makes is to change the cadence in the recapitulation (cf. m. 83), landing on the tonic, not the dominant.

[33] E.g. Hob. XVI: 8/i and XVI: 10/i. Recapitulations which are literal (if tonally modified) repetitions of their expositions also occur in some early string quartet movements, though not with bifocal closes. Op. 1 No. 4/i, iii, and v (mm. 1–71) follow a procedure somewhat akin to a bifocal close. In the exposition, the opening section ends on the tonic, with the dominant tonicized immediately at the beginning of the 'transition' section. In the recapitulation, the opening section is repeated without change, while the dominant section is transposed down a fifth: e.g. Op. 1 No. 4/i: mm. 1–16 = 101–16; mm. 17–58 = 117–58 (transposed).

[34] The tendency to rewrite at least some of the recapitulation, even when a complementary bifocal close was used, can be found in genres other than the symphony, particularly works composed after the 1770s. For example, in the Keyboard Sonata Hob. XVI: 41/i, there is a clear bifocal close in the exposition in m. 20, with a complementary close in the recapitulation in m. 116. Presumably, Haydn could have made mm. 117 ff in the recapitulation a precise transposition to the tonic of mm. 21–55 from the exposition. But he diverges from the model in m. 129.

the form. The form of the second movement is different from that of the first because its premises are different.

Following a slow interior movement in Haydn's three-movement symphonies, there were but two possible continuations: a quick finale (Nos. 1, 2, 4, 10, 12, 16, 17, 19, 27, 30, and 107 (= 'A')) or menuet or tempo di menuet (Nos. 9, 18, 26). As with the first two movements, an essential principle of adjacent multimovement relationships seems to be contrast: compared with the second movement, the finale is in a different key (the tonic versus the subdominant), employs a different meter (3/8 versus 2/4), proceeds at a faster tempo (Presto versus Andante), returns to full orchestration, and has a new and completely different arsenal of thematic ideas. In the early symphonies, the quick finales (like that of Symphony No. 1) were usually sonata forms, but the final movements were generally somewhat less complicated and shorter (in terms of absolute time, if not in the number of measures) than first movements.[35] A comparison of the exposition and recapitulation of the finale of Symphony No. 1 suggests that its form is far simpler than that of either the first or the second movement (see Table 2.3).

TABLE 2.3. *Symphony No. 1/iii: Correspondences between Exposition and Recapitulation*

Exposition (mm.)	Recapitulation (mm.)
1–14	49–62
15–16	—
—	63–5
17–32	66–81 (transposed)

Given the relatively straightforward nature of the form of the finale, one might be tempted to ignore it altogether, as it includes none of the complications posed by either the first or the second movement. But the very fact that this movement is so apparently simple presents us with an interesting problem: What is there in the premises of the exposition that dictates such a schematic formal response in the recapitulation? If, as we saw in the first two movements, the complications in form were a consequence of the premises of the exposition and the development, then, here too, we should expect the overall simplicity of the form to be rooted

[35] The balance between the movements underwent considerable change during Haydn's career. See Bernd Sponheuer, 'Haydns Arbeit am Finalproblem', *Archiv für Musikwissenschaft*, 34 (1977), 199–224.

in the particular kinds of premises employed in the beginning half of the composition.

The exposition divides neatly into a tonic definition region (mm. 1–6), a transition (mm. 7–21), and a dominant confirmation section (mm. 22–32). Although each of these three sections concludes with an authentic cadence, no prominent pause follows the first two. While not devoid of motivic connections to the tonic region (cf. mm. 4 and 22), the material in the dominant region is distinct from that of the tonic section. The dominant key is first suggested in m. 13 and confirmed a few measures later. The development section is tiny and never strays far from the dominant, in which it begins and on which it ends.

As a result, the recapitulation is virtually predetermined. The sonata principle suggests that the entire dominant confirmation section should return transposed to the tonic. It does: mm. 71–81 = mm. 22–32. This same principle dictates that the transition section must be rewritten in order to prevent the dominant from being confirmed. It is: m. 63 cancels the tendency toward the dominant, and thus the latter half of the 'transition' in the recapitulation is a transposition of the end of the transition in the exposition: mm. 17–21 = 66–70. The unity principle would indicate that everything in the recapitulation should be derived from previously heard material. It is: every measure is either a literal repetition, a transposed repetition, or a slightly modified repetition. The redundancy principle would encourage the avoidance of excessive repetition of cadences or themes—but there is no redundancy to avoid. Even if we forget, for a moment, the greater redundancy that seems to have been characteristic of finales, neither the cadences nor the themes present any problem. The three cadences of the exposition do all return, yielding three authentic cadences in the tonic in the recapitulation. But since the first two of these cadences are not followed by marked pauses, they do not seem redundant in the recapitulation. Similarly, the thematic ideas of the dominant region in the exposition are sufficiently different from those of the tonic region that even when they are transposed back to the tonic, there is no thematic redundancy.

Simple—even simplistic—we might say. And with such a judgment, we would tend to ignore this movement, consigning it to a benign oblivion. But before we dismiss this work, we should note two tiny details in the development section, details so apparently insignificant that they might escape our attention. I am referring to mm. 37 and 46–7 (see Ex. 2.7). Is it possible that more consequential factors are at work?

On the face of it, m. 37 is unexceptional—simply a return to the tonic, a typical procedure at the beginning of Haydn's early development sections. This unobtrusive harmony is transformed immediately into a V/IV—also hardly shocking. Motivically, it is nondescript.

Ex. 2.7

What is odd about this measure is its rhythm, in particular the sudden agogic emphasis on the middle of the measure. This rhythmic pattern occurs nowhere else in the movement. So too, the triplets decorating the closing dominant chord of the development section (mm. 46–7) seem disjunct, having no rhythmic antecedent in the movement. Nor do they appear again.

It would be easy to dismiss these rhythmic anomalies as insignificant details, and perhaps they are. But it seems peculiar that in the context of a rather carefully controlled movement in which nothing else seems to be out of place, there are two ever so slight deviations from intra-opus norms.

Clearly, the very discontinuity of their rhythm means that these events do not—cannot—refer to anything in the finale. But is it possible that they could refer to anything else? I would like to consider the possibility that there may be connections with the first two movements.

The triplet sixteenth-note motive was, of course, the principal motive of the Andante, pervading its every corner. Normally, I would be loath to ascribe any particular significance to the appearance of such a common rhythmic figure in two movements. But the very fact that the triplet rhythm at the end of the development section of the finale was unprecedented within that movement might lend some credence to the connection with the Andante.

Even more suggestive is the other rhythmic anomaly, mm. 36–7. A crucial moment in the form of the first movement was the deflected cadence in m. 22. There, as here, an unprecedented rhythmic figure placed a startling emphasis on a weak beat. Again, while we might otherwise pay little notice to a figure like that in m. 37, the unprecedented nature of its appearance in the middle of the development section in the finale recalls one of the most significant events of the first movement.

We must, of course, be very skeptical of these connections. For one thing, it is all too easy to read into music ideas that reflect the biases of our own time—and it is a particular fetish of our age to hunt for unity in music.[36] And, in any event, we will scarcely be convinced by an isolated example.

If we are to approach this problem in a logical manner, we need to describe the basic principles of Haydn's multimovement organization and adopt procedures by which we could test the significance of putative relationships. To the extent that it is possible, this should help attenuate the inherent subjectivity of the whole endeavor. Although I do not want

---

[36] Modern ideas about intermovemental relationships differ considerably from 18th- and 19th-cent. notions, at least as expressed in the theoretical and aesthetic literature of the time. See Wilhelm Seidel, 'Schnell–Langsam–Schnell: Zur "klassischen" Theorie des instrumentalen Zyklus', *Musiktheorie*, 1 (1986), 205–16, and Webster, *Haydn's 'Farewell'*, 179–82.

to seem to be stealing a march on myself by anticipating the discussion of this topic that will occur in later chapters, where we will encounter multimovement relationships far less equivocal than those of Symphony No. 1, it would be useful to outline the central criteria of one of the two methods through which Haydn fostered multimovement unity and against which we can test the significance of relationships we discover. (The other method is not really applicable to Symphony No. 1 and will be discussed in Chapter 3.)

Haydn related apparently separate movements together by structuring the individual movements in such a way that they cannot be completely understood in isolation. An important feature of one movement is incomplete, or unsatisfactorily resolved, or anomalous, and is completed, or resolved, or explained only in a subsequent movement. The degree to which these multimovement relationships are musically significant is dependent on at least three factors: (1) the extent to which the anomalous events are disruptive within the movement in which they occur—the more extraordinary the events, the greater difficulty there is in understanding their role within the movement in which they appear, and the greater the potential importance; (2) the centrality of the event(s) to which they relate in the other movements—the more central the event(s), the more significant the relationship; (3) the extent of the similarity between the events—the greater the similarity, the more important the connection.[37]

If we test our observations about Symphony No. 1 against these criteria, we find that the proposed relationships are not convincing. To be sure, the two rhythmic anomalies cannot be completely understood within the finale itself, for they seem to relate to nothing within the movement. But it would be a gross exaggeration to state that they are exceptionally disruptive—they might better be described as a modest deviation from the intra-opus norms, a barely noticeable ripple in the flow of the movement. The events to which they supposedly relate are certainly central to the first and second movements—the extraordinarily important deflected cadence in m. 22 of the first movement and the omnipresent principal motive of the second. But what about the third criterion—the extent of the similarities? Can we really say that the similarities between the two anomalous events in the finale and the passages in the other two movements are especially strong? Certainly the difference in tempo

---

[37] Multimovement unity in Haydn's instrumental music has received increased attention of late. See my 'Haydn's Altered Reprise', *Journal of Music Theory*, 33 (1988), 335–51, and 'Remote Keys and Multi-movement Unity: Haydn in the 1790s', *Musical Quarterly*, 74 (1990), 242–68. The topic of multimovement unity, through-composition, and cyclic integration is thoroughly discussed in Webster, *Haydn's 'Farewell'*. I do not propose to duplicate Webster's exhaustive (and excellent) treatment of the subject, but will instead focus on how we may evaluate the strength of the relationships.

between the slow triplets of the Andante and the racing triplets in the finale should give us pause before we make too much of that relationship. And the minimal extent of the other anomaly—the odd rhythm is confined to a single measure—militates against assigning it much musical significance. Even more telling, perhaps, is the fact that the supposed anomalies occur in the final movement, making it impossible for them to be resolved by a later movement.

Where does this leave us? Are the movements related? We should not, I think, try to respond as if we were in a jury that was expected to hand down an unambiguous verdict ('related' or 'not related'). Since there is no external evidence (letters, theoretical works, interviews) that could be used to corroborate the hypothesis that Haydn planned multimovement relationships in this symphony (or in any other work), we must necessarily rely entirely on internal evidence, on relationships that we perceive in the music—which means that whatever evidence we advance is dependent on our subjective biases. Although everyone, presumably, would agree on a few obvious cases (like the recall of the Menuet in the finale of Symphony No. 46), most examples are not so clear-cut. The criteria outlined above should help to provide a basis for making objective judgments about the degree of relatedness, but they do not enable us to give an unequivocal, factual answer, at least for an isolated example. Rather, we might do better to rate the connections between movements on a scale (non-existent, weak, moderate, strong), reflecting our evaluation of the relationships. In my judgment, the connections between movements are, at best, extremely weak in this symphony.[38]

Although generalizations are particularly dangerous in Haydn's music, it is fair to say that the approach to form in the three movements of Symphony No. 1 is typical of what one is most likely to find in many of Haydn's early symphonies (those composed before the late 1760s). The recapitulation is usually a tonally adjusted, moderately varied, restatement of the exposition.[39] Generally speaking, there are no major interpo-

---

[38] It is important to keep in mind that there could be a number of different reasons why these connections appear so weak: (1) the relationships were intended by the composer, but were not intended to be a particularly important feature of the work—thus the degree of the relationship (weak) was intentional; (2) the composer intended to relate the movements to one another in a strong manner but was slightly inept and thus did not succeed in realizing his intentions; (3) the composer had no intention whatsoever of relating the movements to one another—the connections are entirely fictitious, imposed by a 20th-cent. analyst on the music; (4) the composer had no conscious intention of relating the movements to one another—the similarities are merely accidental byproducts of a composer's unconscious thought processes; (5) the composer intended the movements to be strongly related, but the analyst has found only some of the relationships and has overlooked the really important connections—the analyst is inept.

[39] It has been noted that the recapitulation should not be thought of as a 'repetition' of the exposition. See e.g. Charlotte L. Alston, 'Recapitulation Procedures in the Mature Symphonies of Haydn and Mozart', Ph.D. diss. (Univ. of Iowa, 1972), 37 ff.

lations into the recapitulations of passages that do not have a precise parallel in the exposition. Sometimes (as in the second movement) passages from the exposition do not return in the recapitulation—almost always owing to the redundancy principle. The development sections are generally fairly short, rarely straying to distant tonalities or placing much emphasis on anything more distant than the relative minor. Although some movements (like the finale) are almost completely schematic and predictable, many more are like the first movement, where the subtle and interesting recomposition of the recapitulation is the result of a flexible process of development and growth. And always, the specific shape of the form—what is kept, what is transposed, what is omitted—can be explained, not as a set of arbitrary compositional decisions, but as the consequence of the application of a limited set of compositional principles to the premises of the individual work.

3

Symphony No. 21

(1764)

EVERYTHING—as the saying goes—is relative. If so, then Symphony No. 1 is a typical work, for many of Haydn's symphonies from the late 1750s and early 1760s have similar overall plans and similar treatments of the forms of the individual movements. By the same standards, Symphony No. 21 is an extremely unusual symphony. As such, it is a particularly useful subject for analysis, offering us a valuable opportunity to test our understanding of Haydn's formal procedures against a number of problematic movements.

The most immediately apparent difference from Symphony No. 1 is its multimovement plan. Unlike the earlier work, Symphony No. 21 begins with a complete slow movement.[1] To be sure, by itself that was not remarkable. Seven early symphonies (Nos. 5, 11, 18, 21, 22, 34, and 49) begin with slow movements, and they all have the same approximate overall plan: a slow first movement, a quick second movement, then a menuet, followed by a quick finale. (Symphony No. 18, in three movements, omits the quick finale and closes with the menuet.) Even though this pattern was not particularly unusual, a slow opening movement is always a sign that some important aspect of the symphony is going to be highly unusual, a significant deviation from the norms of his symphonic writing.

Sometimes the unusual feature is the implied genre: the first movements of Symphonies Nos. 11 and 18 are much like trio sonatas, with the first and second violins weaving imitative polyphony above a walking bass; the first movement of Symphony No. 5 is a quasi-concerto for horns, with the first horn even reaching up to a sounding *a″*. In one case, it is the instrumentation that is out of the ordinary: uniquely among his symphonies, No. 22 employs English horns in place of oboes. Or, in two cases (Symphonies Nos. 34 and 49), the works are in minor—and one

---

[1] Landon has described Haydn's symphonies with an opening slow movement as having a plan derived from the baroque *sonata da chiesa* and has speculated that they may have been meant for performance in church. See *The Symphonies of Joseph Haydn*, 217 and 253–4. Neal Zaslaw, in 'Mozart, Haydn, and the *Sinfonia da Chiesa*', *Journal of Musicology*, 1 (1982), 114–15, and *Mozart's Symphonies: Context, Performance Practice, Reception* (Oxford, 1989), 80–3, evaluates the evidence for performances of symphonies in church in general, and questions Landon's suggestion.

scarcely need mention that minor keys were quite rare in Haydn's early symphonies. (The only other minor-key symphonies written before 1770 are Nos. 26 and 39.)[2]

Symphony No. 21 does not make use of unusual instrumentation, nor is it in a minor key. But the genre of the first movement is quite problematic. It appears to start as if it were a concerto for two oboes—short ritornelli, first on the tonic and then on the dominant in the strings, alternating with brief solo passages for the oboes. However, the concerto aspects of the movement disappear fairly quickly and the strings take over. Between mm. 16 and 45, the oboes appear just once, for three measures, in a doubling of the strings. Through the remainder of the movement, the oboes revert to their customary role of loose doubling of the violins with occasional solos—hardly what we might expect from a concerto (see Ex. 3.1).

Even beyond issues of genre, key, and instrumentation, Haydn's symphonies with opening slow movements often make use of atypical formal types—and not only in the first movements. That certainly is the case here, as the second movement has a mirror recapitulation, while the fourth movement is a binary variant of sonata form. But the most unusual form by far is found in the first movement, a formal type unlike any other movement in Haydn's symphonies.

Or perhaps one should ask: Form? What form? For the form of this movement is not only unique, it is recondite, amorphous. Simply put, it does not correspond well to any commonly recognized formal type—it is not easily classified as a rondo, nor as a set of variations, nor as a ternary form.[3] On first hearing (but only on first hearing) one might suspect for a few measures that this could be a slow introduction to a quick movement. But the size of the movement (too long) and its eventual close on the tonic (introductions usually end on the dominant) should effectively dispel that notion.

One could try to consider it a kind of sonata form, but even this does not work particularly well. Although there is a development-like passage approximately in the middle of the work (mm. 29–41), and although the opening theme does return after that point in the tonic key (m. 49), the

[2] Landon surveyed 7,000 18th-cent. symphonies, and reported that only 2% are in minor keys. See his 'La Crise romantique dans la musique autrichienne vers 1770', in André Verchaly (ed.), *Les Influences étrangères dans l'œuvre de W. A. Mozart* (Paris, 1956), 31. This figure is lower than that reported by Roger Kamien in his discussion of style change, in 'The Opening Sonata-Allegro Movements in a Randomly Selected Sample of Solo Keyboard Sonatas Published in the Years 1742–1774 (Inclusive)', Ph.D. diss. (Princeton Univ., 1964), i. 34. Eleven of Haydn's 107 symphonies are in minor keys: *c.*10%. Two other 18th-cent. Austrian symphonists wrote disproportionately large numbers of minor-key symphonies: Gassmann, 9%, and Vanhal (Wanhal, etc.), 11%. See George R. Hill, 'The Concert Symphonies of Florian Leopold Gassmann', Ph.D. diss. (New York Univ., 1975), 102.

[3] Landon remarks that 'the movement is worked out in very free form, almost like a fantasie', and that it is 'one of the most original single movements' of the early symphonies. See *The Symphonies*, 257.

Ex. 3.1

cadences present a serious problem. Normally, we expect the exposition to conclude with an authentic cadence in the dominant and the development section with a half-cadence on the dominant. In this movement, there are no such cadences at the points that we might reasonably consider to be the end of the exposition or the development. Indeed the 'development section' concludes with no cadence at all, but a V_2^4–I^6 progression which leads, not to the opening theme stated in the tonic (that comes only in m. 49), but to a passage that is similar to the first oboe solo

and almost identical to what had sounded like a closing theme in mm. 22–4.

The harmonic plan also cannot easily be reconciled with the general expectations for sonata forms. The dominant is reached fairly quickly and the opening 'ritornello' is restated in the dominant in m. 13, but this restatement is broken off early, and Haydn turns right back to the tonic, restating the opening theme in sequence (mm. 16 ff.). Not until m. 26 is the dominant suggested again. Before it can be confirmed, Haydn launches into another sequence, this one modulatory. When we finally

Ex. 3.2

break out of the modulatory passage at m. 42, we are already back in the tonic key, leading in short order to an authentic cadence in the tonic (m. 48: see Ex. 3.2). Since there has been no extended statement in the dominant key, nothing is subject to the sonata principle, nothing needs to be brought back to the tonic.

What we do find, if not a recognizable formal type, is an exceptionally thorough and continuous development of the principal theme of the movement. Not only is the theme itself (or a subsection thereof) almost always explicitly present, it also can be seen to form the basis of some of the apparently contrasting material. For example, the opening statement in the oboes might appear to be a contrasting theme. But, much like the ritornello theme in the strings, it too begins on the fifth degree of the scale and steadily works its way down in decorated parallel thirds to the tonic.

The lack of a convincing formal model for the first movement is only the first indication that this symphony is atypical. (We will return to discuss some of the other problems raised by the first movement at the end of this chapter.) The formal type found in the second movement is also relatively unusual (see Table 3.1), as the recapitulation begins with something other than the opening theme, which returns instead at the end of the movement.

TABLE 3.1. *Symphony No. 21/ii: Correspondences between Exposition and Recapitulation*

Exposition (mm.)	Recapitulation (mm.)
1–9	— (but see coda)
10–15	66–71
—	71–4
15–21	—
21–42	74–95 (transposed; some variants, e.g. mm. 32–3 and 85–6)
—	95–102 Coda (but mm. 95–9 = 1–5)

When the opening material does not return at the beginning of the recapitulation, but is instead transplanted to the end as a coda, a movement is said to have a mirror recapitulation.[4] This is not a particularly common formal type in Haydn's works in general, nor in the symphonies in particular.[5] And it should not escape notice that the early

[4] Bonds, 'Haydn's False Recapitulations', 286–94.
[5] Other symphonies with this feature are Nos. 15/i (Presto), 31/i, 59/iv, 44/iv, 81/i, and (possibly) 87/iv.

symphonies in which it occurs (Nos. 15, 21, 31 ('Hornsignal'), 59 ('Feuer-symphonie'), and 44 ('Trauersymphonie')) are among the most striking and unusual of Haydn's symphonies.

Whether or not a specific movement is an instance of a usual or an unusual formal type, we would like to be able to explain how its premises support and motivate the form (or vice versa).[6] In the present instance, that means we would like to be able to explain why Haydn omitted mm. 1–9 from the beginning of the recapitulation and transplanted the first five measures to the end of the movement.

The key to understanding the motivation for the use of a mirror recapitulation in this movement lies in the nature of the opening material. The movement begins in a rather distinctive manner. Instead of a complete triad, the opening *coup d'archet* is composed of bare octaves, as are the tutti strokes on the downbeats of mm. 3 and 5 and the aggressive running eighths in between. Even the next three measures (7–9) are very nearly entirely in octaves, as the oboe and lower strings are essentially doublings of the lowest and highest notes of each group of four eighth-notes in the violins (see Ex. 3.3).

What makes this opening particularly striking is the contrast with the continuation. Beginning in m. 10, Haydn turns to full sonorities, leaving the octaves behind. Although there are definite rhythmic connections (and some underlying thematic relationships),[7] the theme beginning in m. 10 is effectively new. As the piece proceeds, we find that this is not merely a local contrast. Not until the closing measures of the movement does the octave sonority or its associated theme return—not anywhere in the exposition, not even in the development section, nor in the recapitulation. The octave sonority returns only in the coda. It appears as if the opening measures are a kind of introduction—not a slow introduction, but a clearly distinct section nevertheless.

Thus the excision of mm. 1–9 from the beginning of the recapitulation is a logical step, given Haydn's compositional principles. As the material of the opening measures had been entirely excluded from the remainder of the exposition and the development section, it would make little sense for it to reappear suddenly at the beginning of the recapitulation, where, given the complete exclusion of the octaves and the opening theme since m. 9, it could seem to be a discontinuous event.

If that is so, why do the opening measures return after the end of the recapitulation as a coda? Certainly, opening slow introductions do not

---

[6] We can make two complementary assertions about Haydn's symphonies: a certain formal type (e.g. mirror recapitulation) will require certain premises (a same-tempo, quasi-introduction); or, certain premises (e.g. a same tempo, quasi-introduction), will cause specific formal structures to result (a mirror recapitulation). However, what motivated Haydn to decide to write a movement with a mirror recapitulation (or any other formal type) is a question that lies beyond the scope of this study.

[7] The underlying stepwise line from A to E in the violins in mm. 1–2 is stated directly on the surface and extended down to C♯ in the topmost line in mm. 10–11.

Ex. 3.3

normally return as codas in Haydn's symphonies—at least not until
Symphony No. 103, written more than thirty years after No. 21.[8]

    There are some crucial differences between slow introductions and the
passage in mm. 1–9. Slow introductions contrast far more sharply with

---

[8] The only exception: the slow introduction of Symphony No. 6/ii does return to close the
movement, but this may have been prompted by the implied genre (concerto). The opening Adagio
of Symphony No. 15/i also returns to close the movement. However, a number of features (the tonal
plan, the absence of the oboes, and its closure of the movement) make it clear that it is no
introduction. See Webster, *Haydn's 'Farewell'*, 251–3.

their following quick movements than is the case in this movement: here, the tempo is the same, the rhythm of the principal theme (m. 10) is the same as the opening, and there are some similarities between the motives. We recognize that the first nine measures comprise an introduction only gradually and in retrospect as it becomes apparent that the change in texture and theme beginning at m. 10 was not a local contrast, but a long-term abandonment of the opening idea. In comparison with the usual slow introduction, this introduction is more integrated into the movement and less separable. As such, the corollary of the unity principle states that it should be brought back somewhere in the movement.

This presents Haydn with a problem in compositional logic. Although the introduction is similar, it is sufficiently different that it cannot be integrated easily into the body of the movement, particularly the recapitulation. But once the sonata principle has been satisfied, once the parallels with the exposition have been completed, and once the recapitulation is over, it should be possible to append the opening material to the form—and, in so doing, satisfy the corollary of the unity principle. Therefore, Haydn returned to the material from the opening bars in a coda, after the movement proper had been completed.

If this hypothesis is correct, if the mirror recapitulation in Symphony No. 21/ii is indeed motivated by its quasi-introduction, then we should expect Haydn's other mirror recapitulations to have similar premises. They do. All of the mirror recapitulations in his symphonies (Nos. 15/i (Presto), 21/ii, 31/i, 59/iv, 44/iv, 81/i, and 87/iv) have precisely the same premise—a quasi-introduction in the same tempo as the rest of the movement and including a texture, theme, or instrumentation that contrasts with the body of the movement and returns at the end of the movement as a coda.[9]

If we turn our attention to an analysis of the compositional logic of the main body of the movement (between the introduction and the coda), we see that, as in Symphony No. 1/ii, the exposition of Symphony No. 21/ii

---

[9] In Nos. 15/i (Presto) and 44/iv, the introductory texture is not entirely absent from the body of the movement, as it returns at the beginning of the development section. In No. 87/iv, the quasi-introduction even concludes with a fermata. In No. 59/iv, the theme returns at the beginning of the recapitulation, but in the strings, not in the unaccompanied horns as at the beginning of the movement. Symphony No. 81/i will be discussed in detail in Ch. 7. Mirror recapitulations also appear, though rarely, in other genres. See the String Quartet Op. 1 No. 1/iii, which—like the symphonies—has a quasi-introduction that returns as a coda. Bonds, 'Haydn's False Recapitulations', 287, identifies the string quartets Op. 2 No. 6/v and Op. 71 No. 2/ii as having mirror recapitulations, as the opening theme of each returns as a coda. However, in both of these cases, the recapitulation begins with the principal theme (or a closely related variant). A similar treatment of the mirror recapitulation occurs in the Keyboard Sonata Hob. XVI: 34/i. Mm. 1–8 close with a fermata, separating this passage off as a quasi-introduction. These measures are excised from the beginning of the recapitulation, but return—partially—as a coda (mm. 124 ff.). Note, however, that m. 9 begins with the same theme as m. 1.

cannot be subdivided into three distinct harmonic regions. Instead, it
divides neatly into tonic and dominant regions (mm. 1–16 and 17–42),
separated by the half-cadence at m. 16—another bifocal close. But unlike
Symphony No. 1/ii, the present work does not have a complementary
half-cadence in the corresponding place in the recapitulation. Instead, as
can be seen from Table 3.1, Haydn excises the passage corresponding to
mm. 15–21—including the bifocal half-cadence—from the recapitulation
before making his way back to the transposition of mm. 21–42 to the
tonic.

Although Haydn's decision to omit the bifocal close is in keeping with
his general tendency to avoid extended literal repetitions (particularly in
the sonata form movements of his symphonies), his motivations here are
more complex. In addition to omitting the bifocal close, he has cut out
the theme that had been stated at the beginning of the dominant section.
Since this theme was a rather prominent event and was stated in the
dominant, we might have thought that it should be subject to the dictates
of the sonata principle and should return in the recapitulation, transposed
to the tonic.

Ex. 3.4

(a)

(b)

But the passage does not return. Simply put, mm. 17 ff (Ex. 3.4*b*) do
not return in the recapitulation because their thematic material is only
slightly different from that of the principal theme beginning in m. 10 (Ex.
3.4*a*). In the exposition, the two passages were in different keys—tonic
and dominant—and therefore did not violate the redundancy principle.
But in the recapitulation, mm. 17 ff would be transposed back to the tonic
and would be so similar to the principal theme that its repetition would
violate this principle.

By comparison with the last movement of Symphony No. 1, and many
other of his early symphonies, the form of the second movement is
certainly unusual. Haydn's decisions to excise the opening measures, to
transplant them to the end as a coda, and to excise part of the exposition
from the recapitulation are intimately related to the details on the surface.
They flow from the same principles and the same compositional logic that

govern form in more 'typical' movements. The difference is not the compositional principles, but the specific premises of the work.

The third movement is a Menuet and Trio.[10] As inherited by Haydn, the menuet and trio was normally structured as a large-scale ternary form with three discrete, tonally self-contained sections, the last a literal repetition of the first (menuet–trio–menuet). While the menuet was always assigned the overall tonic of the composition, the trio was sometimes cast in a closely related key—frequently the parallel minor—although often neither key nor mode was changed.[11] The menuet and trio was not an invariable component of Haydn's earliest symphonies,[12] but by the mid-1760s, it had become standard.[13] In his early symphonies, explicit connections are rarely found between the menuet and its trio, excepting only the occasional use of similar incipits or cadential clichés.[14]

Usually both the menuet and the trio are cast in binary forms—sometimes simple binary, but most often rounded binary with a double return of the tonic and the opening motive approximately midway through the second section.[15] As such, the familial connection with sonata form is

---

[10] Haydn used 'the spelling "minuet" only up to (and including 1760.' Landon, *Chronicle and Works*, i. 230 and 295. From 1761 on, he employed 'menuet' (or 'menuetto'). See Georg Feder, 'Zur Datierung Haydnscher Werke', in Joseph Schmidt-Görg (ed.), *Anthony van Hoboken: Festschrift zum 75. Geburtstag* (Mainz, 1962), 53–4.

[11] For tables showing the key-choice for trios in Haydn's symphonies, see Gretchen A. Wheelock, 'Wit, Humor, and the Instrumental Music of Joseph Haydn', Ph.D. diss. (Yale Univ., 1979), 177.

[12] There is no menuet (or tempo di menuetto) in nine early symphonies: Nos. 1, 2, 4, 10, 12, 16, 17, 19, 27.

[13] When and where the menuet and trio became a standard component of the multimovement cycle and in what manner the four-movement pattern of fast–slow–menuet + trio–fast became normative has been a subject of scholarly debate for more than half a century. See Jens Peter Larsen, 'Some Observations on the Development and Characteristics of Viennese Classical Instrumental Music', *Studia musicologica, Academiae scientarium Hungaricae*, 9 (1967), 115–39, repr. in Larsen, *Handel, Haydn*, 227–49, also repr. in Rosand (ed.), *History of Western Music*, vii. 47–71; see also Landon, *The Symphonies*, 216. For a summary of the possible influence of Johann Stamitz on Haydn's gradual adoption of the 'standard' four-movement plan (fast–slow–menuet + trio–fast), see Wolf, *The Symphonies of Johann Stamitz*, 86–91; for a related discussion see Zaslaw, *Mozart's Symphonies*, 19. The inclusion of menuets in the symphony was not universally accepted—some critics felt it was an inappropriate type of movement for a symphony. For a discussion, see Wheelock, 'Wit, Humor', 47, 90, and *passim*. See also Wheelock, *Haydn's Ingenious Jesting with Art: Contexts of Musical Wit and Humor* (New York, 1992), 33–51.

[14] For a general discussion of this topic and a survey of compositions with motivic connections between menuets and trios, see von Tobel, *Die Formenwelt*, 129–31. Relatively obvious motivic connections between the menuet and trio are occasionally found in Haydn's symphonies, though usually restricted to the first measure or two of each. See Symphonies Nos. 23/iii and 24/iii. Explicit connections between the menuet and trio do occur somewhat more frequently in other genres. See e.g. the Baryton Trio Hob. XI: 51/iii.

[15] For examples of simple binary see Symphonies Nos. 23/iii (Trio) and 33/iii (Trio). Simple binaries are relatively rare in the symphonies and sometimes result from some special compositional or orchestrational technique. In Symphony No. 23/iii, there is no B section in either the Menuet or the Trio, a consequence of the strict canonic writing. There are occasional exceptions to formal regularity (clear binary or rounded binary), usually involving the use of incomplete forms. For example, in the second movement of the String Quartet Op. 9 No. 1, the Trio (in C minor) moves

quite evident,[16] and it is often possible to see the forms of the menuet and
trio as having similar structures.[17] Frequently, however, precisely because
of their shorter dimensions, these forms present compositional problems—and as a consequence demand solution—different in important
respects from those we have seen in the larger sonata forms.[18]

Ex. 3.5

to E flat at the double bar, and then proceeds through a B section which we would expect should
end on the dominant of C, preparing a return of the tonic and opening theme. The expected cadence
on G does occur, but the A section never returns—Haydn goes directly back to the Menuet without
a reprise of the A section. For a similar example, see Symphony No. 50/iii.

[16] Finscher sees Haydn as expanding the rounded binary forms of menuets into what he sees as
genuine sonata form movements as early as the Op. 9 string quartets. See *Studien zur Geschichte*, 214.

[17] Some 18th-cent. theorists treated the smaller dance forms as models for larger compositions.
Koch, for example, took some pains to demonstrate how to expand a simple dance composition into
a larger form. For discussions of this topic, see Leonard G. Ratner, 'Eighteenth-Century Theories of
Musical Period Structure', *Musical Quarterly*, 42 (1956), 439–54, repr. in Rosand (ed.), *History of Western
Music*, vii. 85–100, and Sisman, 'Small and Expanded Forms'. Rosen, though he acknowledges the
role binary forms played in the development of sonata forms, argues that sonata forms have a much
more complicated genealogy, with influences not only from binary forms, but also from aria and
concerto. See *Sonata Forms*, 16–132.

[18] In some cases (as here), the A' section may bear only a rough resemblance to the A section.
Sometimes only the end of the A section is restated in the tonic (Symphony No. 23/iii (Trio)—in this
case, just the cadence formula), other times only the beginning of the A section (No. 11/iii (Minuet)).

That is immediately apparent in the Menuet of Symphony No. 21. In contrast to the typical harmonic plan of a sonata form, which involves a cadence in the dominant at the internal double bar, this menuet closes in the tonic at that point (m. 8). The opening section (mm. 1–8) divides neatly into two parts, the first a four-measure phrase ending on a half-cadence, the second another four-measure phrase, concluding with an authentic cadence in the tonic (see Ex. 3.5).[19]

The harmonic plan of this opening section is but one of three basic plans Haydn normally employed in the A sections of his menuets and trios. The other possibilities include a close with an authentic cadence in the dominant key[20] and, less often, a close with a half-cadence in the tonic key.[21] Although the modulating A section is more common than the other two types, the type with the close on the tonic occurs frequently. And it would be a mistake to assume that because of its apparent harmonic simplicity, the non-modulating A section represents a primitive version that Haydn outgrew—examples of this type can be found at the very end of his career as a symphonist (e.g. Symphonies Nos. 100/iii (Menuet and Trio), 102/iii (Trio), 103/iii (Trio), 104/iii (Menuet)).

Given Haydn's basic compositional principles, each of these types of openings circumscribes a range of possible responses in the latter half of the work. In the type represented by the present case (where the A section does not modulate to the dominant, but remains entirely in the tonic, with a perfect authentic cadence at the double bar), the A section could conceivably be repeated *in toto* and without alteration after the B section.[22]

For a description of the different degrees of 'rounding', from non-rounded to sonata form, see Tilden A. Russell, 'Minuet, Scherzando, and Scherzo: The Dance Movement in Transition, 1781–1825', Ph.D. diss. (Univ. of North Carolina at Chapel Hill, 1983), 51–6.

[19] For a discussion of phrase structure in Haydn's menuets, see Wolfram Steinbeck, *Das Menuett in der Instrumentalmusik Joseph Haydns* (Munich, 1973). Following Koch, analyses of menuets often start from a consideration of the phrase structure, regarding four-measure phrases as the underlying (though rarely realized) norm. See e.g. Forschner, *Instrumentalmusik Joseph Haydns*, 138 ff.

[20] In a menuet or trio in a minor key, the cadence before the internal double bar would normally be in the relative major. Exceptions exist: see Symphonies Nos. 37/ii (Trio) and 52/iii (Menuetto) and String Quartet Op. 9 No. 4/ii.

[21] There are occasional exceptional works that do not conform to either of these plans. The Trio of Symphony No. 36/iii is in B flat major, yet at the internal double bar it cadences in D minor. This is a particularly unusual movement (see the problematic reprise—is it at m. 49 or 53?). There may be an antecedent for this event in the second movement (also in B flat), where there is a brief emphasis on D minor (mm. 10–11) in between the opening tonic and the arrival on the dominant.

[22] The (supposedly) standard menuet was sixteen measures long, subdivided into two periods, each consisting of two four-measure phrases. In works of this size, therefore, it would not be possible to repeat, *in toto*, a non-modulating A section (which includes eight measures) after the B section. However, a related formal technique is possible: if the first four-measure phrase (mm. 1–4) concludes with an appropriately final authentic cadence in the tonic, then the final four-measure phrase (mm. 13–16) can be a literal repetition of the first phrase. There are no examples of this formal procedure in Haydn's symphonies, but they do occur in other genres: see the Baryton Trio Hob. XI: 43/ii. In any event, sixteen-measure menuets (or trios) are virtually nonexistent in the symphonies. The exceptions (Nos. 24/iii (Trio), 51/iii (both Menuet and Trio I), 58/iii (Trio)) include some of Haydn's

The lack of a modulation to the dominant means that there is nothing within the A section that would be subject to the sonata principle. And, in many cases where the A section concludes on the tonic, Haydn does indeed repeat it, unaltered, as the A′ section.

It is important to note that there seems to be a substantial difference between the ways in which Haydn treats the non-modulating A section in a menuet and a similar A section in a trio. Generally speaking, in his menuets Haydn avoids making the A′ section a literal restatement of the A section. On the other hand, literal repetitions are quite common in the trios.[23] It appears to have been the norm to make the trio simpler, at least formally.[24] This is further evidence that the redundancy principle was not an absolute compositional principle that was applied the same way in every movement. Rather, its specific threshold appears to have been somewhat dependent on genre, with different standards applicable in different kinds of movements.

This means that in menuets (but not necessarily in trios), Haydn often makes alterations in the A′ section to prevent a literal repetition of the non-modulating A section.[25] This is particularly so where there is redundancy within the A section itself (that is, when the second phrase is based on the same thematic material as the first). For example, in the

most unusual menuets. Where sixteen-measure menuets and trios do occur with some regularity is in genuine dance music. See e.g. the collection of Twelve Menuets, Hob. IX: 11 (−25 Nov. 1792, written for a charity ball in Vienna's Redoutensaal). Eleven of the twelve are in two halves of eight measures each.

[23] A′ sections which are literal repetitions of the A sections are found in the trios of the following twenty-four symphonies: Nos. 6, 9, 18, 26, 28, 34, 41, 53, 54, 56, 61, 62, 71, 72, 74, 75, 76, 78, 79, 80, 85, 87, 90, 103. By contrast, they appear in the menuets of only ten works: 21, 28, 29, 39, 69, 71, 74, 75, 76, 79. The contrast is even sharper than the ratio might indicate. Although trios with literal repetitions of the A sections occur throughout his output, most of the literally minded menuets were composed in a relatively brief period (late 1770s − early 1780s) in works that may have been written in a deliberately simplified or popular style designed for commercial success. It should be recalled that Haydn had renegotiated his contract with Prince Esterházy in 1779 with the express purpose of gaining control of his compositions so that he could bargain directly with publishers for the sale of his works. See Landon, *Chronicle and Works*, ii. 42.

[24] See Wheelock, 'Wit, Humor', 194. In the late 18th cent., in general, trios tended to be simpler than menuets. See Russell, 'Minuet and Scherzando', 230.

[25] Sometimes Haydn makes variations in the A′ section itself (e.g. Symphonies Nos. 18/iii, 14/iii); in other cases, the A′ section is a literal repeat of the A section, but Haydn appends a coda after the A section is complete, or nearly so (e.g. Nos. 8/iii, 9/iii). In some works with non-modulating A sections, there is no double return of tonic and opening theme—these are better thought of as simple, not rounded, binaries. An interesting example of this type is String Quartet Op. 2 No. 6/iv (Menuetto). Although this movement is more akin to a simple binary than a rounded binary (the return of the tonic is not articulated harmonically, rhythmically, or thematically), aspects of the opening measures are retained, even while the passage is completely rewritten. See Webster, 'Freedom of Form in Haydn's Early String Quartets', in Larsen, Serwer, and Webster (eds.), *Haydn Studies*, 524. Simple binary forms are relatively common in Haydn's early works. In some, not only is there no return of A-section material simultaneous with the return of the tonic, but also, not even a 'rhyming termination' occurs. For example, in Symphony No. 3/iii (Trio) (−1762), not a single measure in the second half corresponds precisely to any measure in the first half.

Ex. 3.6

(a)

(b)

Menuet of Symphony No. 20 (–1766), the A section (mm. 1–8), which closes in the tonic, can be subdivided into two phrases, both of which begin with precisely the same material (see Ex. 3.6*a*).

Even though the harmonic structure might suggest that Haydn could repeat the A section without alteration, the redundancy in motivic structure suggests otherwise. Thus, the A′ section is not a literal repetition of the A section, but rather, in m. 27 he diverges from the model of the opening measures, touching on the subdominant (see Ex. 3.6*b*).[26]

When a non-modulating A section is motivically diverse, or when its several phrases are made up of contrasting material (the contrast need not be sharp), or when it is formed of a number of variants of a central idea rather than of an antecedent–consequent pair of phrases, the A′ section can be a literal repeat of the A section. For instance, in the Menuet of Symphony No. 28 in A major (1765), the A section (mm. 1–8) concludes with an authentic cadence in the tonic (see Ex. 3.7). After the half-cadence at the end of the B section, the A section returns, note for note (mm. 25–32). In comparison with the example from Symphony No. 20, there is a little more motivic diversity (cf. mm. 1–4 and 5–8, which are not a

Ex. 3.7

---

[26] Curiously, when Koch used this menuet as an example in the *Versuch*, he used a version in which mm. 23–30 were identical in every respect to mm. 1–8. See *Introductory Essay*, 123.

motivically unified antecedent–consequent pair of phrases), and thus the literal repetition after the B section does not trigger the redundancy principle.[27]

If the different kinds of responses we have seen in the menuets of Symphonies Nos. 20 and 28 can indeed be traced to the motivic structure of their respective A sections, we should then be able to look at the Menuet of Symphony No. 21 and, through an analysis of its A section, be capable of predicting what will happen in the A′ section.

As we see in Ex. 3.5 above, the two phrases of the A section give a fairly clear impression of diversity. The second phrase contrasts sharply in dynamics, in orchestration, in the rhythm of the accompaniment, and in the register of the uppermost voice.[28] This means that this example is similar to the type represented by the Menuet of Symphony No. 28, and thus the A′ section could be a complete and literal repetition of the A section.

And so it is—almost. With the exception of a slight change in the lower voices in the first two measures, mm. 25–32 are a literal repetition of mm. 1–8. (We will discuss the possible significance of that slight alteration in due course.)

By contrast, the phrase structure of the A section of the Trio is much more symmetrical than that of the Menuet. Rather than contrasting phrases, the first two measures of the Trio are immediately repeated, and the second phrase begins in the same manner (see Ex. 3.8).

In a menuet, this kind of symmetry would undoubtedly lead to a recomposed A′ section. But, given the simplicity and symmetry typical of trios in his symphonies, Haydn sometimes repeats the A sections, note for note, which he would not have done had it been a menuet. In this Trio, however, the A′ section is not identical to the A section, probably because of the exceptional redundancy within the latter (see Ex. 3.9).

In the small-scale binary forms that are characteristic of the menuets and trios in Haydn's early symphonies, the B section, the section immediately after the internal double bar, might be seen as roughly analogous to the development section in a longer sonata form. Usually— and particularly in works with non-modulating A sections—Haydn makes sure to touch at least briefly on at least one other key before returning to the tonic, as he does in both the Menuet and Trio of the present work.

[27] Reasons of this sort appear to explain the structure of most (but not all) of those menuets whose A′ sections are literal repetitions of their A sections: in Symphonies Nos. 21, 28, 29, 39, 71, 74, 76 and 79, but not Nos. 69 and 75.

[28] Although contrasting, the second phrase is a kind of echo of the first. It begins as a repetition of m. 2, with the melody preserving four notes in order (D–B–C♯–A) thereby repeating and modifying the broken parallel thirds an octave lower. Notwithstanding this underlying motivic connection, the surface contrast (dynamics, orchestration, the new theme in the horn) between the two phrases is strong enough that a literal repetition would not violate the redundancy principle.

Ex. 3.8

Ex. 3.9

But, given the limited dimensions of the B sections, there is rarely time to explore distant key-centers, or to employ extended motivic development.

As they have miniature development sections, the binary forms we see in Haydn's menuets and trios, particularly those with modulating A sections, might appear to be a small-scale version of sonata form. But the difference in scale has significant consequences that should dissuade us from making a facile equation between the formal types. The smaller dimensions mean that many of the strongest formal motivations of sonata forms are absent. The harmonic stability in movements with non-modulating A sections (or the limited amount of time in the new key in forms with modulating A sections) means that little prominent material can be stated outside the tonic. Therefore, there is normally little or no necessity to invoke the sonata principle in the A′ section as a response to the A section. As a consequence, there is no obligation to make the kinds of cuts and splices that are common in the recapitulations of sonata forms from this period. Similarly, the minimal size of the B section means that the possibilities for emphasis on keys other than the tonic and the expansion of motivic ideas are strongly limited.

Seen in this light, it seems logical that Haydn's symphonic menuet and trio often became the focus of other compositional emphases—a kind of compensation for the inherent limitations of the genre. In some works, we see orchestrational fireworks—often in the trio. In Symphony No. 5/iii, the horns are given some spectacular solos, with the first horn reaching up to a sounding *a″*. In Symphony No. 7/iii, Haydn endeared himself in perpetuity to the most improbable of soloists by giving the double bass a solo. In Symphony No. 67/iii, there is a *scordatura* tuning of the second violin. In other works, he employs canons (Symphonies Nos. 3/iii, 23/iii, 44/ii, 47/iii; there is also a hint of canonic imitation in the present work) and other unusual compositional techniques or styles that are not really suited for an extensive movement, but particularly apposite in a short one.

The finale of Symphony No. 21 is another atypical form. It is a binary variant of sonata form in which the opening eight measures of the exposition do not return in the recapitulation.[29] Instead, the recapitulation begins with a transposed version of m. 9 and continues in transposition to the end, following exactly the model of the exposition (see Table 3.2).[30]

[29] Bonds, 'Haydn's False Recapitulations', 273, lists this as a binary movement because the opening theme does not return in the tonic after the internal double bar.

[30] As in Symphony No. 1, the form of the finale is much simpler and more schematic than that of the first movement.

TABLE 3.2. *Symphony No. 21/iv: Correspondences between Exposition and Recapitulation*

Exposition (mm.)	Recapitulation (mm.)
1–8	—
9–40	59–90 (transposed)

Generally speaking, when a passage that has appeared in the exposition does not return in the recapitulation, one can assume that the most likely cause of the excision is the redundancy principle.[31] That is the case here. The opening eight measures—comprising the entire tonic definition section, ending with a bifocal half-cadence—contain two distinct thematic ideas (a syncopated motive in m. 1 and a scalewise descending motive in m. 2), both of which appear in slightly altered form, transposed to the dominant in the remaining measures of the exposition (in mm. 26 f and 9 f respectively; see Ex. 3.10a and b).[32]

As the exposition includes a half-cadence in m. 8 that marks the end of the tonic section and acts as a pivot to the dominant key (a bifocal close), there is no transition section. Instead, the dominant key is in force immediately at the beginning of m. 9. This means that the sonata principle dictates the transposition of mm. 9–40 back to the tonic in the recapitulation. If the first eight measures of the exposition had been kept as well, there would have been a clear violation of the redundancy principle, for the same reasons that motivated some of the excisions in the first movement.

Having looked at the forms of all of the individual movements in this symphony, it is now possible for us to direct our attention to the work as a whole. Are the movements related to one another in some manner?

Binary variants of sonata form are not particularly common in Haydn's early symphonies; they constitute approximately 11 per cent of the sonata

[31] This might seem to imply that all binary variants are motivated by the redundancy principle. That is not so. For example, in the String Quartet Op. 9 No. 5/iii, the recapitulation omits entirely the equivalent of mm. 1–17. No potential redundancy appears to have motivated this excision. The motivation must lie elsewhere. Two features are prominent characteristics of this work: it is a simple binary form (the return of the tonic is not marked off for special attention, either harmonically, rhythmically, or by means of a clear half-cadence); and immediately after the internal double bar, the opening theme is restated in the dominant. The same two characteristics seem to be essential features of many of the binary variants whose excisions are not motivated by the redundancy principle. For similar examples, see Symphonies Nos. 7/ii and 58/ii. See also No. 18/ii, where the return of the tonic and the point of arrival of the abbreviated recapitulation (m. 62) might at first escape notice because mm. 60–2 is a sequential repetition of mm. 58–60.

[32] For a somewhat similar case, see Symphony No. 65/i.

Ex. 3.10

(a)

(b)

form movements in symphonies written before *c.* 1766.[33] Even these raw
numbers are deceptive, for the majority of the symphonic binary variants
occur in unusual cycles.[34] Although they are relatively common in string
trios and quartets, keyboard sonatas, and divertimenti, these formal types
are actually quite rare in the symphonies.

That fact alone should alert us to the possibility that there might be
significant intermovemental relationships in this symphony. Why this
should be the case is unclear, but it seems as if Haydn's most unusual
symphonies are also the most likely to contain convincing intermovemental relationships, at least in his early works.[35]

Traditionally, the starting-place in searches for intermovemental relationships has been the hunt for similarities between the motives or themes
of the different movements. But, with a few exceptions (Symphony No.
31, where the opening measures of the first movement return in the finale,
and Symphony No. 46, where a passage from the Menuet is interpolated
into the final movement), intermovemental motivic relationships in
Haydn's symphonies are rarely literal quotations.[36] Nor should we expect
them to be literal, for if the themes of the different movements were

---

[33] Webster, 'Binary Variants', 133, places the proportion at 13.5% in symphonies written before
*c.*1766. However, Bonds comes up with a somewhat different total. He deletes (in my opinion,
correctly) three movements that Webster includes, Nos. 3/iv, 8/i, and 32/i. See Bonds, 'Haydn's
False Recapitulations', 273, 287, and 307. On the other hand, Bonds includes in his three categories
of binary variants (binary, mirror, disjunct) two pre-1766 movements that Webster (in my opinion,
correctly) omits (Nos. 19/i, 36/i), omits two others that should have been included (Nos. 9/ii and
24/ii), and includes (I think correctly), but mislabels, one that was omitted by Webster (No. 15/i
(Presto)—it should be included with the mirror recapitulations). The complete list of unambiguous
pre-1766 symphonic binary variants should probably include only twelve movements (Nos. 7/ii, 9/ii,
14/ii, 15/i (Presto), 18/i, 18/ii, 21/ii, 21/iv, 24/ii, 31/i, 37/i, 72/i). If so, the proportion of binary
variants is 11.5% (12 of 104) of the pre-1766 symphonic movements that are, potentially, in sonata
form. In any event, the proportion of non-sonata movements in the symphonies is significantly lower
than that in the other genres cited in Webster's table 2. Of course, for many movements there is often
substantial ambiguity as to whether (and where) the double return takes place—which may explain
some of the differences between Bonds's and Webster's lists. Webster suggests some possible reasons
for borderline cases and cites a number of examples (ibid. 128).

[34] Five of the binary variant movements are found in just three extremely unusual symphonies:
No. 15 (which has a unique ABA form in its opening movement), No. 18 (which, like No. 21, begins
with a slow movement), and the present work. It is probably not coincidental that more than half of
the remaining binary movements in the symphonies (Nos. 7/ii, 24/ii, 31/i, 72/i) are quasi-concertos.
Unless a symphonic movement is a quasi-concerto, or part of a particularly unusual multimovement
cycle (like Nos. 15, 18, and 21), it will almost never be a binary variant. The only other symphonic
binary variants before 1766 are Nos. 9/ii, 14/ii, and 37/i. Binary variants are even less frequent in
works composed after *c.*1766. Interestingly, one post-1766 cycle (Symphony No. 44), like Nos. 18 and
21, includes both a binary variant (third movement) and a mirror recapitulation (finale).

[35] The early symphonies Webster offers as examples of through-composition are Nos. 15 and 25,
two of the most unusual. See *Haydn's 'Farewell'*, 251–9.

[36] Although different movements in the same composition rarely make use of the same theme,
scholars have pointed out that Haydn will often begin different movements with similar incipits.
A. Peter Brown suggests that there are many such relationships in Haydn's early keyboard sonatas
(Hob. XVI: 3, 6, 7, 8, 10, 13, 14, G1, and XVII: D1, all written before 1765, and Hob. XVI: 47,
written *c.*1765). See *Joseph Haydn's Keyboard Music: Sources and Style* (Bloomington, Ind., 1986), 276, 291,
and 435 n.

absolutely identical, there would be no element of contrast between movements—and contrast between adjacent movements seems to have been an essential premise of late eighteenth-century musical aesthetics.[37]

It should come as no surprise (particularly in an age that prizes organicism) that some modern scholars have looked below the surface of Haydn's music and found hidden motivic relationships between the themes of the different movements. This in turn has sparked controversy, for it seems as if no one can agree on what might constitute reasonable criteria for determining when the similarities between two themes or motives are significant.[38] On the one hand, there are some who look at a composition and are convinced that relationships between the movements do exist, advancing as their proof two (or more) passages that they claim to be similar. On the other hand, there are those who approach this issue skeptically and tend to dismiss such claims, either by explaining the similarities as the result of the common use of conventional figures or by rejecting the analytic logic of those who see connections.

For those who find thematic connections convincing, there is some evidence in Symphony No. 21 that might support a hypothesis of intermovemental relationships. The principal themes of the second and fourth movements (second movement, mm. 10–11, fourth movement, m. 2; see Exx. 3.3 and 3.10*a*) are quite similar. And there are other interesting similarities between the principal themes of the first, third, and fourth movements, all of which have an explicit or implicit skeleton of parallel thirds.

In my opinion, such thematic–motivic relationships are not especially effective in tying the movements together. It is not that I am convinced that they are coincidental or fictitious, for it would seem to be unlikely that a composer as careful and as craftsmanlike as Haydn would have accidentally or unconsciously made so many similarities between the different movements, let alone one so explicit as that between the second and fourth movements. Rather, if isolated thematic relationships are the only connections between the movements, then there does not seem to

---

[37] Although contrast was an essential principle of movement-to-movement succession, it posed some interesting problems. See Ritzel, *Die Entwicklung,* 112–34.

[38] See Hans Keller, 'K. 503: The Unity of Contrasting Themes and Movements', *Music Review,* 17 (1956), 48–58 and 120–9; Rudolph Reti, 'The Role of Duothematicism in the Evolution of Sonata Form', *Music Review,* 17 (1956), 110–19; Hans Engel, 'Haydn, Mozart und die Klassik', 71–9; Jan LaRue, 'Significant and Coincidental Resemblance between Classical Themes', *Journal of the American Musicological Society,* 14 (1961), 224–34; Nicholas Temperley, 'Testing the Significance of Thematic Relationships', *Music Review,* 22 (1961), 177–80; Newman, *The Sonata in the Classic Era,* 138–40 and *passim;* Karl Marx, 'Über die zyklische Sonatenform: Zu dem Aufsatz von Günther von Noé', *Neue Zeitschrift für Musik,* 125 (1964), 142–6; id. 'Über thematische Beziehungen in Haydns Londoner Symphonien', *Haydn-Studien,* 4 (1976), 1–20; Meir Wiesel, 'The Presence and Evaluation of Thematic Relationships and Thematic Unity', *Israel Studies in Musicology,* 1 (1978), 77–91; Webster, *Haydn's 'Farewell',* 194–204.

be any meaningful sense in which the different movements depend on one another. If so, the question is not so much the existence of intermovemental relationships, but rather their strength.

In Chapter 2, I described one of two methods whereby Haydn fostered multimovement unity and outlined some procedures we might use to evaluate the strength of intermovemental relationships. Surely it has not escaped the reader's attention that thematic relationships do not fare at all well under the guidelines used to evaluate the anomalies in the development section of the finale of Symphony No. 1. It would border on the absurd to state that the principal theme of the second movement of Symphony No. 21 cannot readily be understood within that movement. Yet without satisfying that first criterion, the remaining criteria are inapplicable.

Obviously we must admit the possibility of another approach to intermovemental relationships. Unlike the method outlined in the previous chapter, this one must start by taking into consideration the importance of similarities between events in different movements.

Fundamentally, the intermovemental relationships outlined in Chapter 2 are dependent on violations of the basic principles of *intra*movemental organization. Infringements of inter-opus and intra-opus norms, if not resolved within the movement itself, can only be understood through *inter*movemental relationships. Simply put, anomalous passages within a movement can be resolved only by reference to passages outside of the movement.

But if we wish to account for such intermovemental relationships as thematic similarities, this method is inappropriate, for similarities between the themes of movements have nothing to do with the violation of the principles of intramovemental organization. Rather, we can account for relationships like thematic similarities only if we formulate a second description that is almost the literal inverse of the first: Violations of the normative principles of *inter*movemental organization can be properly understood only by further explanation in the *intra*movemental structures of the different movements. As was the case regarding the method described in Chapter 2, here too, we need to outline the criteria against which we can test the significance of intermovemental relationships in as objective a manner as possible.

Relationships between movements are the most significant when multiple and mutually supportive similarities exist between the different movements, acting in such a manner as to challenge the normative principles of intermovemental organization. The degree to which these relationships are musically significant is dependent on at least four factors: (1) the extent of the disruption of the normal principles governing different movements—the greater the challenge to intermovemental norms, the greater the potential importance for intermovemental relationships; (2) the centrality of the similar event(s)—the more central the event(s) within their respective movements, the more significant the relationship; (3) the number of mutually supportive parallelisms or similarities—the greater the number of similarities, the more comprehensive the relationships between movements, the greater the potential significance; (4) the extent to which a movement (particularly a later movement) can be seen to respond to (that is, resolve) the disruption of intermovemental norms.

If we test our observations of Symphony No. 21 against these criteria we find that, when we restrict ourselves only to thematic similarities, the intermovemental relationships are not exceptionally strong. The similarities between the themes (and in particular, those between the second and fourth movements) do (to a limited degree) satisfy the first criterion—they challenge the fundamental compositional principle that different movements should employ different themes (though certainly not as much as Symphonies Nos. 31 and 46). Moreover, the thematic similarities involve important and central motives. This is not a case of relating a trivial accompanimental figure, buried in the middle of one movement, to another equally subsidiary event in another movement. Therefore, the second criterion is satisfied as well. If the relationships described to this point fail to convince, it is because they do not satisfy the third and fourth criteria: that is, they are fundamentally separate connections between events in different movements. We do not really hear the later movements as resolving any problem left unresolved by the violation of intermovemental norms.

However, the third criterion implicitly states that no one feature (like thematic similarities) should be considered important in isolation. This does not mean that we must reject thematic similarities as a criterion, merely that if we expect them to be convincing, they must be supported by other features. If so, we should not end our search with thematic relationships, but should broaden it to include other dimensions as well.

I believe that the most significant intermovemental relationships in this composition are a consequence of the extraordinary nature of the multimovement cycle. As I have indicated, binary variants in symphonies are anything but common occurrences. To find two of them in the same composition is well beyond the realm of chance. If we take this as a starting-point, we begin to notice numerous similarities between the ways in which the different movements are treated, similarities sufficiently wide-ranging that they begin to satisfy the third criterion.

Consider for a moment the most obvious parallelism between the second and fourth movements: both are binary variants. A parallelism of this sort might seem trivial, but is it also so trivial that—because of the similarity between the motives and because they are both binary variants—the recapitulations of the two movements begin with what might be described as variants of the same theme?

Having noticed that connection, we should also notice something interesting (and parallel) about the way in which the two recapitulations are prepared. In both cases, the dominant at the end of the retransition is neither emphasized, nor highlighted, nor clearly articulated. In the second movement, the dominant chord is not even in root position; in the fourth movement, although the final beat of the measure is indeed a root-position dominant, it is approached as an arpeggiation from a first-inversion dominant on the strong beat.

As a consequence of the common use of binary variant forms and the virtual suppression of the dominant, the arrival of the recapitulation in both the second and fourth movements is an event that is more glossed over than emphasized. So much so, that on first hearing, and perhaps even after several hearings, one is virtually certain to fail to recognize the beginning of the recapitulation and will realize that it has begun only in retrospect.

If we should be tempted to sound a note of caution and refrain from accepting the significance of the parallelisms between the second and fourth movements out of concern that perhaps intermovemental relationships (excepting thematic relationships) are found only there, we should remember a salient feature of the third movement. It should be recalled that because of its motivic and tonal structure, the A′ section of the Menuet could easily have been a literal repetition of the A section. And, with the tiniest, most seemingly inconsequential exception, it was (see Ex. 3.11 and compare with Ex. 3.5).

At the beginning of the A′ section, the bass, instead of beginning a measure after the uppermost voices with a touch of canonic imitation (as it did in m. 1), begins simultaneously with the upper parts—and not with the root of the tonic triad, but with the third degree. Furthermore, the tonic chord is prepared, not by a dominant in root position, but a V^4_2. If that were not enough, Haydn makes the return of the opening theme in the upper voice into an internal component of an ascending line that began in the previous measure. As a consequence, as in the second and the fourth movements, the seam that divides the development section from the recapitulation is virtually erased. Here too we are almost certain to be deceived on our first hearing and fail to recognize, at least for a moment, the beginning of the reprise.

This brings us full circle, back to the opening movement—a movement that defied easy classification. Even more than in the other movements, Haydn erases the crucial dividing line marking the return of the tonic. Can it be coincidental that at the end of the modulatory section (= development section?), when Haydn returns to the tonic (= recapitulation?), he does so by moving from a V^4_2 to a I^6? Could it possibly be an

Ex. 3.11

accident, unrelated to the second and fourth movements, that when we return to the tonic we hear, not a restatement of the opening theme in the tonic, but the return of another one of the thematic ideas from the opening section (= exposition)?

In short, the intermovemental relationships in this movement are not limited to simple similarities in themes. Rather, there are extensive parallels between the movements.

The similarities and parallelisms outlined above should indicate that a case could be made for some connections between the movements, but at the same time, it should be noted that we have not yet presented any evidence to support the argument that the final criterion (that a later movement should resolve the problems posed by the earlier movements) has been met. Without this, the different movements are not really dependent on one another for their comprehensibility—even if all of them can be understood to share a limited arsenal of motivic and thematic features. Therefore, if we return to the rating scale introduced in the last chapter, we may classify the strength of the intermovemental relationships in this symphony as moderate.

4

Symphony No. 49

1768

HAYDN's Symphony No. 49 in F minor[1] is among those of his works of the late 1760s and early 1770s that, for better or worse, are known as *Sturm und Drang* compositions.[2] Every bit as unusual as we would expect from a symphony that is cast in a minor key and that begins with a slow movement, this work reveals itself to be a highly complex and sophistic-ated composition, both in the structure of the individual movements and in its overall cyclical organization.

Some sense of the extent to which the compositional approach of this movement differs from those of earlier works can be gathered by comparing the correspondences between the exposition and recapitula-tion of the first movement with those of any of the sonata forms we analyzed from Symphonies Nos. 1 and 21 (see Table 4.1 and compare with Tables 2.1, 2.2, 2.3, 3.1, and 3.2). Notwithstanding the diversity of formal procedures encountered in Chapters 2 and 3, one common thread can be discerned (and it is typical of most of his early symphonies): the

[1] Two rather different titles have come to be associated with Symphony No. 49: 'La passione' and 'Il quakuo di bel' humore'. See *Joseph Haydn: Werke*, ed. J. P. Larsen et al. (Munich, 1958–), I/6, foreword, and critical report, 17–20. See Elaine R. Sisman, 'Haydn's Theater Symphonies', *Journal of the American Musicological Society*, 43 (1990), 331–6, for a discussion of some of the possible implications of the latter title.

[2] In keeping with attitudes of his time, an early Haydn scholar attempted to explain the sudden (or so it seemed) explosion of expressive minor-key symphonies in the 1770s by recourse to a biographical hypothesis—a supposed 'romantic crisis'. See Théodore de Wyzewa, 'A propos du centenaire de la mort de Joseph Haydn', *Revue des deux mondes*, 79 (1909), 935–46. *Sturm und Drang* was a German literary movement which had taken its name from the alternate title of a play (1776) by Friedrich Maximilian von Klinger. The appropriateness of the association of Haydn's music with that movement and its title and the existence or nonexistence of a romantic or artistic crisis have been the focus of much subsequent literature. A sampling includes: Larsen, 'Zu Haydns künstlerischer Entwicklung'; Landon, *Chronicle and Works*, ii. 266–84; R. Larry Todd, 'Joseph Haydn and the *Sturm und Drang*: A Revaluation', *Music Review*, 41 (1980), 172–96; A. Peter Brown, 'The Symphonies of Carlo d'Ordonez: A Contribution to the History of Viennese Instrumental Music during the Second Half of the Eighteenth Century', *Haydn Yearbook*, 12 (1981), 43–5; Carolyn D. Gresham, 'Stylistic Features of Haydn's Symphonies from 1768 to 1772', in Larsen, Serwer, and Webster (eds.), *Haydn Studies*, 431–4; Joel Kolk, ' "Sturm und Drang" and Haydn's Opera', in Larsen, Serwer, and Webster (eds.), *Haydn Studies*, 440–5; Rummenhöller, *Die musikalische Vorklassik*, 17–20; Larsen, 'Joseph Haydn, eine Herausforderung an uns', in Eva Badura-Skoda (ed.), *Proceedings of the International Joseph Haydn Congress, Wien, 1982* (Munich, 1986), 18, trans. as 'The Challenge of Joseph Haydn', in Larsen, *Handel, Haydn*, 105–6; Zaslaw, *Mozart's Symphonies*, 261–3; William E. Grim, *Haydn's Sturm und Drang Symphonies: Form and Meaning* (Lewiston, NY, 1990); Sisman, 'Haydn's Theater Symphonies'.

TABLE 4.1. *Symphony No. 49/i: Correspondences between Exposition and Recapitulation*

Exposition (mm.)	Recapitulation (mm.)
1–3	62–4
4–21	—
—	65–6
22–38	67–82[a] (transposed)
—	83–91
39–43	92–6 (transposed)

[a] Mm. 81–2 are a compression of mm. 36–8.

recapitulations of Haydn's early symphonies tend to be tonally adjusted, slightly modified, repetitions of the expositions. Small sections may be excised, transplanted to the end, shortened, lengthened, or otherwise altered. When another genre is suggested (e.g., concerto, aria, trio sonata), the rewriting of the recapitulation may be comparatively extensive (e.g. Symphonies Nos. 5/i, 7/ii, 8/i, 18/i). But with these exceptions, the generalization holds: most of the material in Haydn's early recapitulations is composed of literal or transposed repetitions of the corresponding passages from the expositions.

This is simply not the case in the first movement of Symphony No. 49. As we can see in Table 4.1, the first deviation from the model of the exposition occurs as early as m. 65, after the repetition of only the first three measures of the work. Immediately following, Haydn replaces mm. 4–21 of the exposition with a mere two newly written measures (mm. 65–6). This is radical surgery indeed.

That is not all. In the exposition, the relative major was first suggested in m. 19 and confirmed by the elided, contrapuntal cadence in m. 25.[3] In the recapitulation, when Haydn comes to the passage corresponding to m. 22, the sonata principle would suggest that he should merely transpose back to the tonic everything from that point (m. 22) to the end of the exposition. At first, that is precisely what he does (mm. 22–38 = mm. 67–82, transposed). But in m. 83, Haydn breaks completely away from

[3] According to contemporaneous theory and practice, the relative major was the normative secondary key for a composition in minor. See Rey M. Longyear, 'The Minor Mode in Eighteenth-Century Sonata Form', *Journal of Music Theory*, 15 (1971), 189. Although movements in minor normally proceeded to the relative major for the secondary key, it was not unheard of for the dominant minor to be used instead. See Symphonies Nos. 37/ii (Trio) and 52/iii (Menuetto), both of which come to a cadence on the (minor) dominant before the internal double bar. (However, both movements also cadence on the relative major within their B sections.) In both of these cases, Haydn omits the lowered third from the chord at the cadence, thus permitting the final sonority to be reinterpreted as a dominant (with an implied raised third) when he rounds the corner for the return to the opening. For a discussion of this procedure, see Rosen, *Sonata Forms*, 135.

the model and interpolates a sizeable passage that has no precise counterpart in the exposition. The lack of congruence with the exposition is compounded when, in m. 92, Haydn returns to the very point from which he left, continuing to the end of the movement in transposition (mm. 39–43 = mm. 92–6, transposed)—radical transplant surgery.

Revealing though this tabular comparison of the exposition and recapitulation may be, it only begins to indicate just how unusual the formal structure of this movement really is. Nothing in the table can quite prepare us for the way in which Haydn introduces the recapitulation (see Ex. 4.1).

After a short development section (actually, too short, as we will argue below), Haydn makes preparations for the return of the tonic. In m. 59 he brings the development to a close—or so we might think—with a clearly articulated half-cadence in F minor. By all rights, m. 60 should bring the double return of opening theme and tonic. But, as we can see in Ex. 4.1, the tonic does not return at that point. Instead, Haydn states the beginning of the principal theme in inversion in C minor, the dominant minor. Then, without warning, he breaks off this thematic

Ex. 4.1

statement, stopping on V^6 of the dominant minor. What follows is truly surprising on the first hearing, extraordinary on any hearing.[4] In m. 62, the recapitulation begins, prepared, not by its dominant, but by the first-inversion dominant of the dominant minor.[5] The resultant voice-leading is—to put it mildly—jagged and unorthodox, particularly in the bass, which leaps a tritone to the tonic of F minor, leaving unresolved the leading-tone of C minor. It is almost as if mm. 60–1 were mistakenly interpolated between the end of the development section and the beginning of the recapitulation by an errant copyist.[6]

Even this is not all. The movement begins with a passage that at first appears as if it is to be a four-measure phrase. Instead of closing off smoothly at that point, Haydn places a subtle, but insistent, agogic accent on the middle beat in m. 4, thereby preventing closure. As a result, the phrase continues for two more measures, proceeding on to a half-cadence in m. 6, emphasized by a fermata. The half-cadence, the fermata, and the preceding dotted rhythms all combine, on first hearing, to give the impression that this could be the end of a brief slow introduction (see Ex. 4.2).[7]

---

[4] It is fairly common to refer to certain types of musical events as 'surprises' or 'unexpected'. Certainly, genuine surprise can originate only where there are well-understood norms—and even then, usually only on the first hearing (though if the deviation from the norm is very subtle, one may not realize that one should have been surprised until after repeated hearings). For a discussion of this problem, and how surprise can be understood in music, see Cone, *Musical Form and Musical Performance*, 54–6. For an earlier discussion by the same author, with a step-by-step analysis of how Haydn employs surprise by arousing and defeating expectations in the finale of the String Quartet Op. 54 No. 2, see his 'The Uses of Convention: Stravinsky and his Models', *Musical Quarterly*, 48 (1962), 287–90. For a brief survey of Haydn's use of surprise, see Georg Feder, 'Haydns Paukenschlag und andere Überraschungen', *Österreichische Musikzeitschrift*, 21 (1966), 5–8. On the relationship of surprise to humor in Haydn's music, see Wheelock, *Haydn's Ingenious Jesting with Art*. I will return to discuss the problem of surprise and rehearing in Ch. 11.

[5] Ending the development section with something other than V was not the norm, and in Haydn's hands, such an infringement of norms usually had significant formal consequences. For a survey of Haydn's unusual endings for development sections, see Heino Schwarting, 'Ungewöhnliche Reprisen-eintritte in Haydns späterer Instrumentalmusik', *Archiv für Musikwissenschaft*, 17 (1960), 168–82; Webster, *Haydn's 'Farewell'*, 138–45. For some discussions of this feature in the music of other composers, see Wolf, *The Symphonies of Johann Stamitz*, 154 and 279; Margaret G. Grave, 'First-Movement Form as a Measure of Dittersdorf's Symphonic Development', Ph.D. diss. (New York Univ., 1977), i. 237 and 337; Reginald Barrett-Ayres, *Joseph Haydn and the String Quartet* (New York, 1974), 31. The use of non-dominant chords (in particular V/vi) to conclude the development section may have roots in the baroque practice of concluding movements (generally slow, interior movements) in this manner. See Jan LaRue, 'Bifocal Tonality: An Explanation for Ambiguous Baroque Cadences', in *Essays on Music in Honor of Archibald Thompson Davison by his Associates* (Cambridge, Mass., 1957), 173–84.

[6] Todd sees the approach to the recapitulation as 'an abrupt and unprepared transition that remains perhaps the most unusual event of the entire Symphony.' See 'Joseph Haydn and the *Sturm und Drang*', 179. Webster relates the preparation of the recapitulation to weakened preparations of the tonic elsewhere in this movement and in the composition as a whole, seeing these features as essential aspects of through-composition in the symphony. See *Haydn's 'Farewell'*, 264–7. My discussion of the multimovement relationships in this symphony owes much to Webster's insightful analysis.

[7] Sisman, 'Haydn's Theater Symphonies', 342 n., makes a similar point.

Ex. 4.2

When Haydn resumes in m. 7, it is not with an allegro, not even with a new theme and radically different texture (as in the quasi-introduction of Symphony No. 21/ii). Rather, he simply restates a varied version of the thematic idea of mm. 1–3. After having created expectations of an introduction, he purposely frustrates those expectations, and continues with nothing more than a varied repetition of the beginning. The sense of discontinuity, or misplaced continuity, is reinforced by the voice-leading. Although the voice-leading connections between mm. 6 and 7 are not nearly so abrupt as those between the end of the development section and the beginning of the recapitulation, they are, nevertheless, jarring. Not only is the leading-tone not resolved in register, but also, it leaps down an augmented fifth to A♭. The uppermost voice leaps up a seventh; the bass also skips upwards, moving in similar motion with the uppermost voice to the octave F. This is precisely the kind of disjunct voice-leading one would expect to find at the juncture between a slow introduction and the main body of the movement—not between two consecutive (and similar) phrases within a movement. All of this leaves us with serious questions about the role and function of the opening phrase. Is this an introduction or not? If so, why do mm. 7 ff begin by simply repeating, in varied form, mm. 1–3? If not, what is the purpose of the false start, the strongly emphasized half-cadence, and the fermata? And, in any event, why the disjunction between the two phrases, caused by the voice-leading?

Massive cuts and extensive interpolations in the recapitulation, an unusual harmonic preparation for recapitulation, and an introduction which may not be an introduction—all of these are highly unusual features whose formal functions we would like to be able to understand and to explain. The first clues that will help solve these mysteries are found in the exposition.

The exposition proceeds by a flexible process of motivic transformation, whereby virtually each subsequent event is an easily perceived variation, combination, or conflation of preceding events. I mention it in this context, not because I wish to show that Haydn's music successfully meets some (mythical) absolute standard of compositional excellence (i.e. motivic economy),[8] but because the concision of the motivic structure is a crucial determinant of the form of the movement.[9]

The consequences of this kind of motivic structure for the form are profound. If the exposition is formed, not from several clearly contrasting events, but from passages that are only slight modifications or transformations of one another, then it may be impossible to retain large segments of the exposition in the recapitulation. In a highly repetitive motivic environment, a literal, tonally adjusted repetition of the exposition in the recapitulation is redundant.[10] But if the recapitulation cannot be a modified repetition of the exposition, then what relationship can or should its material bear to the exposition?

That is precisely the compositional problem Haydn posed for himself in this movement. As the phrase in mm. 7–14 is merely a varied version of mm. 1–4, it is obvious that the restatement of both phrases in the recapitulation would be redundant. He must cut one. So he does: mm. 4–14 do not return. (Why he repeats mm. 1–3 and not mm. 7 ff will be discussed below.) Similarly, the upper voice in mm. 15 ff, in the tonic, is highly similar to mm. 23–4 in the relative major (as the lower voices are a varied repetition of mm. 1–3, etc.). In the exposition, where the two statements are in different keys, there is no problem of redundancy. In the recapitulation, they would both be in the same key, and therefore,

---

[8] Janet M. Levy, 'Covert and Casual Values in Recent Writings about Music', *Journal of Musicology*, 5 (1987), 3–27.

[9] Virtually the same motive (G–F–A♭–G) forms the basis of another of Haydn's works from this period, the C minor Keyboard Sonata Hob. XVI: 20 (1771). That work too is characterized by an extraordinarily intense motivic process. See Höll, *Studien zum Sonatensatz*, 174 ff.

[10] Ludwig Finscher sees significant changes in the formal procedures in the string quartets of this period, particularly the Op. 17 set (1771). See *Studien zur Geschichte*, 210. He shows that the excisions in the reprises are a consequence of the motivic economy of the expositions. See his discussion of Op. 20 No. 2/i, ibid. 222–3.

one of the two statements must be cut.[11] One is: mm. 15 ff, from the transition section, are excised.[12]

Although the logic that leads to the excisions in this movement should be familiar, the cuts in this recapitulation are far more extensive than those we have seen in any previous movement—almost half of the exposition does not return. Changes of such a degree effectively become changes in kind. This is so because of a complicated chain of compositional reasoning. The motivic economy of the exposition (a consequence of the extension of the unity principle) causes Haydn to excise large segments of the recapitulation (a consequence of the redundancy principle). The excision of so much of the recapitulation leads to a lack of balance that needs to be corrected (the normative principle).[13] Haydn corrects the asymmetry by adding material to the recapitulation, but he cannot add entirely new material (a consequence of the unity principle). The material that is added to the recapitulation must relate to previous events, yet it cannot be a repetition of something that has been excised because of the redundancy principle. It is just such a chain of reasoning that leads to the sizeable interpolation (mm. 83–91) in the recapitulation of this movement, a passage that interrupts the transposed repetition of the latter half of the exposition, interleaving nine measures between two measures that were adjacent in the exposition (see Ex. 4.3).

The motivic and thematic origins of the interpolated passage are readily apparent—Haydn has simply drawn on material similar to mm. 67–73. He has avoided redundancy by stating mm. 83–91 at a different pitch-level and with different harmonic emphases from mm. 67–73.

Although this explanation is technically correct, the interpolation of such a proportionately large passage in between what were two adjacent measures in the exposition cannot be dismissed merely with the explanation that it is motivically similar to another passage. Nor can it be justified merely by asserting that it was necessary to preserve the symmetry between the exposition and recapitulation. We would expect to find a more comprehensive explanation for the addition of this specific passage in this specific location. But we cannot understand the role of the interpolation without first looking at some other problematic events in the movement.

[11] This procedure can be reduced to a fairly consistent formula: the recapitulation will not normally include more statements of a given theme than occurred in the exposition in the tonic key. For example, if a theme occurs three times in the exposition—twice in the tonic and once in the dominant—it will occur only twice in the recapitulation—both times in the tonic.

[12] There were many precedents for Haydn's tendency to rewrite the recapitulation. Bathia Churgin has remarked that rewritten and reordered recapitulations are present in the symphonies of Sammartini, as well as in those of many other composers, especially Brioschi and Wagenseil. See 'The Italian Symphonic Background', 334. See also my 'Haydn's Altered Reprise'.

[13] The practice of keeping the recapitulation close to the size of the exposition should be understood as an inter-opus norm. Sometimes, but rarely, Haydn permits the recapitulation to remain substantially smaller than the exposition, usually in non-symphonic genres. See e.g. String

Ex. 4.3

We have already examined the unusual nature of the preparation for the beginning of the recapitulation and the ambivalent character of the opening of the exposition. The interpolated passage in the recapitulation is a direct response to those events: it answers and resolves some of the difficult compositional problems that were raised by the non-introductory introduction and by the improperly prepared reprise. Moreover, the problems of the 'introduction' and the preparation of the reprise are not separate issues, but closely related.

We have seen that the preparation for the reprise is highly irregular, proceeding from V^6 of the dominant minor directly to the tonic and the restatement of the opening measures. That is only part of what makes the beginning of the recapitulation so unusual.

The development section is short—too short, lasting a mere eighteen measures, a little less than 19 per cent of the movement or 42 per cent of the size of the exposition. Although some symphonic development sections from this period are nearly as short, and one is even shorter (No. 38/iv: 20.9 per cent of the movement; No. 41/iv: 17.5 per cent; No. 44/iii: 19.5 per cent; No. 48/ii: 21.3 per cent), the norm in Haydn's symphonies of the late 1760s and early 1770s was approximately 23–34 per cent.[14] Because the development section is so short, and because it concludes with a non-dominant sonority, the beginning of the recapitulation scarcely seems solidly grounded—it is as if we have not really reached a significant point of tonal and thematic resolution. This sense of instability is intensified by two other factors: the minimal preservation of material from the exposition and the decision to begin the recapitulation with the equivalent of the first measure of the composition.

As we have already seen, Haydn preserves only the first three measures of the exposition before diverging to a newly written two-measure seam (mm. 65–6). Thus, within moments after a return which is itself none too stable, Haydn is already off in another direction.

Equally perplexing is the decision to begin the recapitulation with the equivalent of the first measures of the movement. Development sections in Haydn's early symphonies frequently begin with the opening theme transposed to the dominant. Therefore, when the development section

Quartet Op. 20 No. 2/i in C major (1772): exposition, 47 measures; recapitulation, 26 measures (the recapitulation is 55% of the size of the exposition). During the late 1760s and early 1770s, Haydn would not normally permit the recapitulation to be less than 60% of the size of the exposition in his symphonies, with most recapitulations lasting 70–90% of the exposition. For an exception, see Symphony No. 34/ii (recapitulation = 56% of exposition). This is a most unusual movement in a most unusual cycle. Mm. 16 ff (in the dominant in the exposition) do not return in the tonic in the recapitulation. Although this passage does have resemblances to other passages that do return in the tonic in the recapitulation (e.g. mm. 35 ff), one would have thought the sonata principle should have been invoked. Perhaps the unusual treatment of the form has some extramusical or programmatic motivations—this is a work whose first movement is slow and in a minor key.

[14] The relative size of the development section offers another means (beyond those cited in Ch. 1) by which Haydn's genres can be distinguished from one another. For example, in the string quartets of this period (and later), there are a number of movements with short development sections, and it is clear that this was not an infringement of norms: Op. 9 No. 1/iii (11 measures in the development section, compared with 30 in the exposition = 36.7%); Op. 9 No. 2/iii (a four-measure transition); Op. 9 No. 3/iii (unclear, perhaps 3 mm.); Op. 9 No. 3/iv (19 mm. = 31% of the exposition); Op. 17 No. 2/iii (11 mm. = 26.8% of the exposition); Op. 17 No. 2/iv (18 mm. = 22.7%); Op. 17 No. 3/iii (9 mm. = 20%); Op. 33 No. 1/iii (14 mm. = 35%). This has obvious consequences for the normative principle and its corollary.

begins with a transposition, not of m. 1, but of m. 7, it is as if Haydn wishes to demonstrate that the ambiguities of the opening measures are now resolved and to show that m. 1 was indeed a same-tempo introduction, separable from the body of the movement. But when the recapitulation begins with the equivalent of m. 1, Haydn throws the whole issue back into doubt.

To summarize: the recapitulation begins too soon, after a development section that is too short, starts with what may be the wrong material (m. 1, not m. 7), breaks away too early (after only three measures), and is prepared by the wrong chord (V^6/V). Haydn has gone to great lengths to weaken the sense of arrival of the tonic and to suppress the functionality of the dominant. If this movement is to achieve a proper sense of closure, the formal problems posed by the beginning of the recapitulation must eventually be addressed.

Haydn does not provide us with an immediate and easy resolution to this smoldering harmonic-formal crisis. Instead, he effectively throws gasoline on the fire and then fans the flames.

After only three measures of the recapitulation, he breaks away from the model of the exposition and does so with a rhythmic idea that has been kept in reserve, unused in any prominent manner since its first appearance: that subtle middle-beat agogic accent which was used to good effect in m. 4 to deflect the close of the first phrase, and extended it for two more measures, until the half-cadence in m. 6 (see Ex. 4.4 and cf. Ex. 4.2).

This rhythmic motive has a similar phrase-prolonging effect in the recapitulation. But this is no time for subtleties. Lest we miss the real point of this passage, Haydn replaces the quiet agogic accent of m. 4 with a violent juxtaposition of dynamic levels in mm. 65–6. The harmonic progression is intensified as well: instead of a vii/V preparing the dominant, a far more powerful augmented sixth chord occurs on the final beat of m. 66.

The effect of these two changes is striking. The sudden forte strokes in mm. 65 and 66 act as powerful agents of discontinuity, forcefully separating this passage from its surroundings and encouraging us to look for other similar events to which it relates.

We do not have to look far. The sudden forte dynamics and the augmented sixth preparation of the dominant chord relate back to the supposed end of the development section (mm. 57–9, see Ex. 4.1). There, as here, a sudden explosion of forte dynamics was interpolated between statements in piano. In both cases, the same stepwise bass-line leads down to the dominant (E♭–D♭–C), and, in both places, the dominant is prepared with an augmented sixth chord.

The connections are unmistakable. Haydn has come back and restored the dominant chord from the abortive ending of the development section.

Ex. 4.4

By recalling its dynamics, voice-leading, and harmonic progression, he has made a complete circuit around the strange problem caused by the mysterious interpolation of C minor and the even stranger harmonic preparation of the recapitulation.

In effect, then, Haydn has restored the dominant, brought it back to life. He now has another opportunity to right the harmonic wrongs wrought by the incomprehensible progressions of mm. 59–62. Having gone to such pains to bring the dominant back into play, surely we must expect this to be followed by a solid V–I progression to confirm the tonic, perhaps even followed by an unambiguous statement of the principal theme (whichever one it is). Since the recapitulation was not prepared by the dominant, there has not been a single clear dominant–tonic progression in the movement since the first half of the exposition (m. 14). Given this background, we should be certain that now is the time for an unequivocal dominant–tonic progression.

Wrong. Rather than a clear V–I progression, Haydn takes the strong root-position dominant chord which had been established in m. 67 and transforms it into a V^4_2 which leads to a relatively weakened I^6. As a result, even though we have already begun the transposed repetition of the secondary key-area of the exposition, there still has been no strong dominant–tonic harmonic progression.

However, we should be certain that one is coming soon. In the exposition, in mm. 31–3, Haydn drew out the dominant of the relative minor for three measures. This was followed by a root-position A flat triad in m. 34. If this is transposed faithfully back to the tonic, as the sonata principle says it should be, there will finally be the harmonic progression we have been expecting (see Ex. 4.5).

Wrong again. Instead of dutifully transposing mm. 31–5 (Ex. 4.5a) down a third, Haydn has purposely, and with malice aforethought, rewritten this passage, violating the intra-opus norms (Ex. 4.5b). The most crucial change is in the bass. (Some of the other alterations in these measures will be discussed shortly.) Instead of the long-deferred and painfully overdue root-position tonic following a root-position dominant, Haydn substitutes a first-inversion tonic chord. Incredible as it may seem when

Ex. 4.5
(a)

(*b*)

we consider that we are approaching the end of the recapitulation, the tonic has not been satisfactorily defined by an appropriate dominant–tonic progression since m. 14.

Furthermore, given the material in the exposition yet to be transposed back to the tonic, the only remaining opportunities for V–I cadences will be the transposed equivalents of the three cadential figures at mm. 38–9, 40–41, and 42–3. Yet, none of these appears to have the requisite strength: the winds drop out in m. 38 and do not return until well after the internal double bar; the dynamics drop back to piano and stay there; the fabric disintegrates into hocket-like fragments. How could these relatively weak and unobtrusive cadences possibly serve to resolve the harmonic tensions of this recapitulation?

They cannot and do not. Instead of a verbatim, tonally adjusted restatement, Haydn interrupts the transposed repetition of the exposition immediately after m. 82 (= m. 38, transposed), and interpolates a striking passage (see Ex. 4.3). This interpolation resolves some of the knotty harmonic and formal problems posed by the movement.

At mm. 82–3 we hear, at long last, a clear, unequivocal cadence in the tonic. This is not merely a transposition of the corresponding passage in mm. 38–9. In m. 83 (the beginning of the interpolation), Haydn adds the winds to the fabric, lending a solidity and stability absent in m. 39, a stability which is supported by the low register of the F in the bass, the lowest tone in the work since the cadence in A♭ at the internal double bar.

Even more striking, and most significant, is the dramatic turn to the submediant in mm. 87 ff. After the cadence in m. 83, the bass rises to the fifth degree and then on to the sixth degree. Suddenly, in m. 87, there is another outburst of forte. The bass moves back and forth between the sixth and fifth degrees through the remainder of the interpolation, the multiple repetitions steadily raising the level of tension. Finally, in an unmistakable reference to the two previous (but never properly resolved) structural dominants (mm. 58–9 and 66–7), Haydn arrives in m. 91 on the dominant, and comes via the same augmented sixth chord. At long last, the strange, recondite, baffling misresolutions of the dominant have been addressed. This process was prefigured in the exposition (mm. 9–10), began in earnest at the end of the development section, and was intensified at every turn in the recapitulation, with Haydn even rewriting the progression at mm. 78–9 to make it less stable. Only toward the end of the movement, as a result of an interpolation at the end of the recapitulation, has the long process come to a denouement, the resolution of a succession of infringements of intra- and inter-opus norms.

This movement has many remarkable features: it begins with an introduction that may not be an introduction; it is economical in its use of motives; it excises half of the exposition's material from the recapitulation; it interpolates an extensive passage between two previously adjacent measures; it blurs the return of the tonic at the beginning of the recapitulation. These are not separable, independent features, but rather, related elements in a grand formal design.

Although this analysis has already been quite extensive, it is worth taking a moment to describe a particularly effective instance of Haydn's employment of the variation principle, a passage where he avoids a mechanical transposition back to the tonic, and in the process creates a formally significant developmental dynamic. We have already seen some of the crucial consequences of the rewriting in mm. 78–9 (see Ex. 4.5). This same passage has other significant alterations. In mm. 32–3, the root of the chord (E♭) and its upper neighbor appear in the first violin, while in mm. 77–8 it is the third of the chord with its upper neighbor. Similarly, in m. 34 the first violin leaps to the third of the (local) tonic triad, but in m. 79 the fifth of the triad is in the first violin.

Haydn has combined the principle of variation with that of transposition. In both cases, the melody line moves from the oscillating F–E♮ (or E♭) and skips up to C. The melody is very nearly the same, but in one case we are in the relative major, in the other, the tonic minor.

In comparison with that of the first movement, the form of the second movement is far less complex. As it has none of the striking formal problems present in the first movement, its recapitulation is far more symmetrical—essentially a tonally adjusted repetition. The extensive cuts and massive interpolations of the first movement are absent (see Table 4.2). None the less, there are some interesting problems that Haydn poses for himself.

TABLE 4.2. *Symphony No. 49/ii: Correspondences between Exposition and Recapitulation*

Exposition (mm.)	Recapitulation (mm.)
1–11	100–10
12–27	—
—	111–16 (similar to mm. 23–7)
28–51	117–40 (transposed)

As always, the form is intimately related to the choice and manipulation of the material presented in the exposition. The tonic definition section lasts only thirteen measures, closing with a sharply articulated half-cadence. In the next measure, without any transition, Haydn leaps directly to the relative major (see Ex. 4.6). Thus, a two-part tonal subdivision (this is a kind of bifocal close), and not Larsen's three-part subdivision, is the most apt description of the tonal plan of the exposition. Haydn has gone to some lengths to etch a sharp contrast between mm. 1–13 and mm. 14 ff: he has separated the two sections with the only grand pause in the exposition, and changed the dynamics, the theme, and of course, the key.

If this is so, then why does no passage corresponding to mm. 12–22 appear in the recapitulation? Beginning in m. 14 we are in the secondary key with a new theme. Presumably, the sonata principle should have been applied here. As there has been no transition, with Haydn leaping directly from the half-cadence in the minor tonic in m. 13 to the relative major in m. 14, the recapitulation could simply have repeated mm. 1–13 *in toto* and then transposed mm. 14–51 back to the tonic.[15]

---

[15] Had Haydn done so, this would have yielded a complementary bifocal structure. In his symphonic sonata movements, however, Haydn never has a completely literal transposition of the

Ex. 4.6

(continued)

Ex. 4.6 continued

The answer lies in the nature of the thematic material beginning at m.
14. It is not entirely new. Unlike the material from later in the secondary
key (mm. 28 ff), this is very much like the accompanimental line from the
opening measures. In the exposition, there was no problem of redun-

---

passage that follows the complementary bifocal close. Even beyond the excision of the equivalent of
mm. 12–22, not everything is transposed verbatim: cf. mm. 23–7 with 111–16 and 33–6 with 122–5.
Given the differences between the interval-order of the major and minor scales, the passage in mm.
34–6 could not have been transposed literally because no equivalent exists for the succession E♭–E–F
when transposed to F minor (C–C♯ ?–D♭?). Haydn makes a virtue out of a necessity: in mm. 122–3,
unable to make a literal transposition of m. 34, he generates a statement of the principal motive of
the composition. Not all differences between expositions and recapitulations are compositionally
significant. Some changes are more practical. In many works, Haydn has to adjust the transposition
in the recapitulation to account for the usual range of the violins—in his early symphonies, they did
not normally play beyond *e′′′*.

dancy because the two statements were in two different keys. But in the recapitulation, a literal transposition back to the tonic would be too much like what had preceded it and is quite reasonably omitted.

Although the internal form of the second movement is not as complicated as that of the first movement and does not at first appear to raise as many problematic issues, specific details of its structure raise the question of the strength of the relationships between the movements. The first piece of evidence that would likely be considered is the similarities between the principal themes of the first and second movements, both of which have similar principal motives, beginning on the fifth degree, and then moving on to the sixth and fourth degrees (the 'x-motive').[16] To be sure, as was asserted in Chapter 3, thematic or motivic relationships are not particularly effective in fostering intermovemental connections if they are isolated and otherwise unsupported. If the connections between these movements were dependent solely on motivic similarities between two themes stated only at the beginnings of their respective movements, the connections between the first and second movements would be adjudged to be superficial. Before we dismiss the connections between these movements as weak, however, we should take note of two factors that militate for the exact opposite conclusion.

One is the very pervasiveness of the opening motive in the first movement. We might rate connections between movements as weak when the similarities are limited solely to thematic relationships between the principal themes. But in the first movement of this symphony, the x-motive penetrated to virtually every possible corner. The same is true of the second movement. The other factor is the simple fact that the thematic similarities are not limited to these two movements. Rather, the principal themes of all four movements (including the Menuet and the Trio) are based on the same underlying motive.[17] As a result, it may be unwise to dismiss the motivic similarities as insignificant. These are not isolated connections that are limited to a few measures, but central ideas for all four movements, involving both principal themes and underlying motives.

Another type of evidence that we should find compelling is the striking similarity between the treatment of the two movements' tonal and harmonic emphases. In the first movement, the central problem of the movement was its (purposeful) failure to articulate the arrival of the recapitulation, as the reprise was preceded by a brief statement of the theme in C minor, not by the dominant. This failure was reflected in a

[16] Webster, *Haydn's 'Farewell'*, 265.
[17] Many of these were pointed out by Landon, *Chronicle and Works*, ii. 290. See also Webster, *Haydn's 'Farewell'*, 263.

succession of weakened dominant–tonic progressions and was corrected only through a sizeable interpolation in the recapitulation.

In the second movement, the arrival of the recapitulation is also disguised and is also preceded (though not immediately) by the statement of a subsidiary theme in C minor, the principal key-area of the development section (mm. 63–71 and 85–94). Moreover, in a number of prominent places, the arrival of the root-position tonic from the root-position dominant is purposely frustrated, much as in the first movement (e.g. mm. 111–15 and 117–21). Finally, just as in the first movement, the opening phrase of the second movement is extended for an additional measure by a V–VI progression—a very significant progression, as we have seen.

Thus, the connections between the first and second movements are not restricted merely to similarities between the themes. And as we shall see shortly, Haydn employs yet other means of relating the movements to one another.

An obvious difference between the symphonies written around 1768 and those written around 1760 is in the size of the movements. The initial fast movements of Haydn's symphonies from the late 1750s and early 1760s were, on average, a little less than 100 measures long in 4/4 meters, a little more than 100 measures in 3/4, and slightly less than 200 measures in 2/4, 3/8, or alla breve meter.[18] Approximately a decade later (*c.* 1767–72) the size of the first movements had almost doubled.[19]

At the same time, Haydn had begun to standardize the movements of the symphony. In the late 1750s and early 1760s, neither the number nor the type of the movements was fixed. The earliest symphonies have a broad variety of movement plans, forms, and types. The menuet and trio—if included at all—might well be the finale and not an internal movement (e.g. Symphony No. 9).

By the late 1760s, this diversity had begun to diminish. From approximately 1769 on, Haydn's symphonies invariably consisted of four movements: a first movement in fast or moderate tempo, a slow internal

---

[18] Initial fast movements composed before 1763: Symphony No. 107 ('A'): 113 mm., 3/4 (–1762 [–?1761]); No. 1: 86 mm., ¢ (– 25 Nov. 1759); No. 2: 193 mm., ¢ (–1764 [–?1761]); No. 3: 122 mm., 3/4 (–1762); No. 4: 96 mm., ¢ (–1762 [–?1760]); No. 5/ii: 134 mm., 3/4 (–1762 [–?1760]); No. 6: 112 mm. (excluding introduction), 3/4 (?1761); No. 7: 139 mm. (excluding introduction), 3/4 (1761); No. 8: 247 mm., 3/8 (?1761); No. 9: 137 mm., 2/4 (?1762); No. 10: 90 mm., ¢ (–1766 [–?1761]); No. 11/ii: 162 mm., ¢ (–1769 [–?1760]); No. 27: 108 mm., ¢ (–1766 [–?1761]); No. 32: 181 mm., 2/4 (–1766 [–?1760]); No. 33: 149 mm., 3/4 (–1767 [–?1760]); No. 37: 168 mm., 2/4 (–?1758). See also the statistics relating to the growth in size of sonata-allegro movements in the mid-18th-cent. keyboard sonata in Kamien, 'The Opening Sonata-Allegro Movements', i. 35–7.

[19] No. 35: 177 mm., 3/4 (1 Dec. 1767); No. 26: 133 mm., ¢ (–1770); No. 38: 194 mm., 2/4 (–1769); No. 41: 202 mm., 3/4 (–1770); No. 42: 224 mm., ¢ (1771); No. 43: 254 mm., 3/4 (–1772); No. 44: 157 mm., ¢ (–1772); No. 45: 209 mm., 3/4 (1772); No. 46: 151 mm., ¢ (1772); No. 47: 159 mm., ¢ (1772); No. 48: 196 mm., ¢ (–?1769).

movement, and a quick finale (the only exceptions: No. 60, in six movements, and No. 45, in five movements—if one considers its closing Adagio a separate movement). The menuet and trio became an invariable component of the multimovement cycle, generally appearing as the third movement.[20]

The expansion in size and complexity of the sonata form movements presented Haydn with an interesting compositional problem for the menuet and trio. If this movement was to preserve anything of its traditional character, then it would have to retain its basic overall ternary design, with binary forms (usually rounded binary) for the individual subsections. But given the expansion in size and scope of the other movements, the overall balance between the movements could be threatened if the menuet and trio remained with only small-scale binary forms as its components.

As a result, clear changes began to take place in the menuet and trio. The most obvious is one of size (though Haydn also tried other means of endowing these movements with more importance).[21] The menuet became significantly longer (see Table 4.3), and so, to a lesser extent, did the trio. In Haydn's symphonies composed before 1767, 71.4 per cent of the menuets are between 26 and 32 measures long. By contrast, in those dating from 1767–74, the menuet is substantially larger—68.2 per cent are between 34 and 56 measures long.

These changes are even more significant than they might at first appear, for most of the increase in size takes place after the internal double bar. Throughout the works covered in Table 4.3 (composed up to the mid-1770s), most A sections are between 10 and 20 measures—there is little significant difference between earlier and later works. This means that the increase in size is weighted to the latter half of the menuet's form.

That is immediately apparent in the Menuet of Symphony No. 49. Its second 'half' is almost twice as long as the first. The A section is eighteen measures long, and is divided into three four-measures phrases, each

[20] The menuet and trio occurs as the second movement rarely in symphonies composed after the 1760s. Two exceptions: Symphonies Nos. 44 (–1772) and 68 (–1779 [?*c.* 1774/5]). The fixing of the order of the movements in the symphony came earlier than in the string quartet. See László Somfai, 'Vom Barock zur Klassik: Umgestaltung der Proportionen und Gleichgewichts in zyklischen Werken Joseph Haydns', in Gerda Mraz (ed.), *Joseph Haydn und seine Zeit, Jahrbuch für österreichische Kulturgeschichte*, 2 (Eisenstadt, 1972), 64–72 and tables after p. 160.

[21] The use of canonic devices in the menuets of Haydn's symphonies (as in Nos. 3/iii [–1762], 44/ii [–1772], 23/iii [1764], and 47/iii [1772]) may be a manifestation of the effort to impart more weight to the menuet and trio within the four-movement cycle. A similar point has been made in relation to the music of Mozart (Symphonies K. 110 (74b), K. 130, K. 550): 'This application of learned canonic devices to the insouciant ballroom minuet may be considered an attempt to render the dance more "symphonic" '. Zaslaw, *Mozart's Symphonies*, 212. The historical context for the use of canonic devices in menuets is traced in Kirkendale, *Fugue and Fugato*, 148–9. Russell provides a list of canonic menuets and summarizes (and critiques) the various hypotheses that have been advanced to explain their purpose. See 'Minuet, Scherzando', 76–97. See also Wheelock, *Haydn's Ingenious Jesting with Art*, 64–9.

TABLE 4.3. *Comparative Lengths of Menuets in Haydn's symphonies: −1767 and 1767–74*

Length (mm.)	−1767:	28 menuets	1767–74:	22 menuets
	no.	%	no.	%
16	0	0	1	4.5
18–24	1	3.6	2	9.1
26–32	20	71.4	2	9.1
34–40	5	17.9	8	36.4
42–48	2	7.1	4	18.2
50–56	0	0	3	13.6
58–64	0	0	1	4.5
66 +	0	0	1	4.5

extended to six measures by a two-measure echo.[22] In contrast to the Menuet from Symphony No. 21, this has a modulating A section that cadences in the relative major. The three phrases conform neatly to our adaptation of Larsen's three-part tonal division of a sonata-form exposition: tonic definition (1–6), transition to the secondary key (7–12), confirmation of the relative major (13–18). The x-motive not only forms the principal theme, but also, as in the two previous movements, appears throughout the fabric in various transformations (see Ex. 4.7).

The B section is quite short, only eight measures, moving quickly through the subdominant minor to prepare the half-cadence in the tonic minor as a preparation for the reprise. Given the premises of the A section, the A′ section can repeat the first phrase (which it does: mm. 1–6 = 27–32), but Haydn must rewrite the next two phrases to close in the tonic. As all three phrases of the A section were formed from versions of the x-motive, he must shorten and rewrite in the A′ section to avoid redundancy.

So he does. The second phrase of the A′ section remains in the tonic, closing with a 'rhyming termination', a transposition of the end of the A section back to the tonic. But Haydn has to rewrite the beginning of the phrase (mm. 33 ff) to avoid a literal transposition of mm. 13 ff (because of the redundancy principle—it would be identical to mm. 27 ff).[23] At the

---

[22] Perhaps a reminder of the opening six-bar phrase of the first movement?

[23] Because of its motivic and harmonic premises, this Menuet is subject to compositional procedures similar to those found in Haydn's larger 'sonata forms'. The A′ section responds to the premises with the same kinds of excisions and rewritings that we find in the recapitulations of sonata forms. Finscher has pointed out that in Haydn's contemporary string quartets (Op. 9, 1769/70, and Op. 17, 1771), the menuets and trios were also the focus of explorations in form, and this was revealed most clearly in Op. 17 by the non-literal reprise: 'Kein einziges der sechs Menuette und nur

Ex. 4.7

downbeat of m. 40, all the outstanding formal issues should have been resolved, and the Menuet should conclude there with an authentic cadence in F minor.

It does not conclude at m. 40. Instead it continues for an additional twelve measures (see Ex. 4.8). Haydn has added a coda.[24]

Given the massive codas we encounter in compositions from the end of the eighteenth century and the beginning of the nineteenth century (those of Beethoven are undoubtedly the best-known), it would be easy to overlook the seemingly modest twelve-measure addition to the body of this menuet and underestimate its importance. To do so would be to misunderstand an essential feature of the composition.

A proper understanding of the significance of this coda should begin with the recognition that codas are rare events in Haydn's works in general, and in his early symphonies in particular. That being the case, we must operate from the presumption that a coda is, *ipso facto*, a significant event, a significant deviation from the composer's inter-opus norms. It is also a significant infringement of intra-opus norms to add twelve measures to this movement after all of the tonal and formal obligations have (apparently) been satisfactorily and completely resolved.

In the second edition of his book *Sonata Forms*, Charles Rosen advanced the hypothesis that 'the classical coda is closely related to an anomaly in the main body of the work'.[25] This view can be supported by numerous examples in the literature, as is amply demonstrated by Rosen. But in the present case, it is untenable. What anomaly in the main body of the Menuet could possibly motivate this coda? Indeed, the coda does not relate to an anomaly elsewhere in the movement; it is the coda itself that is (emphatically) the anomaly.[26]

eins der Trios (Nr. 3) hat eine genaue "Reprise"; statt dessen werden die Reprisen verschleiert und variiert, erweitert, verkürzt oder durch neue durchführungsartige Abschnitte, die aber zur Tonika zurückleiten, ersetzt.' See *Studien zur Geschichte*, 214. For further discussion of changing formal procedures in the menuets in Haydn's String Quartets, see Wolfram Steinbeck, 'Mozart's "Scherzi": Zur Beziehung zwischen Haydns Streichquartetten op. 33 und Mozarts Haydn-Quartetten', *Archiv für Musikwissenschaft*, 41 (1984), 208–31.

[24] For a survey of Haydn's codas, see Jürgen Neubacher, *Finis coronat opus: Untersuchungen zur Technik der Schlußgestaltung in der Instrumentalmusik Joseph Haydns, dargestellt am Beispiel der Streichquartette* (Tutzing, 1986), 128–50.

[25] P. 301. There had been no chapter on codas in the 1st edn. (New York, 1980). Perhaps as a result of some of the critical reviews (notably by LaRue and Kerman), Rosen added an extensive chapter in the rev. edn. (1988, 297–352). Given their size and importance, Beethoven's codas have received substantial attention. See Joseph Kerman, 'Notes on Beethoven's Codas', in Alan Tyson (ed.), *Beethoven Studies*, 3rd edn. (Cambridge, 1982), 141–60, and Robert G. Hopkins, 'When a Coda is More than a Coda: Reflections on Beethoven', in Eugene Narmour and Ruth A. Solie (eds.), *Explorations in Music, the Arts and Ideas: Essays in Honor of Leonard B. Meyer* (Stuyvesant, NJ, 1988), 393–410.

[26] Although this coda cannot be explained by Rosen's hypothesis, many others do indeed resolve anomalies from the main body of the work. In Symphony No. 43/iv, a huge coda (mm. 162–202) is appended after the repeat signs at the end of the recapitulation. This coda resolves some significant anomalies and ties together some important strands: (1) the cadence at the end of the recapitulation was unsatisfactory; (2) there was no dominant immediately preceding the beginning of the

Ex. 4.8

Consider its content. One would be hard pressed to find anything here that relates directly back to the main body of the Menuet. The opening motivic idea (m. 41) is new. Its pattern of stresses (amphibrach) is entirely . unprecedented. The texture is completely different. Its two cadential phrases do not correspond to any of the cadences in the main body of the movement. All of this is a clear violation of the unity principle. Here is a passage that begins after the body of the movement has already concluded, and yet Haydn goes out of his way to form this coda out of motives, textures, rhythms, and cadential patterns that have not previously appeared in this movement.

Therefore, the coda of the Menuet should cause us to formulate a second hypothesis, this one a mirror image of Rosen's: in some of Haydn's codas, it is the coda itself that is the anomaly, a significant infringement of norms. It can be properly understood only by reference to something outside of the movement.

That is the case here. The coda cannot be understood in the context of the Menuet, as everything about it was intentionally structured to be anomalous. The coda can be understood only if we recognize its relationships with events outside of the Menuet. There are two aspects to this: connections with the Trio on the one hand and with the other movements on the other.

The Trio is, typically for Haydn, shorter and simpler than the Menuet.[27] Cast in the parallel major, it has a non-modulating eight-measure A section, a tiny four-measure B section, and an A' section that is, with the exception of the final arpeggiation of the tonic chord, a literal repetition of the A section. As is also typical of Haydn's trios, the winds and horns are given their most exposed solos anywhere in the symphony. Careful attention should be paid to the eighth-note figure in m. 55 and the first oboe's solo after the internal double bar (see Ex. 4.9).

We should recognize these ideas. The solo is none other than a version of the unprecedented motive that had been introduced in the coda of the Menuet (moved a beat to the right—see Ex. 4.8), and m. 55 is a literal

recapitulation (the last chord was a C minor triad); (3) virtually the entire development section was in C minor; (4) the false reprise in the first movement was preceded by V of C minor; (5) in the third movement the Trio closes in E flat, but seemed to begin in C minor (both the A and A' sections—there is no B section). The coda in the finale addresses these issues by strengthening the final cadence (virtually the entire coda is a prolonged and intensified cadential formula) and by reinterpreting C minor as part of the elaboration of V (mm. 166–71).

[27] As a general rule, the trio was usually shorter than the menuet. See Russell, 'Minuet, Scherzando', 229. Robert J. Nicolosi reported that, in the works of other composers of this period, when the final movement was a menuet and trio the trio was normally longer than the menuet. 'Formal Aspects of the Minuet and "Tempo di Minuetto" Finale in Instrumental Music of the Eighteenth Century', Ph.D. diss. (Washington Univ., 1971), 31.

Ex. 4.9

(continued)

Ex. 4.9 continued

transposition of the figure in m. 45.[28] Thus, on the most basic of levels, the anomalous coda of the Menuet relates directly to the Trio.

That is not all. The motive of the coda of the Menuet (Ex. 4.8) is also another variant of the principal motive of the entire composition—the x-motive. That is clearest in mm. 43–5, when the motive is transposed up to include the same three pitch-classes that formed the x-motive in its initial appearance in every movement: B♭–D♭–C. This particular registral disposition reflects the evolution of the x-motive over the course of the composition. The version of the motive that appears in the coda of the Menuet is not that of the first movement, but that of the second movement, with the B♭ displaced by an octave to a higher register.

In short, the coda of the Menuet is a prototypical example of the first of our two types of intermovemental relationships. It fulfills, in a thoroughgoing manner, the criteria outlined at the end of Chapter 2: there is an event that cannot be understood within the Menuet itself, but only by reference to events outside it. Within the Menuet, it is highly disruptive and needs to be explained and resolved; the events to which it relates in the other movements are central (the principal motive), and the similarities are unmistakable.

Much the same as that of the second movement, and in marked contrast to that of the first, the form of the finale is (apparently) relatively straightforward (see Table 4.4). As can be seen, most of the material of the exposition is preserved in the recapitulation. Haydn merely repeats

---

[28] Explicit relationships between menuets and their trios become more and more common from this point in Haydn's output, not only in the symphonies, but in other genres as well. See Finscher, *Studien zur Geschichte*, 214.

TABLE 4.4. *Symphony No. 49/iv: Correspondences between Exposition and Recapitulation*

Exposition (mm.)	Recapitulation (mm.)
1–17	87–103
18–24	—
—	104
25–50	105–26 (transposed, with some minor rewriting)

mm. 1–17, splices past the now redundant cadence in m. 20, and proceeds directly to a transposition of mm. 25 ff.

What makes the finale so interesting is its pivotal role in the inter-movemental structure. Most obvious are the thematic connections that bind the principal theme of the finale together with the previous movements. As in every other movement in this composition, the appearances of the x-motive are not limited to the principal theme, but are suffused all across the movement (e.g. mm. 57–61, bass).

A little less obvious, but no less widespread, are other similarities to the first three movements. In the finale, the dividing line separating the recapitulation from the development is compromised, much as it was in the first two movements. As in the first and second movements, the development section places emphasis on the dominant minor—a particularly unusual key-area for a development section. As in the second movement, the exposition makes a sudden leap from a cadence in the tonic key directly to the new key (cf. the finale, mm. 20–1, with the second movement, mm. 13–14). Finally, the first section of the finale is extended slightly by deferring the expectations for a cadence by means of the deceptive progression (see mm. 15–16), exactly as it was in the first movement (mm. 9–10) and second movement (mm. 4–5).

The connections between the movements go much deeper than motivic connections and formal parallels. The central problem of the first movement was the entirely unorthodox and inexplicable preparation of its recapitulation. It is not entirely contradictory to state that while this problem was resolved on one level—through the retrieval and eventual proper resolution of the dominant in the interpolation—it remained unresolved on another level. That is, at a critical point in the movement's structure (the end of the development section and beginning of the recapitulation) a perfectly proper dominant of F minor was inexplicably followed by an episode in C minor. Effectively, the leading-tone (E♮) was (improperly) led backwards to the lowered seventh degree (E♭). At no point in the several C minor episodes in the first and third movements was the E♭ ever corrected and led back to the leading-tone of the

Ex. 4.10

dominant. The finale comes back to this longstanding problem and—
finally—resolves it.

After the development section has gone through several keys, it arrives
in mm. 70–1 (perhaps slightly too early—as in the first movement) briefly
back in the tonic. This time, however, the development section will not
end prematurely. Haydn immediately pushes away from the tonic, and,
in mm. 75–8, breaks suddenly into octaves. With one very important
exception (in the second movement), this is the only such octave episode

in the entire four-movement composition.[29] Its motivic material, though somewhat similar to mm. 45 ff, is not precisely like any earlier place in the movement (see Ex. 4.10). The appearance of this novel passage so late in the composition, only moments before the recapitulation, is a stark challenge to the unity principle.[30] To what end?

Once again, Haydn has established C minor—that troublesome key of the preparation for the reprise in the first movement—and, as was the case there, the C minor episode follows directly after the premature arrival of the tonic key. In yet another extraordinary parallel to the development section in the first movement, he restates the principal theme of the movement in C minor—*déjà vu* all over again (mm. 79 ff).

This time Haydn is intent on resolving the long-deferred problem of the first movement. The restatement of the principal theme in C minor is cut short after six measures (another reminder of the first movement). When Haydn repeats the head-motive in m. 85, the C minor triad has been transformed into C major—the dominant of F minor. The Eb has ascended to E♮, becoming the leading-tone. This leading-tone leads directly into the tonic, which is found at the beginning of the reprise in m. 87.[31] The problem has finally been solved.[32]

The finale, therefore, is the culmination of the entire composition. It is related to the prior movements, not only by thematic similarities and formal parallelisms, not just by the common use of the minor dominant, not merely through their blurring of the dividing line between the development and recapitulation, but through its role in the resolution of a series of difficult and seemingly inexplicable formal and harmonic problems. As such, Symphony No. 49 is the most strongly unified cycle we have examined so far.

[29] See mm. 70–1 of the second movement. Significantly, there too the octaves are in a passage in C minor.

[30] Most striking challenges to the unity principle within a movement (i.e. violations of intra-opus norms) have—as here—obvious connections with other events in the work. There are, however, some puzzling exceptions. In Symphony No. 38/iv, toward the end of the recapitulation, Haydn suddenly and unexplicably touches upon the parallel minor (mm. 134–8), an event that (as far as I can see) has no antecedent either in the finale or in the previous movements. Perhaps the mixed genre of the movement (symphonic finale and oboe concerto) has something to do with this, but I am at a loss to explain how.

[31] Note that as in m. 67 of the first movement the dominant is the V_2^4. Haydn is continuing to draw parallels with the earlier movements, purposely avoiding an unequivocal root-position V leading to a tonic, and thereby deferring the most complete resolution until the closing measures of the piece.

[32] The dominant minor figures prominently in the intermovemental relationships in another minor-key symphony from approximately this period, Symphony No. 39 in G minor (–1770 [?1765]). The dominant minor first appears—inexplicably—in the middle of the recapitulation of the first movement (mm. 95–6), with a restatement of the principal theme. The dominant minor next appears in the B section of the Menuet (mm. 13–18), where it forms a tonally closed passage—a most anomalous passage for a B section. There are obvious motivic connections between the melody in mm. 13–14 and the principal theme of the first movement. The dominant minor returns in the finale, toward the end of the development section. It is followed by the 'correct' version of the dominant, which leads directly into the reprise. Thus (as in Symphony No. 49/iv) the final appearance of the dominant minor serves to resolve the problems raised by that key in the earlier movements.

5

Symphony No. 55

(*1774*)

WITH the exception of the first movement of Symphony No. 21, every one of the movements analyzed to this point has either been a sonata form or a menuet. This is neither accidental nor the result of a purposefully skewed selection. Although other formal types do make occasional appearances, the plain fact is that sonata forms (including binary variants) and menuets constitute the overwhelming majority of Haydn's early symphonic forms.[1] Beginning with works from the 1770s, other formal types start to take on increasing prominence. (Surely it cannot be coincidental that the gradual rise in the use of these formal types is mirrored by the almost total disappearance of binary variants.) Symphony No. 55 in E flat (1774)[2] is symptomatic of this trend: although the first movement is a sonata form and the third movement a menuet, the second is a set of variations and the fourth a 'hybrid variation'.[3] Analyzing this symphony, therefore, will permit us to continue to study the evolution of Haydn's treatment of sonata forms and menuets, but will also allow us to examine his treatment of two additional formal types.

Although a few, exceptional, movements from approximately this period or slightly earlier (e.g. Symphony No. 49/i) have extensively rewritten recapitulations, that of the first movement of this symphony (like most of its contemporaries) is a fairly straightforward, tonally modified repetition of the exposition (see Table 5.1). Given the premises of the exposition (contrasting themes, several cadences in both keys, lack of extensive repetition), the compositional logic that led to the rewriting of mm. 19–28 in mm. 169–78, the excision of the prominent authentic cadence that occurred in m. 22, and the transposition back to the tonic

---

[1] The only symphonic movements composed before 1774 that are not sonata forms or menuets and trios are: Nos. 2/iii, 3/iv, 15/iv, 20/iv, 21/i, 30/iii, 31/iv, 34/iv, 40/iv, 42/iv, 47/ii, 51/iv, 64/iv, 72/iv. This list does not include composite movements in which at least one of the component segments is in sonata form (Nos. 6/ii, 15/i, 25/i, 45/iv).

[2] The nickname for this work, 'Der Schulmeister', is not authentic. See *Joseph Haydn: Werke*, I/7, Critical Report, 17.

[3] Even so, these forms were still relatively rare. Of the twelve movements in the three other symphonies Haydn wrote in 1774 (Nos. 54, 56, 57), only one movement (No. 57/ii) is neither a sonata form nor a menuet.

TABLE 5.1. *Symphony No. 55/i: Correspondences between Exposition and Recapitulation*

Exposition (mm.)	Recapitulation (mm.)
1–18	151–68 (but added vn. 1 line in mm. 166 ff is derived from mm. 61 ff and 84 ff)
19–28	—
—	169–78
29–66	179–216 (transposed)

of mm. 29–66 (= mm. 179–216) is easily reconstructed using the sonata, redundancy, and unity principles (as explained in detail in previous chapters), and thus need not detain us here (the essential data are outlined in Table 5.1).

What should attract our intense interest is the development section, for the steady increase in the average size of movements has continued apace, yielding, in this case, a movement of more than 200 measures (in 3/4). As the development section normally constitutes between a quarter and a third of the movement, it might in this case be expected to last between fifty and eighty measures (see Table 5.2). In fact it lasts eighty-four measures, making up 38 per cent of the movement.

In early works, where the development section was relatively short and often followed a fairly predictable formula, there were some inherent limitations on its possible roles. Generally speaking, the typical development section in an early symphony began in the dominant (frequently with a restatement of the principal theme), moved directly to the tonic (often with another statement of the principal theme),[4] then proceeded with the development proper, modulating to closely related key-areas (most often vi, frequently emphasized with an authentic cadence), before a retransition to the tonic key and a half-cadence to prepare the reprise.[5]

Harmonically, then, the development section would place most of its emphasis on the dominant and the submediant. Motivically, it could only state, often in only slightly varied form, the principal ideas of the exposition a limited number of times. Given the typical dimensions of an early development section, there was little opportunity to do much more than this.

---

[4] See Bonds, 'Haydn's False Recapitulations', 307 and 308, for lists of symphonies in which a statement of the principal theme in the tonic occurs shortly after the beginning of the development section ('disjunct' and 'precursory' recapitulations).

[5] Andrews, 'The Submediant', 465–71.

TABLE 5.2. *Lengths of Development Sections in the First Fast Movements of Haydn's Symphonies, 1759–63 and 1774–7*

Symphony‡	Date	Length	Development	
		mm.	mm.	% of mvt
*c.*1759–63*				
1	–25 Nov. 1759	86	19	22.1
2	–1764 [–?1761]	193	64	33.2
3	–1762	122	33	27
4	–1762 [–?1760]	96	24	25
5/ii	–1762 [–?1760]	134	34	25.4
6	?1761	112	37	33
7	1761	139	43	30.9
8	?1761	247	80	32.4
9	?1762	137	40	29.2
12	1763	157	33	21
13	1763	87	27	31
14	–1764	100	17	17
15†	–1764 [–?1761]	78	20	25.6
40	1763	139	37	26.6
107 ('A')	–1762 [–?1761]	113	37	34.6
1774–7				
54	1774	215	66	30.7
55	1774	216	84	38.8
56	1774	272	65	23.9
57	1774	200	61	30.5
61	1776	201	50	24.9
66	–1779 [?*c.*1775/6]	154	42	27.3
67	–1779 [?*c.*1775/6]	259	73	28.2
68	–1779 [?*c.*1774/5]	158	35	22.2

*This section includes only symphonies that Feder definitely dates *c.*1759–63: see his worklist in *The New Grove*. Thus e.g. No. 10 is omitted, although it may have been written during this period.
†Presto; no precise dividing line between end of exposition and development.
‡First movement except where otherwise specified.

With the dramatic increase in its size, the tried and true development section formulas of earlier days became inoperable. Instead, Haydn had to address a series of interesting and challenging compositional problems.

Since the development sections could now be as long as entire movements used to be (or longer), the simple harmonic emphasis on the dominant could no longer be the sole harmonic strategy—it would lead to violations of the redundancy principle. Inevitably, it follows that other key-areas had to be given prominence—but which key-areas, and why?

So too, the greatly extended dimensions presented problems with respect to the treatment of the motivic material. Because of the unity principle, Haydn was normally constrained from introducing new material in the development section.[6] If he was to avoid introducing new material, it follows that he had to use the same limited motivic resources for a substantial period of time. That, in turn, could create possible problems with the redundancy principle if he were to remain in just one or two key-areas. Here too, the solution involved moving to various areas other than the dominant. That renews the question: which key-areas, and why?

Instead of following the more or less formulaic harmonic and motivic patterns of the early works, Haydn's development sections began to elaborate more remote secondary key-areas for longer periods of time, and to subject the motivic material to more developmental operations. To that end, Haydn increasingly relied on what I will term 'redirected continuations'. That is, the development section unfolds through a succession of events, each of which is derived from some passage in the exposition. But instead of following the patterns laid down in the exposition, the music is redirected along a different path of development, both motivically and harmonically. On first hearing, some or all of these redirected continuations might evoke varying degrees of surprise;[7] on subsequent hearings, the listener is impelled to try to understand the relationships that have been created by the juxtaposition of events and to make sense of the overall course of the development. It is at the seams between two events that the development section creates distinctive thematic and harmonic patterns, and it is through the succession of key-areas that the large-scale harmonic goals are revealed.

The development section of this movement is a particularly apposite example of these compositional techniques. It begins, not with a transposition of the principal theme to the dominant, but with the final

---

[6] When he did introduce dramatically different material, as he did in Symphony No. 45/i, it was an extraordinary, anomalous event that could not be resolved within the movement itself, and was thus crucial for the intermovemental strategy. See Webster, *Haydn's 'Farewell'*, 13–112, and also his 'The D-major Interlude in the First Movement of Haydn's "Farewell" Symphony', in Eugene Wolf and Edward Roesner (eds.), *Studies in Musical Sources and Style: Essays in Honor of Jan LaRue* (Madison, Wis., 1990), 339–80.

[7] The surprise is not occasioned by the fact that the music diverged from the patterns of the exposition. On the contrary, such deviations were expected in the development section. The surprise results only from the specific direction of the continuation. Given the restatement in the development section of some idea from the exposition, we can be sure that, at some point, Haydn will diverge from the version as stated in the exposition. What we do not know is when he will break away and to where he will go. It is in the specifics of the redirection that the surprise resides—but, even then, only on first hearing.

hammerstroke chords (V) of the exposition restated on V^7/vi (a harmonic juxtaposition that would soon become a virtual cliché at the beginning of Haydn's development sections). This redirected continuation has three consequences: it nullifies any expectations of a continuation in B-flat major; it creates a distinctive harmonic juxtaposition (a B flat triad with a dominant seventh chord on G); it forms a new set of local expectations—for a continuation in C minor (see Ex. 5.1).

The next step after a redirected continuation is normally a temporary realization of the new expectations (although Haydn often immedi-

Ex. 5.1

ately follows with a second, redirected continuation even before realizing any of the implications of the first). In this development section,
Haydn follows up instantly on the suggestions of C minor: a version
of the principal theme is promptly restated in this key. But notice his
sleight of hand. The bass is absent and the violins begin alone in
parallel thirds. Thus, although this is supposedly in C minor, the
upper voices are identical to the beginning of the theme in the exposition.[8] This bit of legerdemain is crucial for the next redirected continuation.

After only one phrase in C minor, the melody appears to be preparing
for a second, complementary phrase, but the bass moves down a step to
B♭. Although the melody is the same, suddenly, we have been directed
away from the continuation in C minor and are back in E flat major (the
tonic), with a partial restatement of the principal theme. As a result, we
have nullified expectations (for a continuation of C minor), a distinctive
juxtaposition (C minor and dominant seventh on B♭), and new expectations (for a continuation in E flat major).

As the development section unfolds, it becomes evident that its larger
organization is determined by the juxtapositions of dominant, submediant, and tonic key-areas presented in the first few measures after the
internal double bar. In a sense, the development section is a succession
of attempts to return to the tonic, only the last of which (appropriately)
is properly executed, with each failed attempt (confirmed by a redirected
continuation) raising the level of tension and the desire for a proper
resolution.

The first attempt to establish the tonic (m. 73) comes much too soon
(almost immediately after the internal double bar) and is improperly
prepared (it arrives directly from the submediant without a genuine
intervening dominant). This kind of return, like the 'immediate reprise'
in Haydn's early symphonies, acts as a reminder of where we came from
and where we are headed. The tonic, however, has not yet been properly
approached. As if to demonstrate that this was not the real recapitulation,
the continuation is quickly redirected away from E flat and rushes
through hints of A flat, G minor, and D minor, none of them given any
stability.

Haydn does not go very far afield (only to D minor) or for very long
(only to m. 97) before abruptly returning to E flat and the principal theme
(with an enharmonic shift on the way—the German sixth of D minor is

---

[8] The ambiguity of the statement of the theme in mm. 69 ff is given another wrinkle when the
development section and recapitulation are repeated. Here the purposely deceptive statement in mm.
69 ff follows only a few measures after the concluding cadence in E flat. Our analyses often overlook
the role of the repetition. For a discussion of this problem, see Jonathan Dunsby, 'The Formal
Repeat', *Journal of the Royal Musical Association*, 112 (1987), 196–207.

rewritten as V⁷ of E flat in m. 94; cf. mm. 78–80 and 111). This has been termed a 'false recapitulation'.⁹

Once again, this return to the tonic is still too early and improperly prepared. Even on first hearing, we should be suspicious and recognize that this is probably not the final, definitive, return to the tonic (see Ex. 5.2). This is the case because the development section in Haydn's symphonies composed before 1774 is normally about 60 per cent of the size of the exposition. In the present case, the development section (up to the false recapitulation at m. 97) is only 45 per cent of the length of the exposition—too short.

In any event, what has this told us? Is it not irrelevant? On second and all subsequent hearings an alert listener cannot possibly be fooled by this 'false' recapitulation, unless he or she adopted the dubious approach of trying to forget that there was a premature return. On second hearing, the listener knows what is coming, knows that it is not the 'real' recapitulation, and will not be surprised. If so, how should we understand the supposedly false recapitulation? It is important to address these issues of musical perception and understanding if we are to respond appropriately to this development section.

There are several issues which must be distinguished. One is the question of the likely response of the first-time listener, that is, his or her ability to determine whether or not m. 97 marks the beginning of the recapitulation. Another is the question of what the possible musical meaning of the false recapitulation is in a second hearing.

Even if we wish, temporarily, to limit our discussion to first-time listeners, we are immediately beset by complications. Who is this hypothetical listener? Is it an educated listener or an ignorant listener? How educated? Is it a listener from the late twentieth century or a contemporary of Haydn's? Undoubtedly, we could reach a number of completely different conclusions, depending on the identity of the listener.

As a central premise of the normative principle is the composer's calculation of the listener's expectations, we must assume that our listener is a highly educated listener from Haydn's time, perhaps another musician or an intelligent amateur with a passion for music. Let us also assume that this listener was very fond of Haydn's music and had many opportunities to hear his symphonies. Let us further assume that this listener had an excellent sense of pitch (and would not be surprised by a false recapitulation in the wrong key). How would this hypothetical listener react to the return of the tonic and principal theme in m. 97? Would he or she be fooled into believing that the recapitulation had begun?

⁹ For a discussion, see Bonds, 'Haydn's False Recapitulations', 316.

Ex. 5.2

The statistics cited above indicate that our hypothetical listener probably would not be fooled, even on first hearing, because the expectations
of this listener would necessarily be conditioned by what he or she was
accustomed to hearing. That would not normally include, in the first
movement of a Haydn symphony, a development section that was less
than 45 per cent as long as the exposition.[10] Rather, the first-time,

[10] Short development sections are scarcely anomalous in other genres, including the baryton trios.
A few (of many) examples: Hob. XI: 49/i (the development section is 16% of the length of the

educated, late eighteenth-century listener may well recognize that the return of the principal theme in the tonic in m. 97 was too early.

The issue of timing is absolutely crucial to our hypothetical listener's success in recognizing the false recapitulation. As our listener knows much of Haydn's pre-1774 symphonies, he or she is well aware that episodes in the tonic shortly after the internal double bar are quite frequent, but this listener also knows full well that they are not definitive. What he or she does know (on the basis of hearing many of Haydn's symphonies) is that the genuine, functional, return of the tonic will normally take place only after the development section has lasted around 60 per cent as long as the exposition, and sometimes much more.

But the issue is not so clear-cut. Although it is certainly true that the development section normally is at least 60 per cent as long as the exposition, there are a number of cases where this is not so. If we limit ourselves only to symphonic movements written at about this time or earlier, we find some prominent examples in which the development section is 45 per cent (or less) of the length of the exposition (see Table 5.3).[11] Could these not be advanced as evidence to support the hypothesis that the highly educated first-time listener to the first movement of Symphony No. 55 might have mistaken m. 97 for the beginning of the genuine recapitulation? I think not. In fact, the data supports precisely the opposite conclusion.

It is particularly noteworthy that the vast preponderance of the shorter development sections seen in Table 5.3 occur, not in first movements, but in internal slow movements and finales. In the symphonies composed before No. 55, there are only three first movements whose development sections are 45 per cent or less the size of the exposition: Nos. 14/i, 16/i, and 49/i. Thus, shorter development sections, though perhaps a plausible option for slow inner movements and finales, are highly rare and irregular in first movements. With the exception of Symphony No. 49/i, no first movement has a development section shorter than 45 per cent in any Haydn symphony composed after approximately 1763—more than a decade before Symphony No. 55.[12] But could not Symphony No. 49/i be offered as support for the hypothesis that a short development section would not trigger the normative principle?

movement, 35% of the exposition); Hob. XI: 6/iii (16% and 42%); Hob. XI: 66/i (20% and 46%). We presume that our listener knows the differences between genres and would recognize that the appropriate length of a development section for a baryton trio would be different from that of a symphony.

[11] Excluded from this list are forms like Symphony No. 4/ii, in which there are no double bars. Short development sections were normative in these. (For a later example, see No. 87/ii.) Also excluded is No. 60, whose highly irregular forms probably can be ascribed to its origins as a theater composition.

[12] The development section in No. 70/i (1779) is only 45.1% as long as the exposition in terms of measures (37 vs. 82), but there are two fermatas in m. 113.

TABLE 5.3. *Symphonic Movements, Composed 1774 and Earlier, with Short Development Sections (Approximately 45% or Less of the Length of the Exposition)*

Symphony and movement	Date	Length of development section as % of exposition
25/iii	−1766 (−?1761)	43.5
17/iii	−1766 (?c.1760–2)	35.3
16/i	−1766 (?c.1760–3)	42.6
14/i	−1764	38.6
21/iv	1764	45.0
29/iv	1765	35.8
49/i	1768	41.9
59/ii	−1769	35.6
41/iv	−1770	39.1
44/iii	−1772	40.0
46/iv	1772	33.8
50/ii	1773	21.4
52/iv	−1774	38.9

Having just spent a good part of a chapter wrestling with the paradoxical form of Symphony No. 49/i, we should be well prepared for this argument. In that movement, the end of the development section and the beginning of the recapitulation might have elicited surprise—not just at the point of the seemingly premature arrival of the recapitulation, but afterwards, when the recapitulation continued on, every step making it clearer and clearer that this was no temporary episode in the development section, but the definitive return of the recapitulation. Upon encountering the recapitulation, the highly educated first-time listener would at first doubt that the recapitulation has begun—indeed, might feel it could not possibly have begun. This listener would assume that this was a temporary episode in the tonic in the middle of the development section (a not uncommon feature) and would then be more and more surprised as the recapitulation continued on. Only after the recapitulation was well under way would the listener conclude that this was no mistake after all—this was the Real McCoy.

From the preceding, I must conclude that false recapitulations like that in No. 55/i probably would not have fooled an alert, educated, contemporaneous, first-time listener.[13] And it should be noted that I have

---

[13] Even if the listener was fooled, he or she would have had an immediate opportunity to correct that mistaken impression once the repeat was taken. If so, the effect of the surprise would not persist even throughout the first hearing of the work. See Dunsby, 'The Formal Repeat'.

purposely taken the one false recapitulation in the symphonies that—by far—would have had the best chance at deceiving that listener. All of the other false recapitulations in the symphonies begin much sooner. In no other of these works does the proportion of development section preceding the false recapitulation even exceed 28 per cent of the length of the exposition (see Table 5.4).[14] Therefore there are ample precedents in Haydn's symphonies (before 1774) of returns to the tonic and principal theme in the development section which in no way would be mistaken for the definitive recapitulation by a first-time listener.[15]

TABLE 5.4. *Haydn's False Recapitulations: The Span from the End of the Exposition to the Beginning of the False Recapitulation*

Symphony and movement	Date	Length as % of exposition
11/ii	‑1769 [‑?1760]	27.6
22/ii	1764	15.8
36/iv	‑1769 [?c.1761‑5]	12
38/iv	‑1769	19.4
41/i	‑1770	21.5
42/i	1771	8.6
43/i	‑1772	14.3
46/i	1772	22
48/iv	‑?1769	20
55/i	1774	45.5
71/i	‑1780 [?1778/9]	25
91/i	1788	26.3

[14] The works listed here are those in Bonds, 'Haydn's False Recapitulations', 316. In his table, he indicates that Nos. 11/ii, 22/ii, 36/iv, 38/iv, and 46/i might be considered a hybrid of false and precursory recapitulations.

[15] The normative sizes of development sections are different for Haydn's symphonic and sonata styles. We have already cited examples from string quartets and baryton trios. Short development sections also occur fairly frequently in keyboard sonatas. Some examples: Keyboard Sonata Hob. XVI: 21/ii (development section = 11 mm., 39% of the length of the exposition, 17% of the movement); XVI: 27/i (29 mm., 51% and 20%); XVI: 29/ii (5 mm., 31% and 14%). Because the normative principle would not be invoked when development sections in keyboard sonatas were short, Haydn could not play with the expectations of the listener (or amateur performer) by the 'early' arrival of the reprise. To achieve similar goals, he employed other tactics. In the Keyboard Sonata Hob. XVI: 25/i, the tonic returns, following a clear root-position dominant seventh in m. 39, after only eleven measures of the development section—too early for the first movement in a symphony, but making a plausible size for the development section in a keyboard sonata. However, this return is not to the opening theme; instead it restates the equivalent of m. 8. For at least two and a half measures, Haydn keeps the listener (or performer) wondering whether this could really have been the

To be sure, many a (first-time) listener would be deceived by the false recapitulation in Symphony No. 55/i, both in the eighteenth century and today. Most often, however, that surprise would probably be the result of some degree of ignorance. A listener might know enough to know that sonata forms have recapitulations, but not enough to know that precursory recapitulations (and other episodes in the tonic) are common in Haydn's development sections, and thus would automatically assume that the return of the tonic in m. 97 was definitive. Or, perhaps, the listener has heard only a few of Haydn's symphonies and is unaware that the typical development section is normally approximately 60 per cent or more of the length of the exposition, perhaps confusing norms of symphonies with norms of sonatas. Or we could assume a listener who does not have a particularly good ear. That listener might well not recognize that we have returned to the tonic or could be deceived by a 'false recapitulation' in the wrong key (e.g. Symphonies Nos. 51/i, m. 108, or 53/i, m. 164). Yet another listener might have a bad enough memory or be sufficiently inattentive, so that the false recapitulation would pass by completely unnoticed. But do we really want to treat as normative an analytical hypothesis that rests on the lowest common denominators?

From all of this, we must conclude that the educated first-time listener of Haydn's circle in the late eighteenth century would not have been surprised by this false recapitulation. Indeed, that listener, knowing that m. 97 was too soon for the beginning of the recapitulation, would hear the return of the tonic and principal theme as a temporary (and destabilizing) event, expanding the development section and deferring the definitive arrival of the tonic and principal theme.

There is an additional reason to believe that Haydn intended no surprise with this false recapitulation—and that brings us back to the issue of multiple hearings. Even if we accept the contention that surprise would characterize the first hearing of a false recapitulation, that reaction would not be elicited from future hearings. If so, how would the formerly surprised listener understand the false recapitulation on subsequent encounters with the movement?

Upon rehearing and further study, this listener would find that he or she should not have been surprised by the false recapitulation in the first place. Rather, it should have been recognized that it was too early for a recapitulation and that the dominant was inadequately prepared. This

---

reprise, only resolving the doubt by returning to development-section material in mm. 42–50 and concluding that section with a V/iii chord. He then leaps back directly into the reprise (equivalent of m. 1) with no intervening V. Thus, the challenges to expectations and violations of the normative principle are not dependent on the length of the development section (as in Symphony No. 49/i), but on the return at first to the 'wrong' material from the 'right' chord, then to the 'right' material from the 'wrong' chord. Incidentally, as m. 8 was restated in the tonic in the development section, it is excised from the recapitulation.

means that upon rehearing, this listener should eventually come to the same conclusion that the alert, educated listener came to on the first hearing: m. 97 does not mark the beginning of the recapitulation. In other words, the more that listener studies the movement, the more he or she realizes that the 'surprise' reading was invalid.

Contrast this with our experiences in a work where the first hearing might have occasioned surprise—and properly so. As we saw in Symphony No. 49/i, the misunderstanding of the first hearing turned out to be absolutely crucial for a proper reading of the piece. That is, trying to understand why it was that the recapitulation began too soon (and was prepared by the wrong chord) is the key to the entire movement (actually, all four movements). On first hearing Symphony No. 49/i, the listener *should* have been surprised by the recapitulation. Subsequent hearings should in no way reduce the impression that the preparation for the recapitulation was anomalous—indeed, the preparation for the recapitulation was most emphatically anomalous, and the development section was unquestionably too short. As our experience with Haydn's inter-movemental relationships indicates, an anomaly within a movement will be addressed—either within the movement itself, or between the movements. In short, the improper resolution and too-short development section in No. 49/i should stimulate the listener to resolve this structural problem.[16]

Similarly, the educated (unsurprised) listener of Symphony No. 55/i sharpens and refines his or her initial (and correct) image of the development section on each subsequent rehearing. Instead of having to change completely the very foundations of his or her perspective of the movement, as the surprised listener must do, the educated listener continually improves his or her understanding of the flow of the development section. What should that mean in this case?

The essential organizing features of this development section are the multiple, inconclusive returns to the tonic. Haydn moves back to the tonic three times, and none of these is quite satisfactory. The first time is much

---

[16] In Symphony No. 52/iv, the recapitulation seems to begin in m. 101, leaving the development section at 38.9% of the length of the exposition. Clearly, for a first movement this would be too short, but it is a plausible length for a finale. Yet the context makes it clear that Haydn intended this to be an unsatisfactory and inconclusive return—much like that of Symphony No. 49/i. The recapitulation follows directly after a III⁶ chord—the dominant is absent. Immediately after the restatement of the opening theme, a sequential and modulatory passage (mm. 112 ff) leads to a strong dominant (mm. 128–30). This is followed by the transposition back to the tonic of a passage that was in the relative major in the exposition (mm. 46 ff). But the perceptive listener should be highly troubled: this is the wrong passage—Haydn has skipped past and apparently omitted a prominent thematic section from the exposition that was in the relative major (mm. 28 ff). Not to worry. In m. 154 the motion suddenly halts—one of Haydn's famous GPs. Immediately after, Haydn brings back the equivalent of mm. 28 ff, restating the missing theme in the tonic as per the sonata principle. Thus the slightly short development section contributes to the impression that the return was unsatisfactory, but it does not create that effect on its own.

too early and comes directly from the submediant. The development must continue, and it does, but not for nearly long enough. Instead, having lasted only thirty measures and having barely tonicized any other key-area, the development section returns to the tonic. Again, this is too early, and the dominant preparation is insufficient—the chord becomes the dominant only in retrospect, once we hear the resolution to E flat and not to D. This cannot be the final return. Instead of remaining in the tonic area and completing the recapitulation, Haydn creates another redirected continuation. He makes up—with a vengeance—for seeming to have suggested that this would be a short development section. He returns and devotes considerable effort to expanding upon the sub-mediant (mm. 111–31)—the very key that had begun the development section. The submediant region is prolonged for a very long time, drawing this development section past the point where it would be equal in size to the exposition. Finally, the submediant is left, and the retransition brings us back to the tonic. Even here, Haydn plays with the sense of return one last time: the tonic arrives, but not with the principal theme and again with inadequate dominant preparation. Only after he abandons this line of thought and establishes a solid dominant does the principal theme return, this time as the definitive point of arrival. Everything about this development section has acted to impel the motion forward to this point. The several, inconclusive returns to the tonic do not diffuse the sense of arrival of the tonic at the beginning of the recapitulation. Rather, they intensify our expectations for its final and definitive return.[17]

The forms of the second and fourth movements are two different types of variations. Variations of any sort were quite rare in Haydn's early symphonies, appearing in only two composed before 1770 (Nos. 72/iv and 31/iv).[18] Beginning in the 1770s, however, Haydn made increasing use of variations, both strophic (as in the second movement of the present work) and hybrid (as in the fourth movement).[19]

The second movement is a set of strophic variations. As the theme in such a set normally constitutes a tonally complete form (usually a rounded

---

[17] For another interpretation of this development section, see Rosen, *Sonata Forms*, 276–80. For another work with a development section with a compromised return of the reprise, see the String Quartet, Op. 17 No. 4/i, mm. 75–80.

[18] For a list of variation movements in Haydn's symphonies, see Elaine R. Sisman, 'Haydn's Variations', Ph.D. diss. (Princeton Univ., 1978), 120. For a slightly amended list of these and a comprehensive list of variation movements in other genres, see her *Haydn and the Classical Variation*, 265–70.

[19] Sisman points out that 'in the late 1750s and 1760s, Haydn was one of a number of composers working in and around Vienna who occasionally included variations as first movements or finales in instrumental compositions.' But, as she notes, in 1772, in Symphony No. 47, 'Haydn moved the variation set into the interior slow movement, the first known to me. He would not have taken such a step lightly.' *Haydn and the Classical Variation*, 109 and 135.

TABLE 5.5. *Symphony No. 55/ii: Formal Plan*

Section	mm.	Comments
'Theme'*		
A	1–8	
A¹	9–16	written-out, varied, repetition of mm. 1–8
B	17–24	
B¹	25–32	written-out, varied, repetition of mm. 17–24
'Variation 1'		
A²	33–40	repeat signs
B²	41–8	repeat signs
'Variation 2'		
A³	49–56	
A⁴	57–64	written-out, varied, repetition of mm. 49–56
B³	65–72	
B⁴	73–80	written-out, varied, repetition of mm. 65–72
'Variation 3'		
A⁵	81–8	repeat signs
B⁵	89–96	repeat signs
'Variation 4'		
A⁶	97–104	no repeat signs
B⁶	105–12	no repeat signs
'Variation 5'		
A⁷	113–20	repeat signs
B⁷	121–8	repeat signs

*Neither the theme nor any of the variations are so labeled in the score. This was not unusual for Haydn. See Sisman, 'Haydn's Variations', 145 ff.

binary), which is immediately repeated in its entirety, it is obvious that the variation principle needs to be invoked in each adjacent repetition.

The equal lengths of the strophes, the nearly identical harmonic plans, the constant reiteration of the same melodic outlines—these features could be (and often were) the most deadly of compositional premises in the hands of a *Kleinmeister*. From formal, harmonic, and structural points of view, strophic variations face the very real danger of repetitiveness.[20]

[20] Strophic variations have been oft criticized for everything from excessive repetitiveness through their alleged lack of organic unity, to the problem of closure. Sisman offers a penetrating critique of

One way of defeating the potential tautology inherent in the genre would be to find some means to group the reiterative units into larger spans of time, and this is one of Haydn's common solutions.

A simple, but effective, technique used to attenuate the repetitiveness can be seen in the large-scale plan of this set of variations. Haydn actively varies the large-scale pattern of repetitions (see Table 5.5). Instead of writing a theme (with repeat signs) which is then varied in each of the formal variations, he begins the variation within the theme itself, writing out, in varied form, its repetitions. He adopts the same procedure in the second variation. By contrast, in the first, third, and fifth variations, the repeat signs are retained. Only the fourth variation breaks this regular plan, as it has neither a written-out, varied repetition, nor repeat signs.

Much more fundamental (and effective) in providing a forward-moving dynamic to this set of variations is the manipulation of orchestrational, rhythmic, and chromatic elements. In effect, the second variation acts as a kind of modified return, while the final variation functions not just as the last variation in an undirected chain, but as a synthesis of previous variations (see Ex. 5.3).

At least three factors contribute to creating a sense of return in the second variation. One is the orchestration. The theme is for strings alone (Ex. 5.3*a* and *b*); after the addition of winds in the first variation (*c*), the second variation returns to the texture for strings alone (*d*). Another is the rhythm. The second variation, like the theme, has written-out repetitions, in which A^3 and B^3 (dotted notes) are most like A and B, while A^4 and B^4 (sixteenths and thirty-seconds) are most like A^1 and B^1, in contrast to the first variation (repeat signs) with its mixed values and offbeat accents. The third factor is the dynamic level: the theme and second variation are

Ex. 5.3
(*a*)

Adagio, ma semplicemente

con sordino e piano

the aesthetic assumptions that lie behind some of the criticisms of variation form. See *Haydn and the Classical Variation*, 1–18.

(b)

entirely piano, while the first variation juxtaposes forte, full-orchestra outbursts with piano, strings-alone passages.

Having established a sense of return in the second variation, Haydn then moves on in variations 3 and 4 to diverge more substantially from the original model. Variation 3 changes the bowing in the bass to legato, introduces syncopated rhythms in the upper parts, and, working within the limitations of the theme, infuses a fairly extensive amount of chromaticism (passing- and neighbor-tones). Variation 4 continues the chromaticism and syncopations of its predecessor but adds an additional element—constant grace-notes in the melody.

The fifth variation takes most of the elements presented thus far and wraps them together, making this final variation the culmination of the lines of development initiated by the individual variations (see Ex. 5.4). The beginning of the melody is like the theme in its first appearance, but the legato bass is like variation 3. The addition of the winds is like variation 1, but they drop out entirely in mm. 121–4, recalling the theme and variations 2 through 4. The sudden forte outbursts and offbeat accents recall variation 1, while the syncopations and chromatic tones bring to mind variations 3 and 4. The one prominent feature of the earlier variations that is absent from the final variation is the use of diminution: the faster note values (sixteenths and thirty-seconds), present in the varied repetition of the theme and variation 2, do not return. Even this has a useful formal function, as the unfigured variations in the latter half of the movement provide for 'an overall arch construction and a large-scale contrast with the figured (diminished) interior variations'.[21]

[21] Sisman, 'Haydn's Variations', 236.

(*c*)

The formal plans of both the Menuetto and Trio need little comment, as their logic is similar to that which we have already encountered in previous examples.[22] The A section of the Menuetto is non-modulating

---

[22] Although neither the Menuetto or Trio is particularly adventuresome in this symphony, that is not the case for other movements from this period. In the Menuet of Symphony No. 42 (1771), the A section ends on the dominant, prepared by an augmented sixth chord. The next six measures expand the dominant, leading directly to a return to the tonic and material vaguely resembling the opening. But this turns out to be a false reprise. The 'real' reprise arrives thirteen measures later. It

(d)

and contains contrasting elements. Thus, it can be (and is) repeated without significant alteration after the B section. The brief coda that follows (mm. 37–40) is merely an echo of the final measures of the A section (and, thus, unlike Symphony No. 49/iii, is without exceptional formal significance). The modulating A section of the Trio needs to be rewritten after the B section. Accordingly, the beginning of the A′ section is adjusted to remain in the tonic, while the ending 'rhymes' with the ending of the A section.

The finale is also a type of variation movement, but is not strictly a set of strophic variations. As it combines elements of strophic variation with other compositional principles, it has been termed a 'hybrid' variation.[23] The particular formal subtype of this movement might be described as 'rondo-variation'—its second couplet is not a variation of the first.[24] Indeed, the two couplets are (at least partially) in different keys (see Table 5.6).

In Haydn's rondo-variation movements, the couplets generally introduce new motivic material or tonicize key-areas other than the tonic, or both. Therefore, the contrast occasioned by the intervening couplets obviates the problems of redundancy encountered in simple strophic variations. In the present case, Haydn employs both of these options: the

---

is undoubtedly not coincidental that the first movement also includes a false reprise and that the last movement has several prominent instances of the augmented sixth chord (mm. 63, 91, 137, 139).

[23] Sisman, 'Haydn's Hybrid Variations', in Larsen, Serwer, and Webster (eds.), *Haydn Studies*, 509–15; see also her 'Haydn's Variations', 130–44 and 246–324.

[24] The movement has also been described as a rondo with variation. See Malcolm S. Cole, 'Haydn's Symphonic Rondo Finales: Their Structural and Stylistic Evolution', *Haydn Yearbook*, 13 (1982), 115. See the graph of this movement's structure: ibid. 120.

Ex. 5.4

(continued)

first couplet is based on a new (though related) theme; the second couplet, while using the principal theme, explores other key-areas.

Both of these techniques for creating variety within the movement present certain compositional challenges and opportunities. The most obvious relates to the issue of overall unity. To be sure (as was outlined in Chapter 1), the unity principle is normally operative only within harmonically complete formal units, not between them. It follows that

Ex. 5.4 continued

there is nothing in the unity principle that would require motivic material from the couplets to be derived from the theme (or the intervening strophic variations), any more than there is a requirement that the Trio be motivically related to the Menuet, or that a second movement relate to the first.

However, as we have seen in Symphonies Nos. 21 and 49 (and are about to see in this symphony), Haydn was most definitely interested in forging relationships between different and putatively contrasting move-

TABLE 5.6. *Symphony No. 55/iv: Formal Plan*

Section	mm.	Comments
Theme	1–30	
1st couplet	31–46	E flat, new motives, with slight similarities to theme
Variation 1	47–76	
2nd couplet	77–94	begins in E flat as if it will be a repetition of var. 1; then transition to G flat
	95–106	G flat major; based on theme; first $\frac{1}{2}$ of a binary form
	107–25	transition back to E flat
	126–33	restatement (unvaried) of A section of theme
Variation 2	134–63	
Coda	164–79	restatement of beginning of theme and final cadence

ments. Those relationships were scarcely limited to (or even primarily based on) motivic similarities or identities. Given the evidence of Haydn's interest in actively relating discrete entities to one another on the level of multimovement cycle, surely it would not be unreasonable to expect to find the same kind of relationships within those kinds of movements, like hybrid variations, that are also formed from the juxtaposition of (apparently) contrasting, harmonically complete sections.[25]

Although it is cast in the same key, the sharp contrast in texture and orchestration in the finale marks the first couplet off from its surroundings in a dramatic fashion, leaving no doubt that mm. 31–46 should be heard as a distinct section. But is it related to the opening theme? When we look at the relationships between the first couplet and the theme, we are apt to feel somewhat ambivalent about what we find.

There are some moderately obscure motivic similarities between the theme and the first couplet. The theme of the refrain might be understood as a scalewise rising succession of broken parallel thirds (G–E♭, A♭–F, B♭–G) from the upbeat to m. 1 to the upbeat to m. 3. So too, at the beginning of the couplet (m. 31–3) there are parallel thirds in the oboes.

[25] Relationships between movements and between discrete sections of a movement might be described as aiming for a kind of unity. However, this is not the same thing as the unity principle described in Ch. 1.

I suspect that only the most orthodox of thematicists would be convinced that the subcutaneous relationships described here are exceptionally significant. If we are to be persuaded that there are important connections between the discrete sections of this movement, we will demand that the relationships satisfy one of the two sets of criteria for intermovemental relationships outlined in Chapters 2 and 3. The motivic similarities between mm. 1 ff and 31 ff, though 'true', seem too weak to support a case for musically significant relationships between the sections. (We will return to this issue shortly.)

No problems concerning motivic relationships should arise over the second couplet. In contrast to the first couplet, the second is based almost entirely on the theme of the refrain. The contrasts provided are not motivic, but harmonic. That means that any search for relationships should start with an attempt to relate the key-areas of the second couplet to the theme and variations.

This is an interesting challenge: the couplet begins in E flat, but moves through F minor before restating the theme in the key of G flat major—a remarkably remote key (the relative major of the—never stated—parallel minor). After presenting the first half of what we might expect will be a binary form (repeat signs and all), the second half of the form is never completed. Instead, Haydn moves through a transition (touching on F minor again) back to the tonic, where he states the first half of the theme, before proceeding to the second variation.[26] (See Ex. 5.5.)

Is this couplet (and in particular its harmonic detour to F minor and G flat major) related to the theme or the variations? Obviously, neither the theme nor the variations modulates to either F minor or G flat, but does either have any emphases that are similar? I think that a case could be made for the existence of some significant connections.

When we look at the first variation and compare it with the theme, we see that Haydn has made a subtle change. He has taken the G♭ out of the inner voice (mm. 11–14, Ex. 5.6*a*) and moved it to the bass (m. 59, *b*). There, its function as the upper neighbor to F is given prominent play.

The second couplet takes this simple idea and expands mightily upon it. The couplet begins in m. 77 as if it is to be a repetition of the second variation. Shortly, Haydn moves out of E flat—to F minor—and gradually comes to an almost complete halt. Leaving the F in the bass, he transforms the chord to the dominant of G flat. In m. 95, the theme commences in G flat—the bass has moved up by step from F to G♭—a large-scale realization of the implications of the subtle changes in the bass of the first variation (Ex. 5.5).

---

[26] It was common for there to be a brief statement of the beginning of the theme between the end of a couplet and the next variation. See Sisman, 'Haydn's Hybrid Variations', 511.

Ex. 5.5

Although the section in G flat starts out as if it is to be a complete tonal form (note the repeat signs, suggesting a binary form), it does not conclude in G flat. Instead, in a further expansion upon the F–G♭ neighbor idea, he returns to F. The bass steps down from G♭ (m. 107) to

Ex. 5.6

C (V of F, m. 113). This, in turn, permits Haydn to return to E flat by executing a virtual mirror image of the departure from E flat at the beginning of the couplet. In sum, the remote key-area of the second couplet can be seen to be a working-out of the implications of a specific aspect of the first variation.

The motivic and harmonic connections between the different sections of the finale are the same kind of relationships that bind different movements together. But are the movements themselves related to one another?

The most immediately obvious relationship is a thematic connection. Compare the A section of the Trio (Ex. 5.7*a*) with the first couplet of the finale (*b*).

It is not just an issue of a similar melodic outline. The texture is remarkably similar (high tessitura, three active voices). With one exception (in the recapitulation of the first movement), this texture appears nowhere else in the symphony. Moreover, in both cases the second

Ex. 5.7
(*a*)

(b)

phrase has a 2–3 suspension (between the upper two voices) followed by an acceleration (in parallel thirds) to the cadence. The similarities between the Trio and couplet add a bit more credibility to other motivic relationships that we might not otherwise take particularly seriously. The most obvious, perhaps, is the similarity of the opening of the Trio to the theme of the second movement.

This is not all. The theme of the first movement has a slightly unconventional feature. In between the first and second statements of the principal theme, Haydn moves to the dominant with a rather convincing tonicization, including a complete, rhythmically stressed, authentic cadence (m. 10), with the new 'tonic' prolonged for nearly three measures with a full orchestral tutti. Immediately after, he slips right back out of B flat and resumes with a repetition of the principal theme in E flat.

This would hardly be worthy of mention were it not for similar progressions in the themes of the Menuet and finale. In both cases, the mid-point of the A section is marked by a tonicization of the dominant, a tonicization that, like that of the first movement, is promptly canceled by the return of the tonic.

We could continue to cite other common features of the different movements (such as the tonicization of C minor after the double bar in all four movements, including the second movement), but the principal similarities already cited are sufficient to make the point. The different movements are loosely bound together by a network of thematic, harmonic, and textural parallels. Compared with those in Symphony No. 49, the connections are not particularly strong (the movements do not seem to depend on one another for their comprehensibility), but they are extensive enough to warrant attention.

6

Symphony No. 75

(–1781 [?1779])

NONE of the symphonies analyzed thus far has begun with a slow introduction or ended with a rondo—until 1770 both features were rare.[1] In works composed after that point, one encounters, with increasing frequency, slow introductions to the first movements and rondos as finales. Symphony No. 75 has both.

Slow introductions occupy an uncertain position between independent movement and dependent section. By their very nature, of course, introductions are not complete movements—they cannot stand alone. Part of the reason for this is that they are harmonically incomplete, ending (usually) on the dominant. Moreover, Haydn's introductions are normally so short (between ten and thirty measures) that they rarely have enough musical space to tonicize both a primary and a secondary key. As a result, they can do little more than establish the tonic and end on (not in) the dominant—hardly enough harmonic foundation to permit them to function as an independent movement.

At the same time, introductions do have some of the characteristics of independent movements. Successive movements rely on the principle of contrast, typically differing from one another in tempo, theme, and meter. Haydn's slow introductions (up through the Paris symphonies) are invariably in a markedly different tempo from the main body of the movement, employ a contrasting meter, and are based on different motives and themes. As such, the slow introduction would eventually prompt Haydn to pose an interesting compositional question: How can a section of a movement with a particular theme, tempo, and meter be successfully integrated with another section that is based on a contrasting theme, tempo, and meter, particularly if the thematic material of the introduction never returns?

---

[1] Only three symphonies dating from before 1770 employ slow introductions, Nos. 6, 7, and 25. As for rondos, they are 'employed in only five of the forty-six symphonies dated prior to 1771'. See Cole, 'Haydn's Symphonic Rondo Finales', 114. Stephen Fisher suggests that three other movements may be considered to have rondo finales (pre-1770): Symphonies Nos. 9/iii, 30/iii, and 26/iii. See his 'Further Thoughts on Haydn's Symphonic Rondo Finales', *Haydn Yearbook*, 17 (1992), 90–1. Although Fisher indicates that Nos. 9/iii and 26/iii 'could be rejected as straightforward minuets with trios', he argues that No. 30/iii 'must be considered a rondo' because it has the design of ABCA + coda.

In his slow introductions before the Paris symphonies (and in Symphony No. 75 in particular), I see no evidence that Haydn had any interest in solving this problem, or even that he considered it to be a problem. In any case, there are very few introductions in Haydn's early symphonies, and those that do exist occur most often in works with programmatic associations and in works originally intended for the theater.[2] In the present work (and in the preceding symphonies with slow introductions), I can see no convincing evidence that Haydn was trying to relate the introduction to the main body of the movement.[3]

Although slow introductions are not all cut from the same cloth, there are stereotypical features that occur quite frequently: slow arpeggiations of the tonic triad, slashing upwards runs which lead to massive tutti chords, successions of dotted rhythms, a double statement of the opening theme with the second cast in the parallel minor, an extended pedal-point on the dominant, and a closing fermata. The introduction of Symphony No. 75 employs quite a number of these standard devices, which—perhaps—explains why there are no obvious connections with the main body of the movement.[4]

Turning to the main body of the movement, we see that the extent of the recomposition of the recapitulation in Symphony No. 75/i exceeds anything we have encountered to this point. Substantially less than half of the recapitulation is a repetition (literal or transposed) of an equivalent passage in the exposition (compare Table 6.1 with similar tables in Chapters 2–5).

From Table 6.1, it can be seen that only four of the first thirty-two measures of the exposition return unaltered in the recapitulation. Although we normally expect the recapitulation to cut some of the material

---

[2] At least four of the seven (or possibly nine) slow introductions written before Symphony No. 75 are in works with extramusical associations. (According to Feder's worklist in *The New Grove Dictionary*, Nos. 6, 7, 25, 50, 54, 57, 60 were definitely written before No. 75; Nos. 53 and 71 probably were.) The slow introductions of Nos. 6 and 7 are in avowedly programmatic compositions. The first two movements of No. 50 are adapted from the overture to the marionette opera *Der Götterrat*. So too, No. 60 was written as incidental music for a play (*Der Zerstreute*), the first movement, with the slow introduction, being the overture. See Stephen C. Fisher, 'Haydn's Overtures and their Adaptations as Concert Orchestral Works', Ph.D. diss. (Univ. of Pennsylvania, 1985), 11. The slow introduction in No. 54 may have been added as an afterthought. See Landon's comment in *Joseph Haydn: Critical Edition of the Complete Symphonies*, v. p. xv.

[3] The slow introduction and main body of No. 73/i share a common rhythmic motive: repeated, upbeat eighth-notes, leading to the following strong beat. However, there seems to be nothing else of significance binding the introduction to the Allegro.

[4] For a thorough discussion of the slow introduction, see Marianne Danckwardt, *Die langsame Einleitung: Ihre Herkunft und ihr Bau bei Haydn und Mozart* (Tutzing, 1977). Danckwardt argues (p. 125) that the very nature of the stereotypical material of the early introductions made it difficult for there to be motivic connections between the slow introduction and the fast portion of the movement. But, as we will see in the discussion of Symphony No. 85, even an introduction filled with stereotypical devices can, none the less, be integrated into the main body of the movement.

TABLE 6.1. *Symphony No. 75/i: Correspondences between Exposition and Recapitulation*

Exposition (mm.)	Recapitulation (mm.)
24–37	—
38–41	121–4
42–55	—
—	125–8 (similar to mm. 33–4)
56–65	129–34 (transposed, but correspondences with mm. 56–65 not exact)
—	135–58
66–8	159–62 (transposed)

from the exposition, what happens in Symphony No. 75/i might appear to be hacking away with a machete, not trimming delicately with scissors. But it is the very nature of the material in this exposition that necessitates such a radical response.

In the exposition, the opening theme appears in a double statement: a four-measure phrase ending on the tonic (mm. 24–7), followed immediately by a second, slightly varied statement of the theme (mm. 28–31), which is elided to the continuation and extended until a powerful half-cadence in m. 37—the end of the tonic definition section (see Ex. 6.1).

When Haydn picks up after the half-cadence in m. 37, he begins, not with a new theme, but with a second statement of the opening theme (mm. 38–41), this time forte and with a new bass-line (as per the variation principle) but with only one statement of the theme (as per the redundancy principle). This is followed directly by the tonicization of the dominant (see Ex. 6.2).

Given Haydn's normal application of the redundancy principle, these two statements of the theme (one of which is itself a double statement) cannot both be retained in the recapitulation. As we can see from Table 6.1, he chooses to eliminate entirely the first double statement (mm. 24–37). But why did he make this choice? Why not eliminate the restatement at mm. 38–41? As either excision would satisfy the dictates of the redundancy principle, we should like to find some justification for Haydn's specific decision.

The reason for this choice seems to stem from a convention relating to dynamics. For obvious reasons, if there is a double statement of the theme in the exposition, Haydn generally cuts one of those statements in the recapitulation. When a movement begins with a double statement of the theme, one piano and the other forte, then in the recapitulation Haydn

Ex. 6.1

(continued)

Ex. 6.1 continued

generally excises the piano statement of the theme and begins with the forte statement, as he does in this case.[5]

As a result, the opening double statement (plus extension) is excised completely, and Haydn merely restates mm. 38–41 at the beginning of the recapitulation (mm. 121–4). But in the exposition, the second statement of the theme was followed almost immediately by the tonicization of the dominant (G♯ first appears in m. 44). Therefore, in the recapitulation, Haydn must break away from the model of the exposition shortly after the four-measure restatement of the opening theme. In place of the transition to the dominant section, he substitutes a brief passage (mm. 125–8; see Ex. 6.3) that is similar to a passage that had been excised (mm. 32 ff.; see Ex. 6.1).[6]

Although the logic may be simple, the consequences are not. As a result of the excision of the opening double statement and shortened rewriting of the transition, Haydn arrives, in m. 129—a mere eight measures after the beginning of the recapitulation—at the equivalent of the dominant confirmation section of the exposition. If he were simply to transpose everything from this point (the equivalent of m. 56) to the end of the exposition (m. 68) back to the tonic, following the sonata principle, the

---

[5] See Symphonies Nos. 53/i, 73/i, 77/i, 99/i. In all of these cases, the forte statement comes second in the exposition. In Nos. 57/i and 102/i, the first statement of the theme is forte and the second is piano; in No. 102/i, only the forte statement returns; in No. 57/i, only the forte statement is complete. In No. 58/i, the first statement (piano in the exposition) is retained in the recapitulation but made forte. In No. 88/i, Haydn retains both statements in the recapitulation, but varies the piano statement and abbreviates the forte statement. If both statements are piano, but the second has greater orchestral forces, only the second statement will return. See Nos. 84/i, 85/i, and 96/i.

[6] Haydn may have omitted all of the transition to the dominant section because he wished to avoid transposing mm. 52–5 back to the tonic. In the uppermost voice in these measures, a version of the principal theme occurs in the dominant, and this would have to be transposed back to the tonic in the recapitulation.

Ex. 6.2

recapitulation would be approximately twenty measures long, less than half the length of the exposition. Given Haydn's formal norms, this radical asymmetry would not be acceptable; something must be added to the recapitulation to compensate.

In mm. 135–58, Haydn interpolates an extensive passage (it is larger than the rest of the recapitulation) that solves the problem of asymmetry, restoring the recapitulation to a size that is only slightly smaller than the exposition. The passage is neither a literal repetition of anything from the exposition (thus avoiding redundancy), nor does it introduce any completely new motivic material (thus avoiding a violation of the unity

Ex. 6.3

principle). Instead, mm. 135–58 act as a kind of second development section, presenting the principal theme in stretto imitation in sequence, a procedure that is vaguely reminiscent of the contrapuntal treatment of the principal theme in the development section (see Ex. 6.4).

The second movement is a set of four strophic variations on a hymn-like melody. As in Symphony No. 55/ii, Haydn employs a number of compositional strategies that reach past the boundaries of the strophes. In Symphony No. 75/ii, he manipulates several variables (melody, orchestration, dynamics, rhythm) to create an interesting developmental progression (see Ex. 6.5).

On the one hand, Haydn structures the overall directionality of the movement by careful manipulation of the rhythm. There is a steady progression in surface-rhythmic speed, as the slow quarter-notes of the theme yield to eighths and sixteenths in the first two variations, sixteenths in the third variation, and sextuplets in the final variation. Yet, toward the end of the movement, even as the surface rhythm has increased to its fastest level, the slower-moving (and largely unelaborated) theme emerges from the background, providing a sense of rhythmic return.

Ex. 6.4

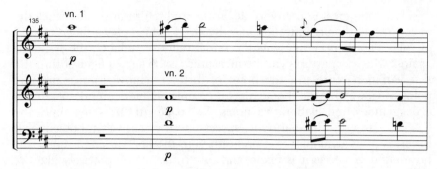

Ex. 6.5
(a)

Poco Adagio

(b)

Variazione I

Haydn also creates a sense of departure and return in terms of melody, in contrast to the orchestration and dynamics, which play a different kind of role. The theme represents the initial point of stability, the standard against which departures can be measured (Ex. 6.5*a*). In light of this, the first variation represents the point of furthest remove from a melodic point of view, with the theme almost completely hidden underneath the arpeggiations and elaborative notes (Ex. 6.5*b*). At the same time, the bass-line (and thus the harmonic succession) is extensively modified. Yet, in terms of its dynamics and orchestration, the first variation represents no motion at all, as it is piano and for strings alone, precisely like the theme.

The second variation begins the process of return from the melodic perspective (Ex. 6.5*c*). The original theme is sometimes plainly evident (e.g. mm. 37–9), although at other times it is still rather disguised (e.g. mm. 41–4). Similarly, the bass-line is closer to the original than that of the first variation. On the other hand, in terms of its dynamics and orchestration, the second variation is the furthest removed from the theme, relying on dramatic contrasts in dynamics and introducing, for the first time in the movement, the winds and brass.

In terms of its melodic profile, the third variation brings us one step closer back to the original point of departure (Ex. 6.5*d*). The melody

(*c*)

is essentially identical to that of the theme; the bass-line retains some differences. But its orchestration presents us with a paradox. It is for strings alone (like the original theme)—but (unlike the theme) for soloists, with the solo cello demanding our attention as a central focus.

(d)

The last variation completes the process of melodic return, as both the melody and bass are, with minor exceptions, identical to those of the theme, while the running sextuplets recede into the accompaniment (Ex. 6.5*e*). But in terms of its orchestration, the final variation (together with the brief coda) acts as a summation, bringing the formerly disruptive and obtrusive winds of the second variation back into the fold, supporting and solidifying the final melodic repetition.

Thus, like Symphony No. 55/ii, the second movement of Symphony No. 75 manipulates the surface in such a manner as to transcend the boundaries of the strophes. Although the sense of strophic variation is never lost, the changes in rhythmic intensity, the departure from and return to the original theme, and the teleological function of the orchestration permit larger groupings.

The third movement is rather straightforward, with both Menuetto and Trio utilizing symmetrical, non-modulating A sections (each of two four-measure phrases) that are repeated, essentially unaltered, after the short B sections. Since the A sections do not modulate, but instead

(e)

cadence in the tonic, it is possible in each case to repeat the A section *in toto*, and without alteration, as the A′ section. However, as we have seen, Haydn often avoids a literal repetition where the A section is itself highly redundant. Given the antecedent–consequent statements in the A sections of both the Menuetto and Trio in Symphony No. 75, one might have thought that he would have been inclined to avoid literal repetitions for the A′ section, at least in the Menuetto (see the discussion of this topic in Chapter 3 above), and would have rewritten, if slightly, the A′ sections. In this case, exceptionally, he does not.[7]

---

[7] As explained above, Ch. 3 n. 23, the symmetry and simplicity of menuets and trios from this period may be a consequence of Haydn's attempts to increase the commercial viability of his works.

TABLE 6.2. *Symphony No. 75/iv: Formal Plan*

A	1st refrain, mm. 1–26 rounded binary a: mm. 1–8 b: mm. 9–18 a′: mm. 19–26
B	1st couplet, mm. 27–50 rounded binary a: mm. 27–34 b: mm. 35–42 a′: mm. 43–50
A′	2nd refrain (variation 1), mm. 51–76 no repeat signs
C	2nd couplet, mm. 77–100 transition, mm. 77–84 quasi-development section, mm. 85–100
A″	3rd refrain, mm. 101–37 a: mm. 101–8 b: mm. 109–29 (much expanded, cf. mm. 9–18) a′: mm. 130–7
Coda	mm. 138–66

The finale corresponds most closely to a formal type that is now commonly labeled as a 'rondo'.[8] Specifically, it might be described as a five-part rondo with coda: ABACA + coda. But characterizing the finale's form with a single term is somewhat deceptive, as it might imply that only

[8] Providing a convincing definition for rondo is as difficult (and futile) a task as finding an acceptable definition for sonata form. It is thus interesting to see that 18th- and 19th-cent. theorists (in treatises) and composers (through the rubrics by which they prefaced works) labeled as rondos works that might not be so labeled today. As Malcolm S. Cole has remarked, 'to theorists of the late eighteenth and early nineteenth centuries the rondo was not just a formal structure but also a concept or a style.' 'Czerny's Illustrated Description of the Rondo or Finale', *Music Review*, 36 (1975), 8. In this book, we will use the term 'rondo' in the more restricted modern sense, to describe a formal idea that involves recurrent statements of a refrain in the tonic, with the refrains separated by episodes or couplets which may be (and usually are) in other key-areas. For further examination of these issues, see Cole, 'Rondos, Proper and Improper', *Music and Letters*, 51 (1970), 388–99. For a comprehensive discussion of the rondo, see Cole, 'The Development of the Instrumental Rondo Finale'. See also his 'The Vogue of the Instrumental Rondo in the Late Eighteenth Century', *Journal of the American Musicological Society*, 22 (1969), 425–55. For a thorough discussion of the problem of establishing a convincing typology for rondos, sonata-rondos, rondo-sonatas, and so forth, see Fisher, 'Further Thoughts', 92–102.

one formal concept is operative, that is, that the movement is constructed merely from the alternation of a tonally self-contained refrain in the tonic, with couplets in closely related keys. As far as it goes, that is an accurate, if rough, description of the movement, but much—too much—is lost in the translation (see Table 6.2).

For one thing, the opening refrain (mm. 1–26) is itself a rounded binary form—internal double bar and all. (This is a common feature in Haydn's rondos.)[9] So too, the first couplet is a rounded binary (in the parallel minor, mm. 27–50). The a section of the refrain concludes in the tonic; as a result, the a' section can be (and is) a literal repetition, with only a slight change in the final measure to make the cadence more solid.[10] In the first couplet, however, the a section ends in the relative major; in response, the latter half of the a' section has to be rewritten to remain in the tonic.

When the refrain returns after the first couplet it is not restated without alteration. Rather, Haydn first varies the orchestration, and then makes some slight variations in the melodic line. That being the case, there is nothing to this point in the movement that would distinguish this rondo from a hybrid variation.[11]

After a brief transition (mm. 77–84), the rest of the second couplet (mm. 85–100) concentrates on the relative minor. Unlike the first couplet (and the two refrains), the second couplet is not itself a complete harmonic unit, but, rather, returns to the tonic and comes to a cadence on the dominant (m. 100).

At this point, if Haydn had restated the refrain in varied form, then the form of this movement could have been classified as a rondo-variation. But the third refrain (mm. 101–37) is neither a literal repetition, nor a strophic variation of the opening refrain. Rather, after a literal repeat of the a section, Haydn conspiciously diverges from the model of the refrain (see Ex. 6.6).

---

[9] When a movement begins with a tonally closed form, such as a rounded binary, and is followed by a contrasting episode that is also tonally closed, then the initial formal unit generally will return, either literally or in variation. That is the case in this movement: mm. 1–26 comprise a tonally closed form and are followed by another tonally complete formal unit—in minor; thus the opening passage is repeated in slightly varied form in mm. 51–76. However, if a composition begins with a tonally closed form, but the following episode is not tonally closed, then there is no necessity for a repetition of the opening section. See Symphony No. 76/iv, where the opening rounded binary form (mm. 1–24) is followed by a tonally open section that modulates to the dominant. Therefore, the opening rounded binary is part of a sonata form, not a rondo. See also Symphonies Nos. 77/iv (opening rounded binary: mm. 1–48) and 88/ii (opening rounded binary: mm. 1–36).

[10] When a rounded binary is used as a component of a larger formal unit (such as strophic variations, hybrid variations, or a rondo), the cadence before the internal double bar is usually on V (in pieces in major), or III (for works in minor). Occasionally—as in this case—there will be no modulation and the cadence will be on the tonic. For an interesting exception to these norms, see Symphony No. 88/iv, where the cadence at the internal double bar is on iii.

[11] Sisman describes this work as a 'rondo with incidental variation' in 'Haydn's Variations', 120, and as a variation-rondo, a fast finale with incidental figurations, in *Haydn and the Classical Variation*, 150. Symphonies Nos. 61/iv, 66/iv, and 68/iv have similar formal plans.

Ex. 6.6

(continued)

What should attract our attention in particular is the way in which Haydn brings the b section to a close and prepares for the a′ statement of the refrain. That is, beginning at m. 118 and continuing until m. 122, he establishes a solid dominant chord in root position. As this b section was already substantially longer than the b sections in the first two refrains, we would be quite justified in expecting the arrival of the tonic and principal theme in m. 123.

Ex. 6.6 continued

What happens in m. 123 is anything but expected. Instead of the tonic and the return of the theme, Haydn follows the root-position dominant of m. 122 with a sudden and jarring (note the dynamics) vii⁶/V. This is no momentary interlude: the applied dominant lasts for a full five measures, replaced by an implied (but not stated) dominant only in m. 128, with the cancellation of the G♯ by a G♮.

The exaggerated frustration of the resolution of the dominant in m. 123 is all the more striking in that it seems somewhat gratuitous. In the two previous refrains (mm. 1–26 and 51–76) and in an identical passage in the first couplet (mm. 39–42), the dominant at the end of the b section was stated clearly enough, but scarcely emphasized. But in the third refrain, Haydn breaks away from the model of the previous passages and expands the dominant to five measures, as if to emphasize its importance. Having gotten our attention by emphasizing the dominant, he then purposefully frustrates its resolution.

The rather self-conscious manipulation of the dominant's resolution is quickly, but only momentarily, forgotten. After the dominant is (implicitly) restored (mm. 128–9), the a′ section returns (m. 130) to complete the refrain (m. 137), after which point Haydn initiates a coda. At first, all of the signs seem to point toward a quick arrival of a concluding cadence (see Ex. 6.7). In m. 146, the surface rhythm slows suddenly, followed, in m. 148, by a vii⁷/V, then a cadential 6–4, and then silence—a measure and a half of silence.

Ex. 6.7

Once again, Haydn has gone out of his way to prepare an important structural cadence, and then, with all due deliberation, has frustrated its resolution. The sense of frustration is compounded by the fact that the chord preceding the cadential 6–4 is very nearly the same chord that thwarted the cadence in mm. 123 ff. But this time, it has been corrected, put in the right place (before the dominant), thereby strengthening the sense that this is to be a definitive cadence. The cadential 6–4 that follows is intense, powerful, unstable, creating strong expectations for the imminent arrival of the structural dominant.

What follows in mm. 151 ff is more than a little odd. We do get a dominant—of a sort—but everything about it is wrong. Instead of a forte, tutti, registrally expanded, complete, root-position dominant seventh chord on the downbeat of m. 150, we get a soft dyad (G/C♯) in the violins in m. 151. As if that were not bad enough, Haydn goes out of his way to make it worse. Instead of resolving this weak dominant to the tonic, he goes in the opposite direction, away from the tonic, at least for a moment.

Three measures later (m. 155) we are back to a dominant, this time in root position. Even this is not the end of this unfolding drama: the dominant resolves not to a tonic chord, but in a deceptive progression to the submediant in m. 156. When we are finally given a proper authentic cadence in mm. 158–9, there is no satisfactory sense of closure as the dynamics are still piano, the tessitura is limited to the lower register, and the winds are omitted. Only after two registrally incomplete statements (for less than the full orchestra) of the beginning of the refrain's theme do we finally get a decisive cadence—in the final measures of the composition.

The events at mm. 123 ff and mm. 149 ff, by virtue of their forceful disruption of expectations and skewing of symmetries, have a strong effect on the form of the movement. On the most obvious level these passages break up what would otherwise be a square and predictable formal plan. But the impact of these cadences goes beyond their disruption of symmetries. Through their infringement of norms (both intra- and inter-opus) the frustrated cadences and deferred resolutions impart a sense of forward motion. As the corollary of the normative principle indicates, a significant infringement of norms will require some kind of compensatory response, something that will resolve the instabilities occasioned by the violation of norms. With its multiple statement of the theme and its emphasis on the final cadence, the coda provides that compensatory response.

The reader who has been comparing the themes of the four movements will long since have noticed that there are no obvious thematic similarities between the movements. Perhaps one might wish to argue that the first four notes of the theme of the second movement are (in transposition) embedded within the theme of the finale. However, I find this very unconvincing, not only on its own merits, but even more so when seen in the total context. Unlike the thematic relationships we have examined in Symphony No. 49, which do play an important role, the supposed relationship is totally isolated—no other even slightly convincing connection could be drawn between any other combination of movements. The themes of the introduction to the first movement are unlike anything significant from the first movement, the first movement is unlike the second movement, the Menuet is unlike the Trio, and both are unrelated to the finale. Therefore, the supposed thematic relationship between the second and fourth movements seems all the more dubious.

Although there do not seem to be meaningful thematic connections between the movements, we should at least consider whether there might be other kinds of connections. Perhaps the best place for us to start is by noting that there are frequent juxtapositions of D major and D minor in this symphony. For example, a prominent feature of the introduction is the turn in mm. 10 ff to the parallel minor. (Although the turn to the parallel minor is a stock figure for introductions, it cannot be completely dismissed merely for this reason.) Haydn has established the juxtaposition of the major and minor modes as an important compositional premise for the movement. As a result, the abrupt (and initially surprising) return of the recapitulation of the first movement may be seen as an elaboration of this idea, for the retransition to the recapitulation comes via a hint of D minor. Moreover, as in the introduction, the juxtaposition of D major and minor is highlighted by a sudden contrast in dynamics.

A comparable juxtaposition occurs in the second movement. The theme of the second movement tonicizes its dominant (D major) at the internal double bar. Immediately afterwards, the B section begins with a D minor chord, another prominent juxtaposition of D major and minor at a central point in the form (see Ex. 6.8). As the second movement is a set of variations, this juxtaposition of D major and minor occurs in each of the variations in precisely the same place. (It should also be noted that this relationship is possible only given the choice of the key of G major for the second movement.)

In the finale as well, the D major–minor opposition plays an important role: the first couplet is in D minor and is thus sandwiched between refrains in D major. Although one might be tempted to dismiss this relationship as trivial (rondos often employ one or the other of the closely related minor keys for the couplets), such a response could be too hasty. Unlike the second refrain (in the relative minor), which begins with a transition from the tonic and ends with a half-cadence in D major, the first refrain is a tonally self-contained entity. Thus, at the end of the first refrain and the beginning of the second refrain, there is an unmediated opposition of D major and minor.

Ex. 6.8

What should our verdict be regarding the strength of these inter-movemental relationships? Unless there are other significant connections that have been missed by the present analysis, we ought to conclude that the intermovemental relationships in Symphony No. 75 are moderately extensive but rather weak. In particular, it should be noted that none of the connections seems to involve the third movement. And even those connections that have been suggested are not particularly prominent, nor are they so strikingly similar as to demand our attention. Finally, none of the movements seems to be dependent on each other for their com-prehensibility. At best, we find only mild resemblances between the movements, primarily the juxtaposition of D major and minor—hardly significant relationships, and ones that scarcely extend beyond coinciden-tal similarities.

7

Symphony No. 81

(-8 November 1784)

IN many of Haydn's later works, significant aspects of the formal organization (both intramovemental and intermovemental) can be traced back to a single event that occurs at the very beginning of the composition. Nowhere is that more easily demonstrable than in Symphony No. 81. Essential features of the structure of all four movements derive from the opening measures of the symphony (see Ex. 7.1).

The beginning of the first movement presents us with an immediate harmonic paradox. For two measures, the opening G major triad seems unequivocal, unassailable, the certain tonic-to-be. But before its tonic potential can be confirmed, the G major triad is promptly and unceremoniously contradicted. An F♮ appears in m. 3, followed in m. 4 by the remaining elements of the dominant seventh chord on G.

Admittedly, the resultant harmonic progression (I–V/IV) is common enough as an opening gambit in eighteenth-century music, scarcely worth singling out for particular attention. But Haydn has gone to some lengths to make the progression as striking as possible, thereby preventing it from receding unobtrusively into the woodwork. The F, the seventh of the chord, is not introduced smoothly by step from the first degree, but is highlighted by the rests that precede it. So too, the bare and starkly dissonant G/F dyad gives this a lean and taut sound. The arrival of the non-chord tone C only makes matters worse, yielding the ambiguous trichord G/F/C before resolving to B. The orchestration contributes to the sense of discontinuity as the bass and the winds drop out after the first chord.

The immediate effect of this progression is to add a subtle twist to the harmonic definition of the passage. The opening G major triad and its extension in the bass clearly creates the impression that G is to be the tonic, but this tonic definition is otherwise unsupported—no other clarifying chords appear before the arrival of the F♮. By adding first an F♮ above the bass and then the remaining elements of the dominant seventh chord on G, Haydn has fostered a shade of harmonic doubt—is the tonality really G? Or could it be something else—C?[1]

---

[1] Charles Rosen has suggested that the beginning of the Allegro of Mozart's Symphony in D Major K. 504 ('Prague'), with its use of the flat seventh degree in conjunction with a tonic pedal, may be

Ex. 7.1

In short order, Haydn resolves this harmonic uncertainty and shows that the dominant seventh on G functions as the V/IV, passing through IV (over the tonic pedal) on to the dominant and then the tonic, G major.

derived from this opening. See his 'Influence: Plagiarism and Inspiration', *19th Century Music,* 4 (1979–80), 89–90. It should be noted that the Haydn symphony, unlike the Mozart, has no slow introduction. This means that the harmonic ambiguity that is central to the Haydn symphony has no real counterpart in the Mozart work, where the introduction clearly and unequivocally establishes the key well before the main body of the movement begins.

In the process, we are presented with the opposition of F♮ and F♯, a juxtaposition of elements that will have significant consequences. These simple ideas—the short-lived and never realized suggestion of C major and the juxtaposition of F♮ and F♯—are the determinants, not only of many of the details of the form in this movement, but also of important aspects of the structure of the remaining movements and the relationships between them.

In the first movement, we find a comprehensive realization of the implications of the opening, not only in the development section, but in the recapitulation and coda as well. Each of these three sections of the movement expands upon a different aspect of the harmonic progressions of the opening measures.

The most obvious attempt to follow up on the implications of the opening measures appears at the beginning of the development section. After the cadence on the dominant at the end of the exposition, Haydn begins the development section with the—by then (1780s)—typical jump directly from V to V/vi, but he does not continue on to the relative minor. Instead, the development trails off in mm. 73–4 with a lone repeated B in the second violins. What follows is a dramatic stroke, a striking, redirected continuation. Using the B as a common tone, Haydn introduces the remaining tones of the dominant seventh chord of C major—the problematic chord from the beginning of the exposition. This time, however, the implications of the dominant seventh chord are amply realized, as Haydn plunges off into C major, staying there until m. 84 (see Ex. 7.2).

On the most obvious level, Haydn has made manifest that which has been latent. In the opening measures, the tonic of G major was challenged briefly by a threat to transform it into the dominant of C major, but C major was only implied, never stated. At the beginning of the development section, Haydn expands upon that idea by realizing the implications of the exposition and tonicizing C major.

Of course, it was hardly unusual for there to be brief tonicizations of a number of closely (and perhaps not so closely) related key-areas within Haydn's post-1780 development sections. But in contrast to all of the other key-areas touched upon in this development section, C major is emphasized by solid dominant–tonic bass progressions. Indeed, within the development section it is the only key-area whose tonic appears in root position, reached from its own root-position dominant.[2] As a result, it has a solidity and sense of local stability accorded no other key-area in the development.

---

[2] In m. 98, F does occur in root position, but the chord tone in the top voice is deferred by a suspension and the chord is approached from an inversion of its dominant.

Ex. 7.2

Ex. 7.3

A further reference to the implications of the opening harmonic progression occurs toward the end of the development section. In m. 105, Haydn states the dominant of G major in root position. Presumably, this ought to mark the beginning of the prolongation of the dominant chord, leading directly to the tonic and the beginning of the recapitulation, but in the following measure, a root-position tonic makes a premature return.

Although it is somewhat unusual, we might not pay heed to this early return were it not for the continuation. No sooner has Haydn reached the tonic chord than he transforms it into a V/IV and moves directly to IV (m. 106, see Ex. 7.3). Haydn has complicated the return of the tonic with the paradoxical harmonic progression of the opening measures of the symphony. Just as the tonic was challenged by its subdominant at the beginning of the movement, so too the return of the tonic is here challenged by the same harmonic progression.

The importance of this passage goes beyond its mere reiteration of the opening progression of the composition. Its placement shortly before the beginning of the recapitulation means that the development section is framed (and thus shaped) by two passages that are direct consequences of the opening harmonic progression. Just as the tonicization of C major at the beginning of the development section was not merely a repetition of the opening progression, but a realization of some of its implications, so too the V/IV at m. 106 does more than restate—it reformulates. By placing the dominant seventh chord with its F♯ in the top voice in m. 105, and following that with the V/IV with its F♮ in the same register, Haydn has made manifest the implicit F♯–F♮ opposition of the opening measures, bringing these two tones into closer temporal and registral proximity. (Further stages in the development of this juxtaposition will follow in the recapitulation in this movement and in the movements to come.)

The return of the V/IV in m. 106 is a subtle violation of the expectations created by the return of the tonic key and the establishment of the dominant. But there is nothing—absolutely nothing—subtle about the next violation of expectations. In m. 110, Haydn returns to the dominant and for the next eight measures it remains as the bass tone. With each passing measure, the level of tension is heightened, helped along in mm. 115–16 by a crescendo. Surely this must be the final preparation for the reprise (see Ex. 7.4).

It is not. In m. 117, Haydn launches into a surprising detour. First, the 6–4 is transformed into minor, and then the bass steps up to E♭, leaving behind the not-yet-resolved dominant. As if that were not enough, Haydn rushes even farther afield, not returning to the dominant until m. 122. There, finally, he states a proper cadential 6–4 (in G major), followed by the structural dominant seventh chord that prepares the recapitulation.

The sudden (if transitory) turn to the tonic minor in m. 117 should stand out as a highly disruptive and anomalous turn of events, one which seems to have neither antecedent nor (with the brief exception of mm. 141–4) consequent in the remainder of the movement. Haydn has done much to heighten the expectations for the return of the tonic (major), but has suddenly and forcefully dashed those expectations by lunging into the

Ex. 7.4

(continued)

(destabilizing) parallel minor. This has some rather significant inter-movemental implications to which we will return in due course.[3]

---

[3] As was shown in the analysis of Symphony No. 1/ii, Haydn treats a turn to the parallel minor, not as a stable equivalent of the parallel major, but as a highly disruptive event, particularly when the minor arrives at the point at which the listener had reason to expect the major. Such destabilizing events need to be addressed in some manner—as per the normative principle. The extraordinary consequences of the turn to the minor in Symphony No. 81/i will be discussed below. For another prominent example from approximately this period, see Symphony No. 79/i. Immediately after the

Ex. 7.4 continued

beginning of the recapitulation, there is a sudden turn to the parallel minor (mm. 106 ff). This anomalous event is not otherwise explained in the first movement. But it has multiple consequences—particularly in the third and fourth movements. See the third movement, where the reprise of the Trio (mm. 57 ff) is anticipated (and destabilized) by the preceding parallel minor (mm. 52–6). In the finale, the tonic minor functions as the first couplet, thus framed (and finally stabilized) by the refrains in the tonic major.

The recapitulation begins in m. 124, not with the opening measures of the movement, but with the equivalent of m. 24.[4] However, the first twenty-three measures are not excised entirely; they reappear, with some modifications, at the end of the movement as the coda. This movement, like Symphony No. 21/ii, has a mirror recapitulation.

As we have seen, binary variants of sonata form were relatively rare in Haydn's symphonies of the 1760s and 1770s (see Chapter 3). By the 1780s they were more than rare—they were virtually nonexistent. Aside from Symphony No. 81/i, the only other binary variant movement in a post-1780 symphony is No. 87/iv (1785).[5]

In the analysis of Symphony No. 21/ii, we saw that its mirror recapitulation was a consequence of the introductory nature of the opening of the movement. The movement began with a passage that was clearly differentiated from the remainder of the exposition, but was in the same tempo and was otherwise inseparable from the main body of the movement. The very same premises are operative in Symphony No. 81/i and function to determine the form: the opening twenty-three measures are unquestionably different from the remainder of the exposition in texture, orchestration, and theme, but are in the same tempo and are not separated by any pause or fermata. As a result of the corollary of the unity principle, the quasi-introduction should return at some point, but cannot do so in the recapitulation proper.[6] Therefore, it is not excised entirely, but returns as the coda.[7]

---

[4] Rosen sees the recapitulation beginning earlier, between mm. 104 and 110. See *The Classical Style*, 158–9.

[5] Symphony No. 87/iv is a binary variant of sonata form with an idiosyncratic mirror recapitulation. As is usual in works with mirror recapitulations, there is a same-tempo quasi-introduction (this one closing with the fermatas in mm. 17–18). The problem is that there really is not much—if any—recapitulation before (or after) the late return of the opening theme. The tonic is solidly reached and confirmed only in m. 156, and when it arrives, it restates the closing theme from the very end of the exposition (cf. mm. 69 ff.), seeming to suggest that the movement is over. But surely it cannot be—primarily for reasons of balance. To compound the problem, the closing theme is followed by an extended passage that is not precisely parallel to anything from the exposition. After coming to a halt with another set of fermatas, the opening theme is finally restated (m. 194).

[6] One might wonder whether the harmonic ambiguity and lack of tonic definition of the opening measures motivates their excision from the beginning of the recapitulation. Such a hypothesis can be rejected by citing a counterexample: in Symphony No. 62/iv, the opening measures outline vii/IV, and the tonic does not arrive until m. 7. None the less, a variant of this same progression returns at the beginning of the recapitulation. (A similar, though less daring, progression occurs at the beginning of the second movement.) In Symphony No. 94/i ('Surprise'), the exposition (which follows a slow introduction) begins with a V/ii proceeding to ii. In the recapitulation, Haydn anticipates the reprise with a passage that includes a return to, and a reiteration of, the tonic chord. This allows the G♯ of the V/ii in the first measure of the reprise to be heard as a chromatic passing-tone from G. In this way, the sense of tonic definition is not challenged, even while a version of the opening measures of the exposition is retained. See Guy A. Marco, 'A Musical Task in the "Surprise" Symphony', *Journal of the American Musicological Society*, 11 (1958), 43. See also Symphony No. 86/i.

[7] In the String Quartet Op. 74 No. 3/i, the opening eight measures (plus two additional measures of GP) constitute a clear same-tempo introduction. As we would predict, they do not return at the beginning of the reprise (m. 128). But, unlike that of Symphony No. 81/i, the opening passage does

TABLE 7.1. *Symphony No. 81/i: Correspondences between Exposition and Recapitulation*

Exposition (mm.)	Recapitulation (mm.)
1–23	(see coda)
24–30	124–30
31–5	131–5 (transposed—tonicizes IV)
36–41	136–44 (similar, but not literal)
42–9	(see mm. 161–6)
50–62	145–57 (transposed)
63–7	—
—	158–60 (extension of mm. 156 ff)
—	161–6 (similar to mm. 42–9)
—	167–79 (coda, begins like mm. 1 ff)

Although the opening measures of the exposition do not return at the beginning of the recapitulation, echoes of the excised passages do appear in the retransition.[8] As we saw earlier (Ex. 7.3), Haydn made a premature return to a root–position tonic in m. 106, compromised by the transformation of the tonic chord into the V/IV, precisely the harmonic progression of the quasi-introduction. So too, some of the thematic material from the quasi-introduction that is to be excised from the beginning of the recapitulation appears as part of the retransition (mm. 110–15).[9] The extensive cutting and rewriting in the recapitulation in this movement is typical of Haydn's practice in the mid-1780s (see Table 7.1).

In the exposition, the abandonment of the tonic was first suggested at the end of m. 35, and the tonicization of the dominant followed shortly

not return as a coda after the recapitulation, probably because there is no need to satisfy the corollary of the unity principle. Although the texture of the quasi-introduction is differentiated from the remainder of the exposition, its motivic material is not. An important component of the principal theme (repeated quarter-notes on the second and third beat descending by leap to the downbeat—see viola, mm. 12–13) is an essential aspect of the quasi-introduction (mm. 1–6). Thus, a repetition of the introduction as a coda would probably violate the redundancy principle.

[8] For a discussion of the retransition, see Beth Shamgar, 'On Locating the Retransition in Classic Sonata Form', *Music Review*, 24 (1981), 130–43, and 'Rhythmic Interplay in the Retransitions of Haydn's Piano Sonatas', *Journal of Musicology*, 3 (1984), 55–68.

[9] In movements where Haydn does not begin the recapitulation with a restatement of the opening measures, or where much of the exposition's material is excised, it is not uncommon (as here) to include some of the omitted material at the end of the retransition. For a brief discussion of this technique, see Rosen, *Sonata Forms*, 95. There are interesting examples in other genres. In the Keyboard Sonata Hob. XVI: 19/i (1767), the recapitulation is prepared by a retransition, mm. 66–8, virtually identical to a passage in the exposition, mm. 16–18, that was excised from the recapitulation because of the redundancy principle. See also the Keyboard Sonata Hob. XVI: 26/i, where mm. 6–8, cut from the recapitulation, appear in the retransition (mm. 55–8). In the String Quartet Op. 2 No. 4/i, the recapitulation does not really begin until m. 75, with the return of I in root position. But virtually every measure of the retransition is equivalent to one of the measures excised.

Ex. 7.5
(a)

thereafter. That being the case, we would expect the recapitulation to break away from the model of the exposition before it reached this point in order to avoid an inappropriate modulation to the dominant. As can be seen in Table 7.1, Haydn does indeed diverge from the model of the exposition before the equivalent of m. 36 (see Ex. 7.5).

What he does, however, is more than a trifle odd. Instead of merely rewriting the transition to keep it in the tonic, Haydn transposes mm. 31–5 (Ex. 7.5*a*) down a fifth (or up a fourth) in the recapitulation (*b*). In other words, he transposes a passage that was already in the tonic (and did not need to be transposed) to a key other than the tonic—a kind of backwards application of the sonata principle. To what end?

The transposition is anything but gratuitous. It permits Haydn to elaborate further on the ambiguous harmonic progression of the opening measures of the movement. By transposing mm. 31–5 down a fifth,

(b)

Haydn has tonicized—if only briefly—C major. In the process, he has effectively transformed the tonic of mm. 124 ff into the V/IV, an idea directly related to and derived from the opening harmonic progression of the composition. At the same time, he has presented a further development of the F♯–F♮ opposition that first surfaced in the initial harmonic progression. In m. 131 and again in m. 133, F♮ in the winds is counterpointed directly opposite the F♯ in the strings, a more direct juxtaposition than we have seen in any of the previous manifestations of this harmonic progression.

Having transposed the end of the tonic region to the subdominant, it would have been possible for Haydn simply to transpose the rest of the transition section down a fifth, thereby ending up where he eventually wanted to be—in the tonic. For a few moments, that is exactly what he appears to be doing, but, once again, he breaks away from the model of the exposition, and in the process touches on G minor (a reminder of the destabilizing turn to the minor before the recapitulation).

As we can see from Table 7.1, Haydn does not merely avoid a literal transposition of the end of the transition from the exposition. Rather, he wields his trusty axe with abandon, cutting out or transplanting a sizeable proportion of the latter half of the exposition.

The last of the excisions—mm. 63–7—is the easiest to explain. As Haydn is planning to restate the opening measures as a coda, he cannot bring the work to a decisive final cadence before that point. The powerful cadential passage culminating in m. 67 (the end of the exposition) would be inappropriately conclusive if transposed to the tonic and placed before the coda. It would give the impression that the movement was over upon reaching the equivalent of m. 67, only to continue on to what would then seem to be a redundant appendix.

The fate of mm. 42–9 is somewhat more complicated. In the exposition, this passage came at the end of the transition to the dominant and included a new thematic idea which was stated in the dominant key. Normally, we would expect prominent material that appeared in the dominant to be restated in the tonic in the recapitulation, as per the sonata principle (see Ex. 7.6).

Ex. 7.6

Haydn cannot do this because of a slight technical problem. In the recapitulations of his symphonic sonata forms, he generally avoids a strong cadential emphasis on the tonic chord before he comes to the transposed equivalent of the dominant confirmation section. This suggests that mm. 42 ff ought to be cut, as there is a strong arrival (in root position) on the local tonic in m. 42 itself. If this passage was transposed to the tonic and restated somewhere after the rewritten transition, it would vitiate the strength of the half-cadence in m. 145. However, if he were to eliminate the equivalent of mm. 42 ff entirely, he would violate the dictates of the sonata principle.

Haydn devises a simple solution for this problem: he transplants a version of mm. 42 ff to the end of the recapitulation, before the mirror recapitulation coda. In so doing, he kills the two proverbial birds—no, make that three—with one stone: he satisfies the sonata principle, he avoids anticipating the half-cadence in m. 145, and finally, he precedes the coda with a passage that is less cadentially definitive (and thus more appropriate) than the equivalent of mm. 63–7.

The first movement of Symphony No. 81 is a representative example of Haydn's techniques of formal organization in the mid-1780s. To be sure, this movement is unique in some of its details—mirror recapitulations were hardly *de rigueur* at this (or any point) in his career. None the less, its essential features—the virtually complete rewriting of the recapitulation, the carefully planned development section, and above all, the profound influence of the opening harmonic progression on the course of the movement—occur in many other works of this period.

The second movement is a set of strophic variations based on a simple binary theme which has a non-modulating A section (it concludes with a half-cadence on the dominant). Four variations follow.

In our previous encounters with Haydn's strophic variations (in Symphonies Nos. 55/ii and 75/ii), we saw that Haydn devised several strategies to override the repetitiveness that could result from stringing together a succession of self-contained and harmonically complete tonal forms. In Symphony No. 81/ii, he adds a new weapon to his arsenal of techniques: the second variation is in the parallel minor. From this point forward, all of Haydn's symphonic strophic variations cast one of the strophes in the parallel minor.[10] Often, as here, the minor variation is only somewhat loosely related to the original theme.

At the same time, Haydn continues to employ the tried-and-true techniques he used in earlier sets of strophic variations. The theme, of

---

[10] None of the pre-1783 symphonies with a strophic-variation movement has a strophe in the parallel minor (Nos. 72/iv, 31/iv, 47/ii, 55/ii, 57/ii, 71/ii, 75/ii); all of the post-1783 symphonies of this type have one (Nos. 84/ii, 85/ii, 91/ii, 94/ii, 95/ii, 97/ii). See Sisman, 'Haydn's Variations', 126.

course, acts as the referential origin, the point of departure. The first variation accelerates the surface rhythm and provides the first steps away from the melodic norms of the theme. The second variation, in the parallel minor, functions as the point of furthest remove. In addition to the sharp contrast in mode, it shows only occasional hints of the original melodic outline. Even its form is different, as it moves to the mediant at the internal double bar, and, with its modified return of its theme, is structured as a rounded binary. The third variation acts as the first stage in the process of return. By coming back to the major mode and returning (approximately) to the surface tempo of the first variation, Haydn brings us back from the relatively distant reaches embodied by the second variation.

In the final variation, Haydn manages to create both a sense of return and the impression that this is the culmination and combination of prior events. The sense of return is provided by the unfigured treatment of both the melody and the bass. These two crucial voices are essentially the same in the final variation as they were in the theme. As they both were varied in the previous variations, their appearance here in their original state (more or less—the bass is pizzicato) functions unmistakably as a return.

At the same time, Haydn makes the final variation a summary of prior events. While the theme and first three variations used various subsets of the orchestral resources, the final variation, uniquely, employs the whole orchestra. Furthermore, although the theme returns in its original note values, the running accompaniment in the second violin is in sixteenths— an echo of the acceleration of the surface rhythm that began in the first variation.

Having looked at the first two movements in some detail, we might take a moment before proceeding on to the third movement to begin consideration of possible intermovemental relationships. We quickly find, as we did in Chapter 6, that if we begin our search for connections between the movements by looking for thematic relationships, we are bound to be frustrated. I see no similarities between the two movements' themes and motives, either overt or disguised.

Before we dismiss the movements as unrelated, I would like to explore one other possibility. In the first movement the striking harmonic progression that opened the composition had a profound influence on the structure of the movement as a whole. Could anything in the second movement be related to this as well?

There is one possible connection. The theme of the second movement begins with a prominent leap upwards to a metrically stressed F♯ (Ex. 7.7*a*). In the (minor) second variation, even though the melodic outline is substantially altered, the melody also begins with a leap upwards to the third degree, that is, F♮ (Ex. 7.7*b*). This means that there is a rather

Ex. 7.7
(a)

(b)

distant, and somewhat tenuous, juxtaposition of F♯ and F♮, perhaps a further realization of the opening progression of the first movement with its opposition of these two tones.

When we evaluate the putative connections in terms of the criteria laid out in Chapter 3, we probably should conclude that this connection is far too amorphous and narrowly based to be particularly significant,[11] but a final verdict should not be issued until we have examined all four movements. Therefore, we will suspend judgment for now and return to this problem at the end of the chapter.

The third movement is remarkable on several counts. Not only are there interesting features in the formal plans of both the Menuetto and the Trio, but there are also unmistakable references to some of the most prominent features of the first movement.

The A section of the Menuetto wastes not a moment before getting right down to business. The harmonic paradox from the opening of the first movement is brought back and, if anything, intensified (see Ex. 7.8).

As in the first movement, the first chord of the Menuetto is a G major triad, here arpeggiated over the course of the first few beats. Precisely as in the earlier movement, the opening triad is not immediately followed

---

[11] In any event, it could be argued that the juxtaposition is trivial because all of the strophic variations in Haydn's symphonies from this point forward have a contrasting minor strophe, which means that the opposition of the major and minor third degrees is a given. This might lead one to ask (with justifiable skepticism) whether all such alterations of major and minor have consequences for the multimovement structure. (They do not.) But there is a response to this objection. In the present case, Haydn could have chosen the subdominant for the key of the second movement. Had he done so, there would still have been an opposition of the major and minor third degrees, but the tones involved would have been E♭ and E♮. One would be hard pressed to show that the juxtaposition of E♭ and E♮ has the same degree (or any degree) of significance in the first movement that the F♮–F♯ juxtaposition has. This would seem to imply that relationship between the first and second movements may be significant, and that it may have determined the key for the movement. Of course, given its significance from the first measures of the first movement, had Haydn chosen the subdominant (C major) for the slow movement, there would have been other connections with the remaining movements.

Ex. 7.8

by a clarifying progression that anchors G as the tonic—quite the opposite. In m. 3, the G major triad is transformed into the dominant seventh of C. Then, in m. 4, going one step beyond what was done in the first movement, the bass leaps from G to C, seeming to confirm C as the tonic. As if to reinforce the tension between the two key-areas—the G we know it has to be, versus the C it appears to be—Haydn pits F♮ and F♯ against one another with biting dissonance at the end of m. 2, the latest instance of the opposition of these two tones.

It does not take Haydn long to redirect the harmonic flow. In m. 5, F♯ returns as a structural tone, reconfirming G as the tonic. But no sooner has he corrected matters than he rushes out of G major, tonicizes its dominant, and comes to an authoritative cadence in m. 8. This is followed by a kind of echo, a soft four-measure phrase, with motivic ideas derived from the opening eight measures, confirming D major as the local tonic.

In a 'normal' menuet, defining the tonic is the first order of business in the A section, after which (if the A section is to modulate) the tonicization of the dominant follows. In the topsy-turvy world of this Menuetto, the tonic is virtually undefined in the A section, caught as it is between the Scylla of C major and the Charybdis of D major. Paradoxically, the place where the tonic is most unambiguously defined is in the following B section (mm. 13–20)—after the internal double bar.

As the B section was rather short (only eight measures), we might expect a quick resolution of outstanding harmonic and formal issues in the A′ section. But given the somewhat bizarre premises of the A section, what precisely is it that we expect?

Surely we would expect that the tonic will have to be reconfirmed, and decisively so. How can that expectation be reconciled with the opening of the A section and its strong gravitational pull toward C major? Certainly something will have to be done to counteract the tendency to establish C major. And what do we expect to be the response to the end of the A section? The echo (mm. 9–12) was clearly in the dominant, but was its material sufficiently different from mm. 1–8 to cause the sonata principle to be activated? Haydn's response to these questions is startling (see Ex. 7.9).

The A′ section begins innocently enough. With the exception of the upbeat, the first four measures of the reprise are identical to mm. 1–4 (up until the augmented sixth chord at the end of m. 24). This means, of course, that we are treated, once again, to the virtual tonicization of C major, and the sharp opposition of F♯ and F♮.

Fair enough—as long as Haydn counters these tendencies with a strong reconfirmation of the tonic, the return of these ideas should not be an insurmountable harmonic obstacle. So, what comes next? First, a quick modulation to the dominant (note the augmented sixth at the end of m. 24), and then—astonishingly—a restatement of the opening theme, transposed to the dominant.

Normally the transposition of the theme to the dominant is a strategy employed in the A section, where the tonicization of the dominant is the usual goal at the internal double bar. But when has it ever been an appropriate tactic to transpose the opening theme to the dominant in the middle of the A′ section—just at the point where we should reconfirm the tonic?

In a bizarre fashion, this not only makes sense, it is eminently logical. The opening theme was unstable; instead of firmly establishing the tonic, it gravitated toward the subdominant. This means that the transposition

Ex. 7.9

(continued)

Ex. 7.9 continued

of this theme up to the dominant should be equally unstable, but should
fall back to the tonic—and thus should establish, through the back door,
the tonic. That is exactly what happens: in m. 34 we come to a solid
cadence in the tonic. Finally, the tonic has been established and
confirmed with a clear cadence. It might seem as if all the loose ends have
been tied up, and the Menuetto can now close.

Haydn disagrees. Not only does the Menuetto fail to close at m. 34, it
continues for another eleven measures, increasing its size by a third. Why
did Haydn feel it necessary to go to such lengths to prolong the
Menuetto? What has been left incomplete, needing this extended response, and what material does he use here?

The thematic material of mm. 34 ff is none other than a version of the
'echo' from mm. 9–12 of the A section. This would seem to indicate that

Haydn felt that the 'echo' was sufficiently distinctive to require activation of the sonata principle. That theory is belied by the facts on the ground. Haydn does not simply take the 'echo' from the end of the A section and transpose it to the tonic—there is no rhyming termination here. Instead, he comes back to the opening harmonic paradox of the composition. Using a version of the echo, stated over a tonic pedal, he takes one more opportunity to revive the G major–C major and F♯–F♮ controversies. G major is never made inoperative, but C major constantly reasserts its presence. As a result, the Menuetto closes with the authority of G major re-established, but resting uneasily against a background of paradoxical definitions and contradictory tendencies.

If the Menuetto is ambivalent in its expression of its tonic, the Trio is almost hamhanded in its near-obsessive reiteration of G. In the A section, for example, the lower strings stay locked onto the tonic chord for six measures, leaving only for the dominant in m. 51 and returning immediately for the cadence.

The most striking event in the Trio occurs after the internal double bar. In mm. 53–60 the B section appears, followed in mm. 61–8 by the A' section (which is a literal repetition of the non-modulating A section). The double bar should be next (at the end of m. 68), initiating the conventional repetition.

The final double bar does not follow. Instead, Haydn manually writes out the repetition of the B section, a drudgery which he usually avoids except if there are to be changes.[12] There are—not in the B section, but in the repetition of the A' section: without warning, the entire repetition of the A' section is cast in the parallel minor (see Ex. 7.10).[13]

The sudden restatement of the A' section in the parallel minor is completely unprecedented in the Trio. Nothing in the Trio, or, for that matter, anywhere in the third movement, could possibly be regarded as a logical motivation for this surprising turn of events.

That is precisely the point. Nothing in the third movement dictates the sudden turn to minor, but there was an important event in the first movement that is directly related to the surprise in the Trio: the equally sudden and equally unprecedented emergence of G minor before the recapitulation of the first movement (see Ex. 7.4).

The emphasis upon the parallel minor in the first and third movements is significant, not merely because similar things happen in two different movements, but because the events cannot be properly understood within

---

[12] There are occasional exceptions. See Symphony No. 61/iv, mm. 101–48.

[13] In Landon's rev. edn. of this symphony, unlike the 1st edn., there are no repeat signs at the end of the Trio, thus indicating that mm. 53–84 should not be repeated. This is clearly the correct reading and is supported by the most reliable surviving sources, including an authentic set of parts (London, British Library, Eg. 2379, fos. 209ʳ–229ᵛ) which Haydn sent to the publishing firm of Forster in 1784. I am most grateful to Dr Horst Walter of the Joseph-Haydn Institut for this information.

their own movements. There is insufficient motivation within the movements themselves to explain and to justify their turn to the minor. In the first movement, Haydn went out of his way to mark the brief episode in minor as something startling and patently out of place. By prolonging the dominant harmony for seven measures, he built up strong expectations for the imminent arrival of the tonic and the recapitulation. Those expectations are dashed by the sudden turn to a G minor 6–4 which acts as a springboard, launching us away from the dominant. It is crucial for an understanding of this passage to realize that there has not been a single reference of any sort to G minor before m. 117. In short, the turn to minor is an incomprehensible moment, one that simply cannot be understood within the first movement, one that challenges carefully nurtured intra-opus norms.

The rewriting of the A' section in the Trio of the third movement is even more disruptive. Here Haydn challenges the stylistic norms of the menuet and trio: given AABA'B, the next step simply has to be A'. Moreover, there is not the slightest suggestion of G minor anywhere else in the third movement. Again, an incomprehensible moment, one that challenges inter-opus norms.

Taken in isolation, neither of these events makes complete sense. Nor—I should emphasize—does the occurrence of one justify the other: two wrongs do not make a right. As both events are disruptive this cannot be the end of the story. The corollary of the normative principle tells us that the problems raised in the first and third movements will have to be resolved in a later movement.

They are. In the finale, essential details of the formal structure are best understood as responses to problematic events from the earlier movements. Effectively, the finale takes the prominent anomalies of the prior movements, recalls them, and then resolves them, causing them to function in a normative fashion within the movement.

The exposition is deceptively simple and straightforward. There is no recall of any of the problematic events from the previous movements: no tonicization of the subdominant, no turn to the parallel minor, no juxtaposition of F♯ with F♮. At the end of the exposition (m. 49), we arrive as expected on the dominant (D).

This is followed immediately by the development section, which begins by jumping down a third to B. This is a harmonic progression we should recognize: in the first movement (the only other sonata form movement in this cycle), the development section began in precisely the same way, with a jump directly from the dominant to the V/vi.

By the early 1780s, however, the jump from V to V/vi was, if not the norm, then certainly a common method of initiating the development section. Could this not simply be another coincidental occurrence of a common figure?

Ex. 7.11

Any suspicions that the similarity might be insignificant or fortuitous should be dispelled by the next passage. Immediately following, Haydn moves to C major, restating the opening theme of the finale in that key. This is precisely the harmonic–thematic strategy employed in the first movement. In stating the theme of the finale in C major, Haydn reveals an interesting property of that theme: at this level of transposition, F♯ and F♮ are in constant opposition (see Ex. 7.11).

So too, the end of the development section is virtually a reprise of what happened in the first movement. In m. 73, Haydn brings us back to the dominant. Although this seems a little early (see the discussion of Symphony No. 55/i in Chapter 5), it is a plausible point of arrival for the pre-recapitulation dominant in a finale. For four measures, Haydn expands on the dominant, with neighbor 6–4s elaborating the dominant seventh. If we had any doubts about the likely formal role for this dominant, they should be set to rest.

However, in m. 77, in a precise analogy to the first movement (and a reminder of the Trio of the third movement), Haydn substitutes the minor 6–4 for the major, and follows this with a step up to an E flat triad. The connections with the first movement could not be closer (see Ex. 7.12).

By recalling the disruptive substitution of minor in the first movement (and, of course, the Trio), Haydn has not resolved the problem. Far from it; the finale has itself been destabilized. In this movement, however, unlike the first and third movements, the instabilities are not allowed to stand.

Ex. 7.12

The problematic passage toward the end of the development section (mm. 77 ff) is a version of a passage first heard in the exposition in mm. 25 ff. As this passage was in the dominant in the exposition, we can expect that in the recapitulation it will have to return transposed to the tonic—which it does (mm. 116 ff).

But mm. 116 ff are more than a simple (transposed) restatement of mm. 25 ff. Because it is restated in the tonic, the passage is also a correction, a smoothing-out of the anomalous and disruptive turn to the minor in mm. 77 ff before the recapitulation. In mm. 116 ff, Haydn has returned to the same material that prepared the recapitulation, but now it is restated in the tonic in an entirely unobtrusive manner. Finally, the significant infringement of norms from the first, third, and fourth movements has received an appropriate response (see Ex. 7.13).

Similarly, other essential details of the recapitulation of the fourth movement can also be seen as a resolution of the harmonic ambiguities

Ex. 7.13

TABLE 7.2. *Symphony No. 81/iv: Correspondences between Exposition and Recapitulation*

Exposition (mm.)	Recapitulation (mm.)
1‒4	96‒9
5‒24	—
—	100‒15 (mm. 100‒2 invert the voices of mm. 5‒7)
25‒32	116‒23 (transposed)
33	—
—	124‒5
34‒49	126‒41 (transposed)

that first appeared in the opening of the symphony. A comparison of the exposition and the recapitulation reveals that, with the exception of an extended rewritten transition, most of this recapitulation consists of literal and transposed repetitions of the exposition (see Table 7.2).

After a brief repetition of some of the opening material of the movement (mm. 96‒9 = 1‒4), Haydn cuts a substantial proportion of the exposition (mm. 5‒24 do not return) and interpolates instead a sizeable newly written passage (mm. 100‒15) for familiar compositional reasons. At this point in his stylistic evolution, rewritten transitions are hardly surprising—it is what Haydn chooses to do in the new transition that is revealing. Again, he brings back reminders of the harmonic progression from the beginning of the composition. In mm. 106‒7 and 112‒13 he makes clear references to the subdominant. As a result, we have further prominent juxtapositions of F♮ and F♯, with the concomitant transitory emphasis on C major (Ex. 7.14).

Even more significant is a subtle deviation from the exposition's patterns that takes place in mm. 124‒5. As mm. 25‒49 were in the dominant, it would have been a simple matter for Haydn to transpose this passage to the tonic in the recapitulation. With one slight exception, that is precisely what he does. But instead of transposing m. 33 to the tonic, he replaces that one measure from the exposition with two measures in the recapitulation (see Table 7.2 and Ex. 7.15).

By diverging from the patterns of the exposition, he draws our attention to this moment, causing us to try to understand its motivations. Crucial for that understanding is the recognition of what Haydn chooses to do at this point: he brings back the progression V/IV‒IV one final time. This time, however, it functions in the smoothest, most unobtrusive manner, as the preparation for a solid cadence in m. 128. At one time this was the most destabilizing of progressions (in both the first and

Ex. 7.14

third movements). But now, finally, it has been brought back into the fold, smoothed over, and resolved—made to function as a simple dominant preparation.

Seen in this light, the finale of Symphony No. 81 is not merely the last movement of the composition, but its culmination. Haydn does not merely recall the problematic events and anomalies of the first and third

movements, he recalls them in order to resolve them, restating them in a context where they are no longer disruptive.

What about the second movement? Does it play no role in the intermovemental relationships?

Earlier, I proposed, with some reservations, one possible avenue by which the second movement could be connected to the first. Given the

Ex. 7.15

rather tenuous nature of those relationships, I also suggested that we defer judgment until all the facts were in.

Perhaps the most sympathetic case for including the second movement within the framework of the intermovemental relationships could read as follows: The opening progression of the first movement directs the formal organization not only of the first movement, but of the intermovemental relationships as well. A prominent feature of that progression is the opposition of the tones F♮ and F♯. The juxtaposition of these tones is a central compositional strategy, realized in a variety of contexts, in the first, third, and fourth movements. In the Andante, three different compositional decisions—(1) the key chosen for the movement (the dominant), (2) the specific shape of the incipit of the theme (a leap up to the third degree), and (3) the use of the parallel minor for the second variation—foster yet another juxtaposition of F♮ and F♯. Given the somewhat remote connection of these two tones, we might not want to accord special status to the connection, were it not for the pervasive importance of the juxtaposition throughout the remaining three movements.

Is this enough? Is the second movement related to the other three, or are these connections the figments of a twentieth-century imagination? To my ear, the strength of the connections between the other movements are so powerful that they make it difficult to dismiss the more rarefied connections with the Andante.

8

Symphony No. 85

(?1785)

WHEN last we had the occasion to examine a slow introduction (in Symphony No. 75), we found no tangible connections between it and the main body of the movement. That was not unusual; in Haydn's (relatively few) pre-1785 symphonies with slow introductions, the absence of significant relationships between the slow introduction and the following fast sonata form movement was the norm.[1] It cannot be happenstance that Haydn's increasingly frequent employment of slow introductions (in eighteen of the last twenty-three symphonies) runs precisely parallel to the increasingly common appearance both of close relationships between those introductions and the movements which they precede, and of connections with the remaining movements.[2] One is tempted to infer that Haydn became interested in the slow introduction only when he realized its potential to create intersectional and intermovemental relationships.

As we have seen, an increasingly important thread in Haydn's formal thinking has been the interest in fostering relationships between seemingly disparate events, most notably between the different movements of a composition. Although the principle of contrast has been (and will remain) an essential aspect of the overall design, Haydn made consistent efforts to relate the different movements to one another without erasing

[1] For a survey of relationships between introductions and the fast movements that follow, see von Tobel, *Die Formenwelt*, 131–40. Von Tobel briefly mentions some of the relationships in Symphony No. 85/i (p. 136).

[2] Although (presumably) everyone agrees that some motivic connections could not possibly be fortuitous or coincidental (e.g. Symphony No. 90/i, mm. 5–8 and 17–20), disagreements over less clear-cut cases are common. The problem of relationships between the introduction and the main body of the movement is similar to that occasioned by separate movements. See Marx, 'Über die zyklische Sonatenform', 142–6, and the response by Noé (ibid. 146). See further Marx, 'Über thematische Beziehungen', 1–20. At the end of this article, Georg Feder wrote a brief rejoinder, taking issue with some of Marx's ideas. For more criticism of Marx's claims, see Raimund Bard, ' "Tendenzen" zur zyklischen Gestaltung in Haydns Londoner Sinfonien', in Christoph-Hellmut Mahling and Sigrid Wiesmann (eds.), *Gesellschaft für Musikforschung: Bericht über den internationalen musikwissenschaftlichen Kongress, Bayreuth 1981* (Kassel, 1984), 379–83. For further discussion of the topic, see Rudolf Klinkhammer, *Die langsame Einleitung in der Instrumentalmusik der Klassik und Romantik: Ein Sonderproblem in der Entwicklung der Sonatenform* (Regensburg, 1971), 43–57. See also Webster, *Haydn's 'Farewell'*, 162–4 and 194–204.

Ex. 8.1

(continued)

Ex. 8.1 continued

their distinctive identity. In Symphony No. 85 (and in other works of this period and beyond), he extrapolates that idea to the relationships between the introduction and the following Vivace.[3]

The introduction may be seen as divided into three subsections: the first, mm. 1–3, with tutti simultaneities alternating with dotted-note, ascending, scale-like passages; the second, mm. 4–6, with quick ascending runs over a throbbing chordal accompaniment; the third, mm. 7–11, an extended and elaborated dominant triad, lasting for nearly half of the introduction, with dotted-note figures over the pedal-tone dominant (see Ex. 8.1).

On the surface, the introduction to Symphony No. 85 is no less a compendium of standard-fare introduction formulas than is the case in earlier works (e.g. Symphonies Nos. 50 or 75).[4] Unlike most of its predecessors, however, this introduction has some obvious motivic relationships with the following movement: many of the most prominent themes and harmonic progressions of the Vivace are derivatives of ideas from the introduction (see Ex. 8.2).[5]

---

[3] The desirability of making (motivic) connections between the introduction and the main body of the work was asserted a few years later in a theoretical treatise. Galeazzi states: 'It is good practice that the Introduction (if there is one) be sometimes recalled in the course of the melody, so that it should not seem a detached section and be entirely separated from the rest, since the fundamental rule for the conduct [of the composition] consists of the *unity of ideas*.' Churgin, 'Francesco Galeazzi's Description', 191.

[4] It has been asserted that Symphony No. 85 is the most 'French' of the six Paris symphonies, and that its introduction clearly stems from the French *ouverture* tradition. See Wolfgang Börner, ' "Was eine Sache nicht im ersten Moment enthüllt": Die Pariser Sinfonien von Joseph Haydn', *Musik und Gesellschaft*, 32 (1982), 140.

[5] Landon, *The Symphonies*, 409, points out some of these connections. He also cites other examples from this period of motivic connections between the slow introduction and subsequent movements (ibid. 408–10).

Ex. 8.2

The exposition (mm. 12–111) begins with a rather extended tonic definition section (mm. 12–41). In this section, Haydn has two complete statements of the opening theme (mm. 12–23 and 31–42), the second a varied repetition of the first—as per the variation principle.[6] Sandwiched

---

[6] For an interesting discussion of the use of variation techniques in this movement, see Sisman, 'Small and Expanded Forms', 474–5. As Sisman demonstrates, the interpolation of contrasting material between a theme and its varied repetition (as here) was a basic technique in expanded forms.

(d)

between these two piano statements of the theme is a forte orchestral tutti (mm. 23–30).

The transition to the dominant section (mm. 42–77) holds closely to the motivic ideas presented so far in the Vivace (and, therefore, in the introduction). For instance, in mm. 42–3, the upwards run and following arpeggiated quarter-notes are a slight transformation of mm. 23–4, with a further development in mm. 45–6. After a brief tremolo passage (mm. 47–51), further transformations surface, first in the bass, then in the descant, with some explicit recollections of the introduction: the C–B♭ runs in mm. 52–3 and 56–7 refer to mm. 4–6 in the first violin, while the descending arpeggio B♭–G–E and the continuation on to F is a diminution of the bass-line in mm. 4–7.

Given the strength of the half-cadence in the dominant in mm. 60–1, we would expect the dominant confirmation to follow directly. Instead, Haydn goes out of his way—far out of his way—to frustrate the expectations he has raised. We would expect the dominant major; instead we find dominant minor. We would expect the dynamics to stay the same, or drop down to piano;[7] instead they are abruptly much louder—the first

---

[7] It was customary for the dynamics to drop immediately after the cadence marking the end of the transition to the dominant. For example, in the other Paris symphonies: No. 82/i, mm. 69–70; No. 83/i, mm. 41–5; No. 84/i, mm. 73–4; No. 86/i, 53–4. In No. 87/i, there is no lowering of dynamics at the beginning of the dominant confirmation section, but neither is there an articulation of the cadence—see mm. 36–7.

fortissimo in the Vivace. Most surprising of all, he quotes the opening theme from the first movement of another work—Symphony No. 45 ('The Farewell'), a quotation lasting a full eight measures (see Ex. 8.3).[8]

When we look a bit more closely, we see that this is a rather clever sleight of hand, an adroit handling of the technique of motivic transformation. Haydn has made a series of slight adjustments to some of the motivic ideas of this movement, and the motives of this work are transformed into the theme from the earlier composition.[9] But even a plausible pedigree cannot (and should not) entirely erase the impression that the 'Farewell' theme is exactly what it first seemed to be: a willful frustration of the expected continuation.

That Haydn meant the quotation to be heard as a detour is made perfectly plain by the continuation. When he has finished with his self-borrowing, he proceeds to a passage (mm. 70–5) that (although still in F minor) is a virtual replay of mm. 56–61, the passage that at first appeared to be the end of the transition (see Ex. 8.4).

After returning from the detour, Haydn arrives, finally, in the dominant major key. He then begins the dominant confirmation section, not with a new theme, but with another (varied) statement of the principal theme, this time in the dominant.[10] Here we have a clear example of what has been termed 'monothematic sonata form', something that has long been recognized as an important type among Haydn's sonata forms.[11]

From a purely practical standpoint of musical cognition, either the statement of a new theme or the transposed repetition of the principal theme could serve equally well to mark the arrival of the dominant section. In either case, the interaction of theme and key is quite effective in delineating the principal harmonic subdivisions of the form.

However, the two methods have palpably different consequences in their effect on the content of the recapitulation. Although a new theme stated in the dominant would be subject to the dictates of the sonata principle and would normally demand transposition to the tonic, a

[8] One could argue that the theme in mm. 62 ff is merely a common figure (a descending arpeggio) and not a quotation from the 'Farewell' Symphony. At least three reasons might be advanced against this opinion: (1) Haydn quotes the 'Farewell' theme in another symphony (No. 60/i, mm. 109 ff), lending additional credibility to the quotation in No. 85/i; (2) themes formed from arpeggios are common in Haydn's works; arpeggios spanning two octaves are not; (3) the similarities extend past the arpeggio: cf. mm. 68–9 from this symphony with mm. 3, 7, 11, and *passim* in No. 45/i.

[9] A brief description of the transformational process from the subsidiary idea in m. 16 to the theme from the 'Farewell' Symphony is given in Georg Feder, 'Similarities in the Works of Haydn', in H. C. Robbins Landon and Roger Chapman (eds.), *Studies in Eighteenth-Century Music: A Tribute to Karl Geiringer on his Seventieth Birthday* (New York, 1970), 191–2.

[10] Sisman, 'Small and Expanded Forms', 474.

[11] In any event, the term is something of a misnomer. As A. Peter Brown has stated: 'More often than not, only a very small portion—at the most the first two or three measures—of the initial phrase will return in a varied form.' *Joseph Haydn's Keyboard Music*, 291. For further discussion, see id., 'The Structure of the Exposition', 108, and Fillion, 'Sonata-Exposition Procedures'.

Ex. 8.3

Ex. 8.4

restatement of the principal theme in the dominant requires no such resolution. Indeed, a transposition of this material back to the tonic may well be redundant. This is a problem that will have to be addressed in the recapitulation.

After the transposed statement of the theme and its transformations in mm. 85–95, Haydn concludes the exposition with a closing section (mm. 96–111). Even here, he does not introduce any completely new material. Rather, most of the new ideas can be seen to be transformations of earlier events.

TABLE 8.1. *Symphony No. 85/i: Correspondences between Exposition and Recapitulation*

Exposition (mm.)	Recapitulation (mm.)
12–22, 31–41	212–22
23–30	—
42–5	223–6
—	227–9
46–69	—
70–95	230–55 (transposed)
96–111	256–76 (transposed and slightly varied, with two-measure phrases substituting for three-measure phrases)

Such are the premises of the exposition. As they are rather complicated and the response of the recapitulation correspondingly so, we will break away from a chronological survey of the movement and leap forward to see how the recapitulation copes with the problems in formal logic posed by the material of the exposition (see Table 8.1).

Given the premises of the exposition, the most immediate compositional problem facing Haydn in the recapitulation is the issue of thematic redundancy. In the exposition, the principal theme appeared a total of three times (mm. 12–23, 31–42, 78–85)—the first two times in the tonic, the last time in the dominant. If all three were repeated in the recapitulation (with the last one transposed back to the tonic) there would be a rather clear violation of the redundancy principle. As we would expect, Haydn excises one of the three statements. But even so basic an issue as the excision of a redundant thematic statement is anything but pro forma.

If we compare the exposition with the recapitulation we see for certain that the last of the three statements of the theme from the exposition (the one that was in the dominant) does return in the recapitulation, transposed appropriately to the tonic (mm. 238–45 = mm. 78–85). With respect to the other two statements, it is by no means unequivocally clear which of the two is retained in the recapitulation—it might even seem as if Haydn has fused them. Although the orchestration suggests that it is the second statement that is retained, the registral placement of the theme in the lower voices implies that it is the first statement that returns. But Haydn has not simply combined the statements of the theme from the exposition into a single statement in the recapitulation, for there is an added voice (second violin) that was present in neither of the statements in the exposition (see Ex. 8.5).

Ex. 8.5

That added voice came, not from the exposition, but from the development section—in fact, from the very first appearance of the principal theme in the development section (mm. 134 ff). In an important sense, therefore, the restatement of the theme at the beginning of the recapitulation is a combination of features not only from the exposition but from the development section as well. Haydn has thus made the return of the principal theme at the beginning of the recapitulation into something far more than a return—it has become a goal, the culmination of prior stages in the development.[12]

Having reduced the first two statements of the theme to a single version, Haydn has solved the problem of redundancy, but he has also created another problem. In the exposition, the first and second statements of the principal theme (mm. 12–23 and 31–42) were each followed by a tutti (mm. 23–30 and 42 ff), the second of which was, at least initially, a variant of the first. In the recapitulation, now that one of the two initial statements of the theme has been excised, the first (intervening) tutti becomes extraneous. In any event, since the second tutti was a variant of the first, there is an added incentive (the redundancy principle) to omit the first tutti—and so Haydn does.

Having made these decisions, Haydn is ready to confront the next formal problem. In the exposition, the second tutti first suggested the tonicization of the dominant at m. 47. Clearly, in the recapitulation Haydn must break away from the model before he reaches the passage corresponding to m. 47. Precisely as we would expect, mm. 223–6 are almost identical to mm. 42–5, but mm. 227 ff diverge from the pattern in the exposition, in order to remain in the tonic key.[13]

This, in turn, brings Haydn to the quotation from the 'Farewell' Symphony. As we can see from the score (and Table 8.1), Haydn decided to excise this passage from the recapitulation.

Why did he do so? It was a prominent theme; it was stated in a key other than the tonic; ergo—it ought to have been restated in the tonic, as mandated by the sonata principle. That Haydn did not retain it in the recapitulation must be an indication that he felt that something about it would have been inappropriate when transposed back to the tonic.

---

[12] A related procedure can be found in the Keyboard Trio Hob. XV: 9/ii (1785), written about the same time as Symphony No. 85. In the exposition, the principal theme is stated twice in the tonic definition section, first with the theme stated by the piano with the strings accompanying (mm. 1–4) and then with the theme stated by the violin with the piano and cello accompanying (mm. 9–12). As the opening theme also appears at the beginning of the dominant confirmation section (mm. 54 ff), the recapitulation must excise at least one of these statements. At the beginning of the recapitulation (m. 136), Haydn combines the two statements from mm. 1–12 into a single statement, with piano and violin stating the principal theme in unison.

[13] Some further connections with the introduction may be seen in the bass. See Danckwardt, *Die langsame Einleitung*, 111.

One reason might relate to the destabilizing effect of the parallel minor. To be sure, in some of Haydn's symphonies (particularly early works), the dominant minor appears after the tonicization of the dominant, providing a touch of contrast with the dominant major. In such instances, it does not have a disruptive function and can indeed appear in the recapitulation, transposed to the tonic minor.[14] But when the parallel minor key appears at a point where expectations have been created for the arrival of the parallel major, the effect is highly disruptive and destabilizing (as we saw in the analyses of Symphonies Nos. 1/i and 81/i and iii). Events of this sort cannot easily be brought back in the recapitulation, and this argues against the return of the 'Farewell' theme in the recapitulation.

There may be other reasons as well. In general, the excision of a passage is—*ipso facto*—evidence that Haydn has invoked the redundancy principle. If we operate from that assumption and imagine what the recapitulation would have sounded like had Haydn retained the 'Farewell' quotation in the tonic, we discover two possible areas of redundancy: cadential and motivic.

In the exposition, the half-cadences at mm. 61 and 76 were the first cadential articulations in the new key, and thus occasioned no redundancy. But in the recapitulation, the return of those half-cadences might be inappropriate; both would be in the tonic key—as are all of the other cadences in the recapitulation—and both would mark off the first half of the recapitulation from the second with strong half-cadences. Our experience with Haydn's music should lead us to conclude that he regarded one of them as redundant.

Similarly, the very nature of the immediate aftermath of the 'Farewell' quotation virtually precludes the possibility of its return in the recapitulation. Haydn uses very nearly the same material to recover from the borrowing as he used to prepare it (cf. mm. 52–9 with 70–4), and that material, although transformed, is a transposition to the dominant of material that was stated in the tonic (mm. 23 ff and 42 ff) An additional two statements in the tonic probably would be redundant on motivic grounds.

[14] Rosen suggests that the excision of the 'Farewell' quote in the recapitulation stems from a tendency to avoid repeating in the tonic minor events that were heard in the dominant minor in the exposition. See *The Classical Style*, 73. But, as he shows, exceptions exist. In the early symphonies, passages in the dominant minor from the end of the exposition dutifully return in the recapitulation, transposed to the tonic minor. See No. 1/i, mm. 29–30 and 76–7; No. 4/i, mm. 24–31 and 83–90. In No. 32/i, the dominant minor in the exposition (mm. 47 ff) does not return in the tonic minor in the recapitulation, but this is a destabilizing event, which is resolved in the recapitulation of the finale when the dominant minor of the exposition is restated in the tonic minor. In later symphonies, the dominant minor occurs far less frequently in the exposition as an element of contrast with the dominant major. But when it occurs, and when it does not figure as a disruptive element, it can return transposed to the tonic minor in the recapitulation. See No. 84/i, mm. 81–92 and 244–9.

Ex. 8.6

Haydn's procedures reveal a fundamental aspect of his compositional thought. When the sonata and redundancy principles come into conflict, the negative principle (redundancy) outweighs the positive principle (sonata). However, even though Haydn will not violate the redundancy principle in order to satisfy the sonata principle, he does find a way to meet the demands of both.

One of the ways in which he solves this problem is quite simple. Something very similar to the 'Farewell' theme is, in fact, stated in the tonic minor, not in the recapitulation but in the development section (see Ex. 8.6).[15]

The passage in question is not quite a literal repetition of the 'Farewell' theme, and the emphasis on the tonic minor lasts only a moment. To complicate matters, it is followed by a phrase that brings back another version of this theme on the dominant minor triad (mm. 148–9). These cavils notwithstanding, the passing reference to the tonic minor does have the desired consequence of restating in the tonic something that is very close to the 'Farewell' theme. Granted, this is not enough to resolve the

---

[15] Rosen, *The Classical Style*, 73, cites similar procedures in two string quartets: Op. 64 No. 3/i and Op. 50 No. 6/i.

problem in its entirety (and, as we shall see, Haydn offers a further solution at the end of the movement), but it appears to be at least part of the answer.

As a result of a series of responses to the compositional premises of the exposition, a new problem has been created—that of balance between the exposition and recapitulation (a violation of an inter-opus norm). Haydn has excised one of the first two statements of the opening theme (a loss of eleven measures) and the intervening tutti (eight more measures), shortened the transition, and excised the 'Farewell' quote (a net loss of twenty-one additional measures). If the recapitulation were to conclude merely by transposing the remainder of the dominant confirmation section of the exposition (mm. 96–111) back to the tonic, the hundred measures of the exposition would be answered by only sixty measures in the recapitulation. A potential disparity of this degree normally prompted Haydn to make some correction. As we can see from a comparison of the remainder of the exposition (mm. 96–111) with the remainder of the recapitulation (mm. 256–76), he does indeed compensate slightly for the excision of so much material in the recapitulation.

He does so in a rather interesting way. The end of the recapitulation sounds longer than the end of the exposition, not only because five measures are added (which, given the disparity, is not all that much), but because Haydn substitutes two-measure phrases for three-measure phrases (cf. mm. 100–2 with mm. 259–60; mm. 105–7 with mm. 263–4) and a three-measure phrase for a four-measure phrase (compare mm. 96–9 with mm. 256–8).[16] The effect is, at one and the same time, an expansion and an acceleration. The end of the recapitulation has more phrases, so it seems longer; some of those phrases are shorter, so it seems to rush to its final cadence.

In the process of expanding the closing section of the recapitulation, Haydn also takes the opportunity to address a formal problem that has resulted from an earlier compositional decision: the abrogation of the sonata principle by the excision of the 'Farewell' theme from the recapitulation. In mm. 269–76 he states closing material that is similar—but not quite identical—to the closing material of the exposition. The descending arpeggio in m. 269 prepares the subdominant and dominant in m. 270; these two measures are then repeated in mm. 271–2; and finally, the one-measure arpeggio of the tonic chord is extended to two measures in mm. 273–4 (see Ex. 8.7).

When Haydn extends the arpeggiation through two octaves, he effectively transforms the closing material into the 'Farewell' Symphony theme. (Perhaps that is not overly surprising, as both the 'Farewell' and closing themes are transformations of the motives first stated in

---

[16] This feature is pointed out in Alston, 'Recapitulation Procedures', 119.

Ex. 8.7

the introduction and then reformulated in the Vivace.) By slightly reshaping the closing flourish, and transforming it into a version of the 'Farewell' theme, Haydn has brought that theme back to the tonic, and in so doing has addressed the outstanding demands of the sonata principle.

The development section of the Vivace lasts a hundred measures (mm. 112–211)—this in a movement with a total of 265 measures. In both its absolute size and the proportion of the movement that it occupies, the scope of this development section is greater than that of any of the movements we have encountered up to this point.

It is not only its size that marks the section as so significant. Its tonal structure is extremely complicated, quite problematic, and demands careful attention, for it is impossible even to begin an analysis from the (historically reasonable) assumption that the development section functions as an expansion of the dominant. Any such assumption would be contradicted immediately and continuously by the harmonic trajectory of this remarkable section, which neither begins nor ends with the dominant, nor for that matter gives the dominant any emphasis during its entire span of a hundred measures.[17]

Haydn begins the development section with an abrupt harmonic shift, countering the F major triad from the end of the exposition with a succession of tutti dominant seventh chords in G minor. Instead of continuing to G minor, he makes a deceptive progression to E flat (m. 114), and for the next twenty measures, while developing the 'Farewell' theme, stays mostly within the orbit of E flat. He follows this by coming to a dramatic halt in mm. 132–3 with four tutti E flat major chords, which are immediately reinterpreted as the dominant of A flat.

This is followed by an extended passage (from m. 134 to about m. 170) in which Haydn works through various transformations and variations of the principal theme, while traversing quickly a number of keys (A flat, B flat minor, and C minor) but giving emphasis to none of them. The tonal wandering comes to an end in m. 170, where, following an augmented sixth chord, Haydn re-establishes G minor. With the exception of a brief excursion away from this key in mm. 182–8, he remains in G minor for the next forty-two measures—an extraordinarily extended span. And, within this prolonged G minor section, emphasis is placed, not on the G minor triad itself, but on D major, the dominant of G minor.

The conclusion of the development section heightens the emphasis on the dominant of G minor. Rather than returning to the dominant of B flat and then proceeding with the recapitulation, Haydn moves directly from the prolonged statement of the D major triad straight to the tonic and the recapitulation, with no intervening dominant (see Ex. 8.8).

Taken as a whole, the development section might be seen as an extended—an extraordinarily extended—prolongation, not of the dominant, but of the dominant of the relative minor. The development not only begins and ends with the V/vi, but spends nearly half of its time on the dominant of the relative minor.

---

[17] Excepting only mm. 143–4, where a quick V–I progression (in B flat minor) permits Haydn a statement in the tonic minor—discussed above.

Ex. 8.8

By some important measures, therefore, the tonal emphases of this development constitute a challenge to harmonic and formal norms. Whereas a movement whose development section prolongs the dominant can be immediately understood in the context of the basic axioms of late eighteenth-century tonal theory and the norms of Haydn's treatment, the prolongation of a non-dominant sonority demands a more contextual explanation of the harmonic function and meaning of the development section.

Most intriguing of all—no gesture anywhere else in the movement seems to explain, justify, or comment upon the harmonic emphases that frame the development section. Simply put, the prominent stress on V/vi seems to be a purposeful and powerful anomaly—unresolved, unexplained, and not otherwise followed up within the first movement itself.

The Romance is a set of strophic variations on a popular folk-tune.[18] As this movement displays features that we have already examined in some detail in previous analyses, we can dispense with a close analysis here. Three features are worth brief mention. The variation in the parallel minor stays much closer to the melodic outline of the original than is normally the case.[19] At the same time, the second half of that variation is a different length from the second half of the theme: twelve measures instead of the usual fourteen, divided into five and seven, instead of the usual six and eight. Finally, Haydn adds a brief coda (mm. 116–26), which functions both to strengthen the finality of the close and to act as a kind of orchestral summary of the movement.

The third movement has some remarkable formal features, but, from its opening, one would scarcely suspect anything untoward was about to happen. The Menuetto begins innocently enough with an eight-measure, non-modulating A section, closing with an authentic cadence on the tonic. After the internal double bar, the brief B section in mm. 9–16 touches in passing upon a few closely related keys and concludes, as expected, with a half-cadence in B flat.

Given these rather straightforward premises, it would be reasonable to presume that the Menuetto would continue with an additional eight-measure period, ending in the tonic. Since the A section concluded with a perfect authentic cadence in B flat, it should be possible for Haydn to repeat those measures more or less without alteration, particularly as there was not a high degree of motivic or thematic redundancy within the A section itself. So he does: with the exception of some minor changes, mm. 17–24 are a literal repetition of mm. 1–8. However, these are not the final measures of the Menuetto; it continues on to a coda (mm. 24–38). As this coda is rather substantial (it increases the size of the Menuetto by more than 50 per cent), it should not be ignored or dismissed (see Ex. 8.9).

If we were to hypothesize that the coda was necessary to strengthen the final cadence and to differentiate it from what would otherwise be an identical cadence at the internal double bar, that would sound reasonable enough, but such a theory is contradicted by what Haydn does in many other menuets. In general, he adds a coda to a menuet when the A′ section is a literal repetition of the non-modulating A section, and this often has the effect of strengthening the final cadence, but there are a number of menuets with literal repetitions of their A sections, yet without codas. Some occur in early symphonies (Nos. 21/iii, 28/iii, 29/iii, 39/iii), some in those of the 1770s (Nos. 69/iii, 71/iii), and some even in those of

---

[18] 'La gentille et jeune Lisette.' See Landon, *Chronicle and Works*, ii. 608.
[19] Sisman, 'Haydn's Variations', 128.

Ex. 8.9

the early 1780s (Nos. 74/iii, 75/iii, 76/iii, 79/iii), although none in symphonies composed after 1784.

If we cannot justify the presence of this coda on stylistic or generic grounds, then we must look back at the specific details of the piece, operating from the assumption that an extensive coda will have some formal motivation—either to create an anomaly or to resolve one. Such a search only compounds our puzzlement, for this coda seems entirely and completely unremarkable. It merely repeats, in slightly varied form, material that was heard in the main body of the Menuetto, with no new motives and no unexpected emphases. Furthermore, nothing in the main body of the movement seems even remotely problematic; nothing seems to demand a further response. It too seems so very ordinary.

If mild puzzlement is the appropriate response to the coda in the Menuetto, stupefaction should be our response to the retransition from the B section to the A section in the Trio. After an entirely conventional eight-measure A section, ending with an authentic cadence in the tonic, Haydn begins what at first appears to be a similarly conventional B section. After six measures, he lands on the dominant. At this point, we would normally expect a half-cadence and then a return to the A section, which, given its tonal outlines could be repeated *in toto*, without alteration.

What happens instead is extraordinary. In place of a measure or so on the dominant, Haydn stands on the dominant for no fewer than nineteen measures, almost half of the duration of the Trio (see Ex. 8.10).[20]

If we were slightly troubled by the apparent lack of motivation for the somewhat extended and rather modest coda in the Menuetto, then what can we possibly say about the absurdly overexpanded and totally immodest dominant in the Trio? What plausible compositional motivations could there have been for this turn of events?

There are no credible causes for this event within the Trio itself, nor does there seem to be any motivation within the Menuetto. The nineteen-measure expansion of the dominant in the Trio is a forceful violation of compositional norms—both of the norms established by the specific premises of the rest of this movement and of the norms of late eighteenth-century symphonic practice in general and Haydn's music in particular.

To what end? Is this a joke, a transparent tweaking of conventions? The disproportionate expansion of the dominant may well be a joke, but scarcely just a joke. Rather, it is an essential aspect of the large-scale design of the symphony as a whole, for it is clear that this powerful anomaly can be explained only by events in other movements.

---

[20] Rosen sees this passage as an instance of Haydn's sublime wit and, moreover, asserts that it is 'a retransition—not that one was really needed: it is delightful because it is so absurdly gratuitous.' *Sonata Forms*, 117–18.

Ex. 8.10

(continued)

By the back door, as it were, the expanded dominant in the Trio has solved another problem—the seemingly unjustified coda in the Menuetto. That coda has become necessary because of the events in the Trio. This can best be understood when we look at the normal proportions of Haydn's menuets and trios.

On the basis of the available evidence (almost 100 symphonic menuet movements) it is possible to make some reliable generalizations about the relative lengths of Haydn's symphonic menuets and trios. Generally speaking, the menuet is longer than the trio, sometimes much longer (e.g. No. 24/iii: 44 vs. 16 measures; No. 56/iii: 72 vs. 22 measures; No. 94/iii: 62 vs. 27 measures), but usually only moderately so. Occasionally, the menuet is the same length as the trio (e.g. No. 62/iii). The average for post-1774 symphonies is approximately forty-four measures for menuets and thirty measures for trios. In only eleven cases is the trio longer than the menuet (Nos. 8/iii, 15/ii, 32/ii, 37/ii, 46/iii, 47/iii, 67/iii, 82/iii, 85/iii, 92/iii, 93/iii), but in none of these is it markedly longer, usually surpassing it by only a few measures. The greatest disparity is in No. 8/iii (36 vs. 46 measures).

We may therefore have a reasonable explanation of why the coda of the Menuetto is necessary. (For reasons that will become clear shortly, I am assuming that the Trio with its expanded dominant is the principal point of the movement as a whole and thus is a given.) If the Menuetto were allowed to close in m. 24, the Trio (forty measures long) would be out of proportion. Something has to be added to the Menuetto to bring it more into line with the Trio. From the range of options available to him, Haydn chose simply to repeat, in varied form, material already stated in the main body of the Menuetto.[21]

Although the coda may be necessary in order to right the asymmetries caused by the expansion of the dominant in the Trio, the reverse is not true. Nothing within the third movement justifies the length of the dominant in the Trio. The more we look, the harder we look, the less sense the Trio makes. We should not flinch from this conclusion. It is correct. The expansion of the dominant in the Trio is unabashedly anomalous.

The finale is in what might be termed monothematic rondo form, that is, the couplets do not present new or contrasting material. Instead, they develop the material of the refrain, both harmonically and motivically.[22]

---

[21] Theoretically, other options were available. He could have simply expanded the B section. Or he could have written a completely different Menuet, one which would have been long enough to balance the Trio without having to resort to a coda.

[22] See Malcolm S. Cole, 'The Rondo Finale: Evidence for the Mozart–Haydn Exchange?', *Mozart Jahrbuch* (1968–70), 249. Cole's hypothesis that Haydn adopted the sonata-rondo idea as a result of his contact with Mozart has been questioned in Steven C. Fisher, 'Sonata Procedures in Haydn's

At the same time, the movement has some sonata form characteristics and could also be called a sonata-rondo.[23]

The first refrain (mm. 1–24) is cast as a rounded binary.[24] The first couplet (mm. 25–69) begins in the tonic and moves fairly quickly to the dominant, where it states a related theme (mm. 39 ff) and eventually comes to a fairly strong cadence in the dominant (m. 61 ff). This is followed by an abbreviated version of the refrain (mm. 70–85) leading directly into the second couplet, which is quite extended (mm. 86–163). This section has much of the feel of a development section, moving through several key-areas and concluding with an extended dominant chord. That brings us to a return of the refrain, which has some characteristics of a recapitulation, an impression supported by the appearance in mm. 190–203 of a transposition to the tonic of material previously heard in the dominant (mm. 39 ff). The movement concludes with a brief coda.

Apparently this is a simple form, lacking significant complications. However, this rough sketch of the finale scarcely does it justice. The details, as always, are everything. Haydn does far more than bring the composition to a close with a self-contained movement. Rather, many of the most prominent and problematic formal ideas of the other movements are commented upon, explained, and effectively resolved.

As is frequently the case, the connections that bind the movements together most strongly are not motivic. This is not to say that a case could not be made for at least some motivic connections between the movements,[25] but the motivic relationships pale by comparison with the other methods Haydn employs to bind the movements together. The finale returns to the most problematic issues of the first and third movements and resolves them. The first and third movements are not just related to the finale, but depend on it for their very intelligibility.

The problem with both the first and third movements was the unsatisfactory way in which they treated the dominant. In the first

Symphonic Rondo Finales of the 1770s', in Larsen, Serwer, and Webster (eds.), *Haydn Studies*, 481–7. Fisher expands upon this subject in 'Further Thoughts', 105–7.

[23] For a consideration of the problems surrounding the applicability of the term 'sonata-rondo' for Haydn's music, see Fisher, 'Sonata Procedures' and 'Further Thoughts'. Fisher notes that Haydn's transposition back to the tonic of material stated in the dominant is not automatic, but rather, dependent on the specific character of that material, an observation that is entirely in line with the analyses in the present book.

[24] See Cole, 'Rondo Finale', 247, for a table showing the reprise structures in Haydn's symphonic rondo finales.

[25] E.g. the theme of the finale may be seen as a retrograde of the Menuetto; the octave passage in the finale (mm. 54–5) is similar to the opening measure of the introduction of the first movement; the theme of the Trio shares a similar contour to that of the theme of the finale, particularly beginning with the upbeat to m. 2. The scotch snap of the Menuet may have its origins in the first movement. See Ulrich Busch, ' "Ein brandneues Menuett": Das Menuett beim späten Haydn in Symphonie und Quartett', *Musica*, 36 (1982), 148–51.

movement, the confirmation of the dominant was compromised and disrupted by the sudden turn to the parallel minor and the imposition of a theme from another symphony. Moreover, the entire development section was framed by the V/vi, not V; indeed, the dominant was effectively absent. As a result, the recapitulation was approached directly from the V/vi—not from a briefly emphasized V/vi, but from a long-drawn-out, heavily stressed V/vi. In the Trio in the third movement, there was a complementary problem. The dominant that prepared the reprise of the A section was present, but in a proportion that was totally out of scale with the remainder of the movement. As a result, neither movement makes complete sense by itself. The finale serves to resolve the outstanding problems from the earlier movements and does so through a crucial passage that is strategically located at a comparable point in the form, that is, in the preparation of its reprise.

Haydn begins the process of reconciliation at the beginning of the second couplet (the development section). In the first movement, the exposition ended on the dominant and jumped immediately to the V^7/vi. In the finale, Haydn draws a parallel by interrupting the second statement of the refrain before it can be completed. The refrain runs through its A and B sections without incident, but after an arrival on the half-cadence at the end of the B section (m. 85), the dynamics and orchestration change abruptly. The beginning, but only the beginning, of the theme is heard, transferred to a lower voice, over a dominant pedal. This is immediately interrupted by a restatement in G minor (see Ex. 8.11).

The parallel is subtle, but none the less precise. The development section of the first movement began with the dominant of G minor proceeding directly from the dominant, with the resultant clash of F and F♯. Here, although the connection is from the ordinary dominant of B flat to the dominant of G minor, the same abrupt juxtaposition of D major and F major yields the same sharp opposition of F and F♯ (mm. 87–8). Continuing the parallels with the first movement, the first three key-areas touched upon in the development are identical: first G minor, then E flat major, then F minor (first movement: mm. 112–26; fourth movement: mm. 88–96).

In the finale, a lengthy period of harmonic instability follows, lasting until m. 127, when a more stable region arrives, with a powerful tutti on the dominant of G minor (mm. 130 ff), prepared (as in the first movement) by an augmented sixth chord (mm. 128–9). The arrival on the dominant of G minor and the expansion of this chord should recall the forceful emphasis on the D major chord that governed the end of the development section of the first movement. This time there are none of the harmonic disruptions occasioned by the direct progression of V/vi to I. After standing on the dominant of G minor (mm. 130–5) and stating

Ex. 8.11

the principal theme in that key, G minor is quickly dissolved. Haydn then
pauses with G in the bass (as part of vii/V, mm. 142–4) before proceeding
down a final step to F in the bass (see Ex. 8.12).

   In the first movement, the development section was characterized by
the complete absence of the dominant. Instead, Haydn had prolonged

Ex. 8.12

(continued)

the V/vi, beginning and ending the development section with extended emphasis on chords built on D. In the finale, Haydn recalls that progression, giving prominent emphasis to D major, but this time places D major in the context of the preparation for the dominant. Thus, he comes back to the problematic progression of the first movement and then resolves it, interleaving it back into a straightforward and traditional tonal context in which the relative minor (and its dominant) functions as a preparation for a dominant, not as a substitute for it.

The next passage also functions to address an important unresolved anomaly. In m. 146 Haydn lands on the dominant chord, and he remains there for the next eighteen measures. This prominent expansion is a direct reference to the other unresolved formal problem, the Trio in the third movement and its supererogatory expansion of the dominant.

The prolonged dominant in the finale is far more than a mere reference to an isolated event in a prior movement. In the third movement, the expansion of the dominant was totally out of proportion to the size of the movement. In the finale, Haydn has recalled that event. But by placing it in a movement where an expansion of this sort is proportionate to the size of the rest of the movement, he has not only reminded us of the prior event, he has resolved it. The finale is not just related to the first and third movements—the very intelligibility of the earlier movements is, ultimately, directly dependent on specific details in it. Indeed, although the form of the finale of the Symphony No. 85 is 'simple', without the internal complications we have seen in the first and third movements of this composition, every aspect of its structure, from the content of the theme to the harmonic areas emphasized, is geared to contribute on the highest level to the form of the work as a whole.

9

Symphony No. 96

(*1791*)

In the course of Haydn's two trips to England (1791–2 and 1794–5), and in preparation for them, he wrote (among many other works) twelve symphonies. Carefully tailored to appeal to the London audience, Haydn's last symphonies are, at the same time, among the most profound products of his art, forging an inimitable synthesis between the avowedly popular and the unabashedly recondite.[1]

Although they have attracted substantially more attention than his earlier symphonies, the London symphonies do not mark a radical transformation in Haydn's formal procedures.[2] Therefore, in the present chapter it will not be necessary to document new formal principles nor to describe new techniques. Rather, it will be possible to use the analytical method that has been developed in the preceding chapters and apply it to an extremely interesting symphony—one with a number of problematic passages, particularly in the first movement.

Symphony No. 96 begins, like all but one of the London symphonies, with a slow introduction.[3] In some of the London symphonies, the connections are so explicit as to remove any doubt that Haydn intended to relate the slow introduction directly to the following quick movement.[4] But, in contrast to those of a work like Symphony No. 98, the themes and motives of the introduction and Allegro in Symphony No. 96 might not immediately strike one as being closely related.

---

[1] For an extended discussion of this topic, see Schroeder, *Haydn and the Enlightenment*.

[2] It has been argued that the years 1787–90 represent a critical period in Haydn's career, a period in which his instrumental music was characterized by more experimentation than was normal. See A. Peter Brown, 'Critical Years for Haydn's Instrumental Music: 1787–90', *Musical Quarterly*, 62 (1976), 374–94.

[3] For a general survey of the features of the introductions in Haydn's London symphonies, see Peter Benary, 'Die langsamen Einleitungen in Joseph Haydns Londoner Sinfonien', in Anke Bingmann, Klaus Hortschansky, and Winfried Kirsch (eds.), *Studien zur Instrumentalmusik: Lothar Hoffmann-Erbrecht zum 60. Geburtstag* (Tutzing, 1988), 239–51.

[4] For general discussions of the relationship between the slow introduction and the following quick movement, see von Tobel, *Die Formenwelt*, 131–40; Landon, *The Symphonies*, 408–10, 572–5; Rosen, *The Classical Style*, 345–50; Danckwardt, *Die langsame Einleitung*, 106–8; Raimund Bard, *Untersuchungen zur motivischen Arbeit in Haydns sinfonischen Spätwerk* (Kassel, 1982), 85–9, 117–18, 128–30, 138–47; Webster, *Haydn's 'Farewell'*, 162–5, 199.

Such an impression would be incorrect. Not only is the introduction intimately related to the Allegro, but also features of all four movements can be traced back to it.[5] Furthermore, as in Symphony No. 85, only more so, the connections between the Adagio and the Allegro are not restricted to similarities between an isolated theme here and an isolated theme there. Rather, because of Haydn's careful use of a limited number of motivic, thematic, and rhythmic figures in the Allegro, a connection between one figure in the Adagio and another in the Allegro is effectively a connection—directly or indirectly—with every single phrase in the movement. To take but a single example, consider the rhythmic figure that appears for the first time in m. 2—three eighths leading to the following stressed downbeat. Various versions and transformations of this simple idea virtually saturate the introduction itself.

Furthermore, this figure has even greater consequences for the Allegro. Given the motivic and rhythmic economy of the Allegro, almost every one of its phrases can be related—at least to some degree—to the rhythmic motive of m. 2.

It should be noted that it was relatively easy for Haydn to make explicit rhythmic connections between the introduction and the Allegro because the two sections have the same meter. As we saw in our previous encounters with slow introductions, it was not the norm for the introduction to have the same meter as the following quick movement—quite the reverse. Up through the Paris symphonies, the meter of the slow introduction always contrasted with that of the remainder of the movement—much as it contrasted in tempo and theme.[6] In the later symphonies, most of the slow introductions have the same meter as the following quick movement—making possible the explicit use of common themes, as in Nos. 90 and 98 (see Table 9.1).[7]

---

[5] Many of these relationships have been observed before. See Danckwardt, *Die langsame Einleitung*, 112–13, for an analysis of the rhythmic motive. See also von Tobel, *Die Formenwelt*, 136; Gail E. Menk, 'The Symphonic Introductions of Joseph Haydn', Ph.D. diss. (Univ. of Iowa, 1960), 91; Norma P. Butcher, 'A Comparative-Analytical Study of Sonata-Allegro Form in the First Movements of the London Symphonies of Franz Joseph Haydn', Ph.D. diss. (University of Southern California, 1971), 79–92; Landon, *Chronicle and Works*, iii. 511–12; and Bard, *Untersuchungen*, 83, 90–1.

[6] Menk, 'The Symphonic Introductions', 24. The only exception to this rule, and it is only a partial exception, is Symphony No. 25, where the introduction is in **c** time while the main body of the movement is in the somewhat related meter of 2/4. As Webster has pointed out, 'this Adagio is formally and functionally ambiguous', and the 'overall cyclic form of the symphony is also ambiguous'. *Haydn's 'Farewell'*, 258.

[7] Although works composed after 1788 often have different meters for the introduction and the main body of the movement, they are more closely related than previously. For example, in Symphonies Nos. 94, 101, and 103, the meter of the introduction is 3/4 while that of the main body of the movement is 6/8. This allows Haydn to suggest the meter of the main body of the movement in the introduction or vice versa, particularly when a measure consists entirely of eighth-notes. Even more closely related are the meters of **c** and **¢**—see Symphonies Nos. 99 and 104.

TABLE 9.1. *Haydn's Symphonies with Slow Introductions: Meter of introduction compared with that of main body of movement*

No.	Date	Meter of introduction	Meter of main body
6	? 1761	c	3/4
7	1761	c	3/4
25	−1766 [−?1760]	c	2/4
50	1773	c	3/4
60	−1774	2/4	3/4
54	1774	3/4	¢
57	1774	3/4	c
53	? 1778/9	3/4	¢
71	−1780 [?1778/9]	c	3/4
75	−1781 [?1779]	3/4	c
73	−1782 [?1781]	3/4	c
85	? 1785	¢	3/4
84	1786	3/4	¢
86	1786	3/4	c
88	? 1787	3/4	2/4
90	1788	3/4	3/4
91	1788	3/4	3/4
92	1789	3/4	3/4
93	1791	3/4	3/4
94	1791	3/4	6/8
96	1791	3/4	3/4
97	1792	3/4	3/4
98	1792	¢	¢
99	1793	¢	c
100	1793/4	¢	¢
101	1793/4	3/4	6/8
102	1794	¢	¢
103	1795	3/4	6/8
104	1795	c	¢

Having looked in detail at so many sonata forms in previous chapters, it should be possible for us to dispense with a blow-by-blow account of the Allegro, and jump right to the most problematic aspects of the form. In the exposition, a most curious turn of events takes place after m. 57 (see Ex. 9.1).

In Haydn's symphonic sonata forms, the transition to the dominant is frequently closed off by a strong articulation—often a half-cadence. After

Ex. 9.1

(continued)

Ex. 9.1 continued

that cadence Haydn may introduce a new theme in the new key, or restate the principal theme in the dominant.[8]

That is precisely what he seems to be preparing to do in the measures that lead up to m. 57. In mm. 18–38 the principal theme is stated twice, with a powerful tutti sandwiched between. The dominant key is first suggested in m. 49, and the new key becomes increasingly secure in the measures following—helped along by overreach (D♯ in mm. 54 ff). All that is lacking is a solid cadence to mark off the tonicization of the dominant.

In m. 57 we get that cadence, precisely as we have been led to expect—a striking half-cadence in the dominant key. But, having gone to more than a little trouble to create expectations, Haydn now goes to just as much trouble to frustrate the very expectations he has created.

In the normal course of events, after the first prominent cadence in the new key (like that which we find in m. 57), we expect the dominant confirmation region to follow immediately. Given Haydn's standard practice in the late 1780s and early 1790s, that would be followed either by a restatement of the principal theme in the dominant key, or perhaps a new theme—also in the dominant. Haydn does neither. What he does seems almost willful.

At first, just after the half-cadence, in m. 57, we are thrown totally into the dark. The texture thins suddenly down to octaves, and the harmonic-melodic goal of the new passage is not immediately apparent. There is a chromatic turn around E♮ which then rises to and momentarily pauses on

---

[8] E.g. Symphonies No. 82/i, m. 70; No. 85/i, m. 61; No. 86/i, m. 53; No. 94/i, m. 53; No. 97/i, m. 74; No. 98/i, m. 58.

E♯ (m. 58). But as Haydn begins to work his way upwards, it becomes clear that he is arpeggiating through the dominant of the new key—all of this sound and fury, signifying only that we have gone nowhere; we have never left the E major chord of the half-cadence.

That is not all. In m. 61, Haydn extends the arpeggiation all the way to the seventh of the dominant seventh chord on E. When he gets to that unsupported D, he stops and sustains it for the full span of the measure.

Given the continuous frenetic pace of the Allegro—scarcely missing a single eighth-note attack up to this point in the movement—the sudden grinding to a halt in m. 61 is peculiar enough. When that is combined with violations of normal expectations of form and harmony, this moment seems more than peculiar, it seems downright inscrutable.

It gets more so. Instead of proceeding on to the long-awaited, long-deferred, harmonically expected, formally appropriate, and resolution-producing A major triad (and associated theme), Haydn leaps in another direction entirely.

The seventh (D) of the dominant seventh chord does not resolve; instead Haydn uses it as a common tone—it becomes the fifth of a dominant seventh chord on G. The progression is V⁷ in A major (m. 61) to V of C major (m. 62). Haydn highlights V of C major with a forzando, marking it for special emphasis by lifting it out of the prevailing piano dynamic level.

When the dominant seventh chord on G resolves to a C major triad in m. 63, one scarcely knows whether one ought to be relieved or further mystified. It is about time that something resolved somewhere, but resolving to a C major triad hardly helps matters. We are still waiting for the resolution of the dominant seventh of A major; what possible use is a resolution to C? In any event, Haydn places the dynamic weight on the dominant seventh chord on G, and not on its resolution—as if to emphasize the G and not the C. This is to have important ramifications.

As quickly as Haydn leapt into C, he leaps back out. With chromatic lines slithering downward, first in the bass, then in the upper parts, he slips back toward A—landing on a dominant preparation chord in m. 65 (II⁶), followed by a cadential 6–4 in mm. 67–9, and then in quick succession V in m. 70 and the long-overdue resolution in m. 71. To summarize the events of the exposition in numerical terms: it has taken Haydn a mere forty measures to state the original tonic, complete the tonicization of the dominant, and set up a half-cadence in the new key. It has then taken fifteen measures just to resolve to that new tonic.

The non-arrival of the A major chord after m. 57, the precipitous and completely unexpected detour to C by means of its sharply emphasized dominant, and the instant rebound back to A major constitute a dramatic disruption of the harmonic trajectory of the movement. The sense of

harmonic disruption is compounded by the continuation, for after
returning to A major, Haydn proceeds to the end of the exposition,
making no further references to the striking harmonic detour. Clearly,
nothing in the first part of the exposition—or for that matter the
introduction—could possibly be seen to have predicted or motivated the
momentary detour to C major. It might seem as if the sudden move to
C major was an arbitrary or capricious event.

In this movement, the most immediately obvious consequence of the
detour is found in the development section.[9] Haydn exploits the characteristics of the detour to determine the shape and content of the
development section.

After the internal double bar, Haydn returns, almost immediately, to
the harmonic problem of the exposition. The development section begins
with a quick tonicization of the relative minor, B minor, and a brief
expansion of that key-area. In short order, using variants of the principal
motive, he turns B into the dominant of E and drops down the cycle of
fifths to E minor, arriving upon and prolonging the E minor triad with
double neighbor-figures (mm. 92 ff).

Having arrived on E, Haydn is ready to return to the harmonic
problem he posed in the exposition. In mm. 99–103, by means of a
written-out ritardando, the motion gradually grinds to a halt, moving
from the E minor chord in m. 98 directly to a G major chord—at first
in second inversion (m. 99), then with the seventh added (mm. 100–1),
finally coming to rest on a dominant seventh chord on G in mm. 102–3.
Immediately after, in m. 104, is a transposition, to C major, of mm. 71 ff
(see Ex. 9.2).

On the most obvious level, what Haydn has done is to make a direct
connection with the anomalous harmonic progression from the exposition.[10] C major has become the first prominent point of harmonic
emphasis within the development section, marked for particular attention
by means of the exaggerated interruption of the rhythmic flow—as in the
exposition.

However, Haydn has done more than relate the passages simply
through their common use of C major. The approaches to C major in
the two progressions are virtually identical, moving from a chord based
on E (there E[7], here E minor) directly to a dominant seventh on G, and
from there on to a C major triad. As in the passage from the exposition,
so too here, in the development section, there is a prominent disruption
of the rhythmic flow. If all of that were not enough to draw a parallel, in

---

[9] For a discussion of formal consequences of tonal deflections in the expositions of works by Haydn
and Mozart, see John M. Harutunian, 'Haydn and Mozart: A Study of their Mature Sonata-Style
Procedures', Ph.D. diss. (UCLA, 1981), 109–55.

[10] See Schroeder, *Haydn and the Enlightenment*, 164.

Ex. 9.2

the passage that follows (mm. 104 ff), Haydn restates in C major the very theme that followed the detour in the exposition (mm. 71 ff).

The direct references to the detour from the exposition in mm. 91–108 constitute only the first stage of the development's attempt to come to terms with that disruptive progression. After dwelling on C, Haydn pushes back very quickly to E minor, resting on its dominant in mm. 114–16. Immediately after this, he jumps to a G major chord, as if he were about to use it once again as a dominant to C. This time, he changes direction, pushing the bass down a half-step to F♯ (with E♯ moving to F♯ in the upper voice) and thus arriving at an F sharp chord, the dominant of B minor, which is then drawn out for seven measures (see Ex. 9.3).

The return to the dominant of B minor brings us full circle, for this is precisely how the development section began. As a means of emphasizing the completion of a harmonic circle, Haydn resorts to one of his most famous and dramatic silences: eight complete beats of rest after the half-cadence in B minor.

What comes after the prolonged silence is, perhaps, even more startling than the detour to C major in the exposition. Immediately after the pause Haydn plunges directly into G major, and does so with a restatement of the opening theme of the Allegro—that is, giving the impression of a recapitulation, but, of course, in the wrong key. After a few bars he drops the pretense, pulls back out of G major, and proceeds through a hint of E minor (again!) back to D major and the recapitulation. This emphasis on G—reinforced by the thematic treatment—serves as the final stage in the changing role of G in the course of the movement. Haydn began by using G as the dominant of C in the strange detour of the exposition. G repeats and amplifies this in the prominent passage in the development section. Then G itself becomes the focus of attention—no longer as the dominant of C, but as a key-area in its own right, even to the point of initiating a wrong-key recapitulation. Finally G is reinterpreted, as we knew it had to be, no longer as an independent sonority, but in the context of D major as a preparation for the dominant.

Having brought G back into the context of the overall tonic, Haydn reserves one final and ever-so-subtle touch for the close of the development section. Upon reaching the dominant chord in root position in m. 147, he repeats the chord in the next two measures. Then the lower voices drop out and the first violin ascends to the ninth of the dominant chord, after which it drops back down the scale. It continues down past a complete octave, coming to rest on the seventh of the dominant chord—that is, on G—giving a final and tantalizingly multifaceted touch of emphasis to this tone. G has now been recaptured, fully and pervasively, in the orbit of D—this is, after all, the seventh of the dominant. At the same time, by bringing the development section to close

Ex. 9.3

(continued)

with a passage that fades out, ending with a lone G, followed by silence, Haydn gives us a gentle reminder of the nearly autonomous role this pitch has played throughout the movement (see Ex. 9.4).[11]

---

[11] A similar gambit is used at the end of the development section of Symphony No. 45/i. The development section includes a mightily disruptive episode in D major. But when Haydn ends the development section he does so with an arpeggiation of vii⁷ in F sharp minor, concluding with the violin rising to a lone D, followed by five beats of silence.

Ex. 9.3 continued

Taken together, the emphases of the development section appear, not as a string of unrelated events, not as aimless wandering through various non-tonic key-areas, nor a purposeless succession of thematic references, but as a functional whole. The individual keys chosen, their ordered succession, and the motives assigned work together as inseparable components of the form.

The recapitulation, which begins at m. 154, is—of course—anything but a literal, tonally adjusted repetition of the exposition.[12] Less than a third of the sixty-six measures of the exposition return in the recapitulation, either at pitch or transposed (see Table 9.2).

Given the attention paid to this subject in the previous chapters, the rationale for most of the responses of the recapitulation should be obvious enough. The telescoping of the two statements of the principal theme into one, the rewriting of the transition, the variations made in the closing theme, and so on are all motivated by the same basic compositional principles that have guided Haydn's hand from his earliest symphonies. Two details, however, are worth a moment of our attention.

Measures 171–6 correspond—somewhat loosely, and much condensed—to a transposed version of mm. 49–56. In the exposition section

---

[12] See Eugene K. Wolf, 'The Recapitulations in Haydn's London Symphonies', *Musical Quarterly*, 52 (1966), 71–89. Wolf discusses the recapitulations of the first movements of Haydn's last twelve symphonies, providing a valuable survey of the techniques he employs in varying exposition material. He also offers rational explanations for some of Haydn's specific compositional choices.

Ex. 9.4

this was followed by mm. 57–60 (= mm. 177–80) and then the crucial harmonic detour to C major. As can be seen in the comparable passage in the recapitulation, Haydn most assuredly does not mechanically transpose the passage. Rather, in the recapitulation, the harmonic detour is conspicuously absent (see Ex. 9.5).

It could hardly have been otherwise. The detour from the exposition played an essential role in determining the emphases within the

TABLE 9.2. *Symphony No. 96/i: Correspondences between Exposition and Recapitulation*

Exposition (mm.)	Recapitulation (mm.)
18–31	—
32–8	154–60
39–48	—
—	161–70
49–56	171–6 (transposed and very loosely related)
57–60	177–80 (transposed)
61–83	—
—	181–203

Ex. 9.5

development section. A comparable passage in the recapitulation could have no such function. A harmonic detour would be destabilizing (as it was in the exposition), demanding further explanation. Inasmuch as the emphasis on C in the exposition was essential for the further course of the movement, so too, the omission of this passage from the recapitulation is essential for closure.

At approximately m. 180 we have come to the end of passages that correspond to events in the exposition. Having omitted such a large proportion of the exposition's material, the recapitulation is now substantially shorter than the exposition. As we have seen in other works, if Haydn does not insert something within the body of the recapitulation, he normally corrects the imbalance by adding a coda. And, as is so often the case, the specific content of the coda plays an important role in the overall formal scheme.

In m. 194, after three tension-building measures on the dominant, he reaches the climax of the movement—the only fortissimo. And at this moment he makes a dramatic turn to the parallel minor (see Ex. 9.6).

To what can this refer? There have been no references whatsoever to D minor in the course of the Allegro.

Ex. 9.6

But the parallel minor was a crucial component of the second half of the introduction. By returning to this idea (using the same rhythm—made possible by the same meter) in the coda of the movement, Haydn has made an explicit reference to the introduction.[13]

The coda of this movement may have been motivated by the need for formal balance. In the process of righting the imbalance and giving proper emphasis to the tonic, Haydn makes a virtue out of a necessity. He uses it to do far more than merely reaffirm and emphasize the tonic. Rather, he exploits this opportunity to forge persuasive connections with the introduction—its rhythms and emphasis on the parallel minor.

---

[13] See Bard, ' "Tendenzen" zur zyklischen Gestaltung', 380–1. Bard also points out some connections between the introduction and the principal motives of the second, third, and fourth movements.

The form of the second movement, typical of many of Haydn's later slow movements, resists easy classification. Although the three-part outline (A section, mm. 1–25; B section, mm. 26–45; A' section, mm. 46–89) is, perhaps, the most prominent formal feature, numerous other formal types play a functional role, at least within the discrete segments of the larger form.[14]

The A section (mm. 1–25) is itself a rounded binary (a, mm. 1–9; b, mm. 10–21; a' mm. 22–5) with a non-modulating a section.[15] Since the a section is tonally self-contained and returns after contrasting episodes, a strong sense of rondo emerges. The B section, though mainly in the parallel minor, is harmonically unstable, traversing a number of tonal areas before closing on the dominant, suggesting the development section of a sonata form. Moreover, it contains an extended passage of imitative writing—a fugato. The A' section includes an extensive written-out cadenza (mm. 69–85) as if it were a concerto. Finally (as will be discussed in more detail shortly), none of the numerous restatements of the opening theme (mm. 5–8, 22–5, 46–9, 63–6) is a literal repetition of the initial statement: in every instance, the theme is altered—as in a variation form.[16]

Although numerous formal types leave their imprint on the Andante, this movement is far more than a succession of discrete events and much more than the sum of the effect of different formal types. Rather, Haydn takes great care to integrate the different sections and formal ideas into a functional whole. This can be seen most clearly in the A' section, where mm. 46 ff are anything but a literal repetition of mm. 1–25.

There are two essential differences between mm. 1–25 and 46–89. The two statements of the principal theme in the A' section (mm. 46–9 and 63–6) appear in varied form, and an extended cadenza is inserted in mm. 69–85.

We could simply ascribe the differences between the A and A' sections as originating in the need to avoid redundancy and the desire to break up what might otherwise be a stultifying symmetry. Haydn responds to the dictates of the redundancy principle by excising one of the potential repetitions of the theme (cf. mm. 1–8 with 46–9), and by invoking the variation principle for the remaining thematic statements. In addition, the cadenza breaks up the symmetrical ABA plan.

---

[14] For an analysis of this movement see Bard, *Untersuchungen*, 198–203. Another slow movement which includes references to many different formal types is Symphony No. 76/ii.

[15] This might suggest that the a section should be repeated without alteration. But since it includes two virtually identical statements of the theme (mm. 1–4, 5–8), the a' section reduces this to one (mm. 22–5) as per the redundancy principle.

[16] Rondo-variation characteristics might be seen as well—the various statements of the theme (refrains) are separated by couplets of differing lengths.

Although 'true', these explanations are, ultimately, insufficient, failing to account for the specific details by which the A′ section is distinguished from the A section. When we look at the specifics of the A′ section, and in particular attempt to identify the origins for its divergence from the norms established in the A section, the results are highly revealing.

With the exception of changes in orchestration and the excision of one of the statements of the theme, mm. 46–62 are much like mm. 1–21—the variation of the repetition is very light. But in m. 63, with the arrival of the a section, Haydn breaks away from the slightly varied repetition of the comparable passage from the A section (see Ex. 9.7a) and launches into a more extensive variation of the theme (b).

Ex. 9.7

Ex. 9.7

(*b*)

The variation is a melodic-outline variation, with the accompaniment almost unchanged. It is in constant triplet sixteenths, and its melody spans a broad spectrum of registers. The choice of rhythm and specific aspects of the melodic shape are consequences of earlier events—specifically, the central section of the movement. The B section is clearly distinguished from the A section by its emphasis on long-breathed triplet lines (see Ex. 9.8). Although triplet figures appeared in many guises in the A section, they occurred almost entirely as short bursts of motion, not, as in the B section, extended into running lines. In mm. 63–6, Haydn draws upon the specific content of the B section, transforming the rhythm into a non-stop succession of triplets, exactly like the rhythmic profile of the theme in the B section, and ranging widely across the registers, also as in the B section.[17]

Thus the final section of the movement acts not merely to repeat the first section, but to combine important features of the first and second sections. As such, it functions as a synthesis and a summary of prior events. To state that the statement of the theme in mm. 63–6 is a variation of the opening theme is true enough, but misses the point. To state that mm. 63 ff are a variation of A, drawing upon the resources of B, thereby creating a later event that is the sum of prior events, is to capture something of the sense of forward motion and continuous development that marks Haydn's formal thought.

---

[17] See Bard, *Untersuchungen*, 201.

Ex. 9.8

The cadenza also makes essential contributions to this very process. It ranges quite far afield from the tonic, turning to the flat side (see Ex. 9.9).

The tonal wanderlust of the cadenza is all the more striking given the A section, which was (harmonically) quite tame—mm. 1–25 scarcely leave the tonic. By inserting a written-out cadenza, Haydn takes the opportunity to touch upon key-areas not even remotely suggested in the A section.

Ex. 9.9

(continued)

Ex. 9.9 continued

As was the case with the variation in mm. 63–6, here too, the clear divergences from the model of the opening section are employed in the service of the developmental process. The cadenza turns immediately to the flat side, placing substantial stress on E♭—eventually returning to the dominant by means of stepwise descent in the bass from E♭ to D (see m. 77 in Ex. 9.9 and m. 85 (not shown here)).[18]

This is a virtually literal repetition of the principal emphases of the B section—even including the preparation for its closing dominant, which was also approached from E♭ in the bass. The connection is strengthened by the rhythmic and motivic connections between the varied A′ section and the material of the B section (see Ex. 9.10).[19]

From the foregoing it should be clear that the features of the A′ section that most clearly distinguish it from the A section can be traced to events in the intervening B section, and must be seen as consequences of that section. Tovey once remarked that a fugue is not a form, but a process. The same could be said—should be said—of this Andante.

Given the attention that Haydn has paid in previous compositions to forming relationships between movements, we might expect to find connections between the the first two movements of this symphony. Some obvious relationships are motivic. Most prominently, the principal theme of the second movement, an ascending figure D–G–B–D, is an inversion of the first four notes of the theme in the introduction of the first movement. Similarly, other motivic details in the second movement can also be traced back to events in the introduction of the first movement— the figure in mm. 10–11 of the second movement is remarkably similar to mm. 8–9 in the first; the countersubject in the fugal middle section of the second movement (mm. 26–8) is much like mm. 9–10 in the introduction of the first movement.

Although powerful intermovemental relationships can be found in many of Haydn's symphonies, the relationships, at least to this point, have not always involved all of the movements, at least not in equal measure. Indeed, in the previous four symphonies we have examined, Nos. 55, 75, 81, and 85, a significant trend should now be apparent: the strongest connections are between those movements that are in the same key. The internal slow movement—which is normally cast in a

<hr/>

[18] Only one sketch has survived for this symphony, and it deals entirely with the turn to E♭ in the cadenza. For a transcription, see Landon (ed.), *Joseph Haydn: Critical Edition of the Complete Symphonies*, xi. 219. For a facsimile and transcription, see Schafer, ' "A Wisely Ordered *Phantasie*" ', ii. 6–7.

[19] A clear echo of the approach to the dominant from the end of the B section is preserved at the end of the cadenza, not only through the augmented sixth chord in m. 77, but also through the emphasis placed on the E♭ in the bass in m. 85. At the same time, a hint of a motivic connection is preserved in m. 74, where a distinct recollection of the running triplet theme of the B section appears in the first violin.

Ex. 9.10

contrasting (if closely related) key—has scarcely played any significant role. Therefore, of the symphonies analyzed so far in this book, the only ones that seem to have unequivocal connections between all the movements are those works in which all the movements are in the same key (Nos. 21 and 49). And the symphonies I have chosen as my examples are in no way unusual in this respect—up through the Paris symphonies, when an inner slow movement is cast in a different key, there are fewer significant intermovemental relationships between it and the remaining movements than between those movements which are in the same key. But in Haydn's last symphonies (Nos. 88–104), relationships between the movements are often extended to involve all the movements—including the contrasting-key, slow inner movement. Symphony No. 96 is a case in point.

On the basis solely of the motivic connections described above, one would be hard pressed to justify the claim that the first two movements are strongly related. There are some similarities between the principal thematic ideas of the second movement and the introduction of the first movement. But this is scarcely enough to support anything other than a vague sense that (at best) Haydn made use of an arsenal of moderately similar motivic ideas. Or even, as the skeptic might say, the connections are purely coincidental ('all tonal compositions have triadic outlines of some sort or another'). If we see something here, perhaps we ought to give pause to make sure—to borrow a phrase once applied to the claims of the discovery of canals on Mars—on which end of the telescope is the intelligent life that has been discovered.

I would argue that the connections between the first and second movements are significant. The motivic connections are—on their own— merely the tip of the iceberg. What is crucial is the choice of key.

Normally speaking, the slow inner movement of Haydn's symphonies (in major) would be in the dominant, the subdominant, or the tonic minor. But, as we have already seen, there does not seem to be a convincing explanation for the specific choice from the available options. In Haydn's earliest symphonies, it did seem as if there was a trend for D major symphonies to place the slow movement in the subdominant. But that trend breaks down in the 1770s. Although Haydn's last seven D major symphonies (Nos. 73, 75, 86, 93, 96, 101, and 104) all cast their slow movement in the subdominant, that consistency is probably happenstance (no such consistency obtains for other keys).[20] Therefore, I tend to believe that the choice of key for the slow movement is not predetermined by the key of the composition.[21] Rather, it appears that in Haydn's later symphonies the choice of key for the slow movement (from a limited range of acceptable possibilities) is frequently a contextual decision— determined not by custom, habit, or chance, but calculated to accomplish specific compositional purposes.

In this work, because of the choice of key (G major), the principal theme of the second movement does more than merely mimic the

---

[20] For example, in the six post-1773 G major symphonies (Nos. 54, 81, 88, 92, 94, and 100), half of the slow movements are in the subdominant and the other half in the dominant.

[21] Because they are a different genre, it may or may not be relevant to point out that there is no consistency in the assignment of keys for the slow movements of Haydn's D major string quartets: Op. 17 No. 6, subdominant; Op. 20 No. 4, parallel minor; Op. 33 No. 6, parallel minor; Op. 50 No. 6, parallel minor; Op. 64 No. 5, dominant; Op. 71 No. 2, dominant; Op. 76 No. 5, mediant major.

intervals of the opening of the introduction of the first movement; it also outlines the same octave, D to D. This would not have been possible had Haydn chosen any key other than G major. Similarly, the countersubject in the fugue is cast in G minor, and as a result corresponds precisely to mm. 9–10 in the introduction, where G minor was suggested.

Moreover, by choosing G as the tonic for the second movement, Haydn adds yet one more dimension to the emphasis that was placed on G in the first movement. As we discussed in detail above, G—first as the dominant of C, then as an independent sonority, and finally absorbed back into the dominant of D—took on a central role in the first movement. In the second movement, a choice of G as the tonic serves to extend this relationship, and to expand upon the ideas presented in the first movement.

By choosing G as the tonic Haydn has the opportunity to draw yet another parallel with the role of G in the exposition of the first movement, where G was transformed into the dominant of C and functioned to tonicize C. This is exactly what he does at an important point in the second movement. In mm. 39–41, toward the end of the contrasting middle section, he presents a short tonicization of C minor, with the fugal subject appearing in this key, and then almost immediately transforms C into the preparation for the dominant of G (see Ex. 9.11).

It appears, then, that the motivic relationships are merely a single component of the connections between the first and second movements. Rather than depending merely on an evanescent similarity between their themes, the first and second movements are bound together by a complex matrix of interrelated compositional decisions, of which the choice of key for the movement is one of the most central. To have cast the second movement in any other key than G major would have been to diminish— appreciably—the meaning of the composition as a whole.

In the third movement as well, easily recognizable motivic connections can be found between the themes and earlier events, most notably the introduction to the first movement.[22] The head-motives of the Menuetto and the Trio, both straightforward arpeggiations of the D major triad, relate explicitly to thematic ideas from the first movement.

Formally, the Menuetto has a three-part A section, the first in the tonic (mm. 1–8), ending with a half-cadence, the second modulating to and cadencing on the dominant (mm. 9–14), and the third in the dominant (mm. 15–20). After the brief B section (mm. 21–8), Haydn rewrites the A section, taking care to avoid restating all three of its cadences, reducing them to two (mm. 40 and 52), and transposing to the tonic the final section (mm. 15–20), which was in the dominant.

---

[22] See Marx, 'Über thematische Beziehungen', 12.

Ex. 9.11

The Trio, with a modulating A section (mm. 53–60), has a brief coda, which (perhaps) includes some motivic references to the Menuetto (cf. the first violin in mm. 81 and 83 with m. 49).

The finale, an engaging rondo, has few formal complications—in the couplets Haydn never strays very far either harmonically or thematically from the material of the refrain. Although the movement might best be described as an ordinary rondo (i.e., not a sonata-rondo), this does not mean that the sonata principle is entirely inapplicable. One of the more prominent events of the first couplet (mm. 62 ff) is in F major. A version of this returns, restated in the tonic (mm. 210 ff).

Here too, there are some connections with events in the previous movements. As in the second and third movements, one of the most immediate connections with the first movement is motivic: the principal theme of the movement is similar to the opening notes of the introduction to the first movement.[23] Therefore, the theme of this movement also relates to the themes of the other movements, most explicitly the Trio in the third movement.

Although intermovemental relationships are an important component of its design, Symphony No. 96 is not the most strongly unified multimovement cycle of Haydn's late symphonies. Unlike those of other works we have examined (notably Nos. 81 and 85), the different movements do not depend for their very intelligibility on events that happen elsewhere, nor does the finale serve to resolve anomalies from earlier movements. That said, one should recognize the extent of the relationships that do exist: as we have seen, the motives of the introduction flow logically one into the next; the principal themes of all of the movements are related to ideas that first unfold in the introduction; the harmonic structure of the exposition of the first movement (including the surprise modulation) acts both to establish the emphases of the development section, and to determine the specific content of the recapitulation. And we should pay particular attention to the fact that Haydn has made the slow movement participate in the intermovemental relationships, even though it is not in the same key as the other three movements.

---

[23] Marx, 'Über thematische Beziehungen', 120.

IO

Symphony No. 99

(*1793*)

IN 1794, Haydn returned to England for his second visit. In preparation for this trip, and during the course of his stay, he wrote the last six of his symphonies. Of these, Symphony No. 99 appears to have been the first one composed, written not in London, but in Vienna before his departure.[1]

In Symphonies Nos. 85 and 96, the introduction played an essential role in the formal structure of the composition—not only as the instigator of motivic and harmonic events within the first movement, but as the source of some important features of all four movements. In Symphony No. 99, it plays an even more critical role in the formal process, presenting striking harmonic ideas that have far-reaching consequences for all of the movements.

The introduction begins traditionally enough—tutti chords in forte, alternating with piano statements of a more lyrical theme (mm. 1–4), followed by a passage dominated by the inevitable dotted rhythms (mm. 5–7). In m. 8 Haydn dutifully arrives on the dominant, prolonging it for two measures with the lowered sixth degree (Cb) as its upper neighbor (see Ex. 10.1).

With the arrival of this extended dominant, it might seem as if Haydn has come to the point which should function to prepare the end of the introduction. The prominent dominant chord in root position and the dramatic slowing of the harmonic rhythm are the very features we would expect to see at this stage. The addition of the seventh (m. 9) heightens the tension and the instability—surely the tonic and the main body of the movement are at hand.

Instead of concluding the introduction and proceeding directly with the Vivace assai, Haydn has a startling surprise in store. In m. 10, he steps back up to Cb, and then, instead of returning down to the dominant, freezes on the Cb, drawing out this elaborative tone for a complete measure, which is prolonged even further with a fermata.

This is only the first challenge to expectations. Immediately following the fermata, the Cb is transformed into its enharmonic equivalent, B♮, and

---

[1] Landon, *Chronicle and Works*, iii. 496.

Ex. 10.1

then, as the common tone of a dominant seventh chord (its root), unleashes an astounding, and totally unanticipated, modulation through E minor to C minor. Just moments away from what was expected to be the end of the introduction, the trajectory of the harmony has been violently deflected, ricocheting away from the anticipated dominant.[2]

---

[2] It has been suggested that there may be a connection between Symphony No. 99 and Beethoven's Piano Sonata Op. 7. See Marx, 'Über thematische Beziehungen', 7 and 16.

(continued)

The next few measures compound the surprise and heighten the harmonic tension. Having modulated—implausible as it may seem—through the Neapolitan (minor) and on to the relative minor at the very point where the closing dominant was expected, Haydn gives us all of the usual hints that suggest that the introduction is about to conclude. In m. 14, following an augmented sixth chord, he arrives on the (local) dominant, and he prolongs this sonority for four measures. He comes to

Ex. 10.1 continued

a stop in m. 17 with a forte, tutti statement of octave Gs, drawing this out
with yet another fermata.

On the surface it seems as if this time—even more so than in m.
10—we have really come to the end of the introduction. All of the
appropriate clichés are in place—a powerful augmented sixth chord, a
four-measure prolongation of a dominant chord, in tutti and with a

TABLE 10.1. *Introductions in Haydn's Symphonies that do not Close on the Dominant*

No.	Closing harmony
90	vii$^{6}_{5}$/V
92	German sixth
103	V/vi

throbbing bass, and a dramatic pause on that chord, drawn out by a fermata.

But this is the 'wrong' dominant—the dominant of the relative minor. Could the introduction really end in this key?

For Haydn's music of only a few years earlier, we could have stated confidently that he would not end the introduction at this point, but instead would have returned to the tonic key in order to end with a 'proper' dominant. For a symphony composed in 1793 we can no longer be so certain—three of his late introductions close with something other than the dominant chord, and in Symphony No. 103 (1795—also in E flat) Haydn actually ends the introduction with the V/vi (see Table 10.1).

In Symphony No. 99, Haydn has it both ways. In an extraordinary progression, he abruptly extricates himself from C minor, untying his harmonic Gordian knot with one stroke of the pen. In m. 18, following the tutti on G, Haydn moves directly back to E flat simply by stating its dominant chord. And to heighten the contrast the dominant seventh of E flat is presented piano, in the winds.

By means of this return to the dominant of E flat, Haydn has presented us with interesting harmonic and formal problems, paradoxes, and dilemmas. On the one hand, the jump to the dominant seventh chord has—after a fashion—resolved the outstanding harmonic issues of the introduction. By moving to the dominant seventh in E flat Haydn has completed a bass arpeggiation of the tonic chord (E♭–G–B♭) that has been unfolding slowly over the course of the introduction. At the same time he has also implied the resolution of C♭, the chromatic neighbor of the dominant, left hanging since m. 10.

On the other hand, it would be absurd to assert that anything has been adequately and properly resolved. The quiet, high-register, wind-band sound of the dominant seventh chord scarcely seems substantial enough to act as the resolution for the massive, tutti, low-register sound of the V/vi. Nor could a single chord (let alone one so gossamery) possibly be sufficient to restore the harmonic balance so forcefully disrupted by the tonicizations in mm. 10 ff. Events as powerful and as arresting as the frozen chromatic neighbor, the enharmonic shift, the tonicizations of E and C minor, and the surprise return to E flat must be played out on a much larger stage than is provided by the last measure of the introduction.

The extraordinary harmonic progressions of the introduction exert decisive control, not only over crucial details within each movement, but also over the relationships between the movements. The structure of the introduction is, therefore, of central importance for an understanding of the work as a whole and is a topic to which we will return, time and again, in the course of the following analysis.[3]

In a number of places in the first movement, Haydn recalls the harmonic challenges posed by the introduction. After the straightforwardly diatonic opening theme, he addresses this issue in the transition to the dominant (see Ex. 10.2).[4]

Although there are many prominent differences between the progression in the introduction and the present passage, the connections are significant. The Cb/B♮ which was—in the introduction—first unresolved, then the agent of a modulation to C minor, and finally unsatisfactorily resolved, functions in a less disruptive fashion in the transition. In m. 35, the Cb is introduced as the minor ninth of a dominant chord. To be sure, as was the case in the introduction, it does not immediately resolve back down to Bb, but instead is displaced in the upper register by a C in m. 36. Haydn has transformed the dominant minor ninth into the dominant major ninth, which then resolves, perfectly properly (in m. 37), to a tonic chord. So too, in mm. 39–40, B♮ appears as the leading-tone of the V/vi. As in the introduction, this applied dominant is followed (in m. 41) by the C minor triad. In comparison with that of the introduction, this progression is far smoother and less remarkable (the sudden lurch to E minor is absent), and it proceeds on to the tonicized dominant through the V/V—a distant echo of the cathartic tonicization of C minor in the introduction.

Another step in this process takes place at the beginning of the development section. Immediately after the conclusion (in B flat) of the exposition, Haydn jumps directly to the dominant of C, presenting two statements of variants of the principal theme (see Ex. 10.3).

---

[3] For a brief discussion of some motivic relationships between the introduction and the remainder of the work, as well as a perceptive reading of the implications of Haydn's harmonic plan, see Landon, *Chronicle and Works*, iii. 553. An extended discussion of the relationship between the introduction and the remainder of the work appears in my 'Remote Keys and Multi-movement Unity: Haydn in the 1790s', *Musical Quarterly*, 74 (1990), 254–66. See also Webster, *Haydn's 'Farewell'*, 320–9.

[4] Motivic connections between mm. 34–6, 71–4, and 145–7 are described in Peter Hauschild, 'Liedthema und Entwicklung in den Expositionen von Haydns "Londoner" Sinfonien', in Eva Badura-Skoda (ed.), *Joseph Haydn: Proceedings of the International Joseph Haydn Congress, Wien, 1982* (Munich, 1986), 178–9.

Ex. 10.2

The progression from a B flat triad in root position (m. 89, the end
of the exposition) to a G major triad as the dominant of C (mm. 90–3),
and from there on to a statement of the subsidiary theme in C
major (mm. 94 ff) represents yet another reminder of the harmonic ideas
of the introduction. Haydn presents—in another context, and with some
significantly different emphases (notably, the turn to C major, not C
minor)—essential aspects of the progressions in the second half of the

Ex. 10.3

introduction. Paradoxical though it may seem, the most obvious consequence of this recollection is a further destabilization—not a resolution. Haydn has added a new ingredient, one that will need to be addressed.

Even beyond these two instances, numerous other references to the harmonic problem of the introduction occur throughout the movement—toward the end of the development section, at the transition, in the interpolation within the secondary theme. Taken together, these recurrent statements have the effect of keeping the harmonic problem at the forefront of our consciousness. Be that as it may, in no place is there a satisfactory response to or resolution of the problems posed by the introduction. Unfinished business, indeed.

In the course of this book we have had the opportunity to see a gradual change in Haydn's treatment of the recapitulation, leading (by the mid-1780s) to works in which the recapitulation can no longer be described simply as a tonally modified repetition of the exposition. But no matter how thoroughly Haydn's late recapitulations are rewritten, they still retain—at least partially—the function of restating and reformulating the material of the exposition. Generally speaking, even in his late symphonies, the prominent ideas of the exposition will return, in order, in the recapitulation, unless there is good reason to the contrary. Of course, because of the nature of his material, there are almost always very good reasons to the contrary. As a result, Haydn usually cuts a significant proportion of the material of the exposition from the recapitulation. This in turn motivates him to interpolate or append passages to restore the proper proportions to the movement, giving him the opportunity to make surprising references, sudden changes in direction, startling juxtapositions, and so forth. If one were presented only with the exposition of an early work which one did not know, it would be possible to make fairly accurate (though rarely, if ever, precise) predictions about what would happen in the recapitulation. That is simply not even remotely possible in the later recapitulations. To a large degree, one can still predict which passages from the exposition will likely be excised in the recapitulation, but one cannot predict what kinds of interpolations and additions Haydn will make and where he will place them. Invariably, the sudden, often shocking, deviations from the patterns of the exposition trigger the normative principle, motivating him to make further responses, either within the movement or, frequently, in subsequent movements. The recapitulation of the first movement of Symphony No. 99 is representative of these trends and thus typical of many of Haydn's later sonata forms.[5] Fully two-thirds of the measures of the exposition do not return

---

[5] Other works from this period have recapitulations that are as completely rewritten as that of the present work, if not more so. Perhaps the most extreme case is the recapitulation and coda of Symphony No. 92/i. Much of the impetus for this remarkable movement comes from the premises set forth at the join between the slow introduction and the subsequent Allegro spiritoso. The introduction concludes, not on the dominant chord, but on a German sixth, thus leaving unresolved a neighbor to the dominant (Eb) at the end of the introduction. The Allegro spiritoso begins with an unstable idea, a four-measure expansion of the dominant seventh chord. Throughout the Allegro spiritoso, Haydn brings back this idea again and again, as if he were trying to find a version that would be stable. Some of the unusual (and unpredictable) events of the recapitulation and coda recall the introduction and its frozen neighbor (see mm. 144–6, 211–12). For a perceptive analysis of this movement, see Webster, *Haydn's 'Farewell'*, 167–73.

TABLE 10.2. *Symphony No. 99/i: Correspondences between Exposition and Recapitulation*

Exposition (mm.)	Recapitulation (mm.)
19–26	—
27–36	138–47
37–70	—
—	148–56
71–6	157–62 (transposed)
—	163–78 (but for mm. 163 ff, see end of development; for mm. 166 ff, see mm. 81–4)
76–80	179–83 (transposed)
81–6	—
—	184–99 Coda?
87–9	200–2 (transposed)

in the recapitulation, and perhaps even more significant, approximately half of the recapitulation has no parallel passage in the exposition (see Table 10.2).[6]

At the beginning of the exposition, the principal theme appeared in a double statement (mm. 19–26 and 27–34), the first statement in the strings alone, the second for full orchestra. As we saw in Symphony No. 75, a double statement of this sort is always reduced to a single statement—the forte statement. This means that the passage corresponding to mm. 19–26 is excised from the recapitulation, which begins, instead, with a literal repetition of mm. 27 ff.

By any measure, Haydn's responses to the next events in the exposition are drastic. The simple facts should be sufficient to give an indication of how extensive are the differences between the exposition and the recapitulation: of the passage between m. 34 and m. 70, only the first three measures return in the recapitulation. Everything else is excised entirely, or completely reworked and reordered.

In the exposition, the transition to the dominant section (beginning m. 34) moved quickly away from E flat, passing through a suggestion of C, before the tonicization of the dominant. In the recapitulation, Haydn preserves the first three measures of the transition, taking care to retain part of the passage that recalls the harmonic challenges of the introduction.

---

[6] In a comment sparked by the recapitulation of this movement, Donald Francis Tovey remarked: 'And as to his "recapitulations", why, the very use of the word has blinded historians to the fact that Haydn says in the place of his "recapitulations" what Beethoven says in his codas.' *Essays in Musical Analysis*, i: *Symphonies and Other Orchestral Works* (repr. London, 1981), 356.

Ex. 10.4

(continued)

    As always, he must break away from the model of the exposition before
the point where it began the process of the tonicization of the dominant—in this case, that means before the passage corresponding to m. 42.
Precisely as we would expect, in m. 148 Haydn diverges from the
harmonic patterns of the exposition, and thereafter remains in the tonic
key, proceeding to a strong half-cadence in m. 156.

Ex. 10.4 continued

When he resumes in m. 157 after the half-cadence in the preceding measure, it is with the transposed equivalent of mm. 71 ff—that is, he has lopped off mm. 37–70 almost in their entirety (although the runs in mm. 150–5 that prepare the half-cadence are somewhat similar to mm. 42–3; see Ex. 10.4). What could possibly have motivated an excision of this magnitude?

One might be tempted to offer the redundancy principle as the motivation for this excision, for at m. 48 the dominant region is announced by a transposition of the opening theme to the dominant key. Such a hypothesis has a plausible ring to it, but one has to recognize that other symphonies from this period and earlier begin the dominant region with a transposition of the opening theme to the dominant, yet retain both statements in the recapitulation.[7] Moreover, as we have seen, Haydn has already excised one of the two statements of the opening theme— surely the redundancy principle would scarcely demand the excision of two of the three statements from the exposition. Even if we can justify the excision of the partial restatement of the opening theme, that does not explain why Haydn has omitted a transposed restatement to the tonic of mm. 52–70. This entire passage was in the dominant. Therefore—or so it might seem—the sonata principle ought to have been invoked, and this passage should have been transposed back to the tonic.

That it was not transposed is an indication either that Haydn saw something in the passage that would make its transposed repetition

---

[7] Cf. the analysis of Symphony No. 85/i, Ch. 8 above.

unnecessary, or that the passage is in fact repeated and transposed somewhere in the recapitulation. Both are possible explanations.

In the exposition the restatement of the opening theme at the point of arrival of the dominant was less than solid or stable. Rather, Haydn made it through but two measures of the theme before he revealed that he was treating it as a transitory stage in the developmental progression of the motives derived from it. Generally speaking, when only the incipit of a theme is repeated at the beginning of the dominant confirmation sections and is treated in a more developmental context—as here—Haydn feels under no obligation to repeat this treatment in the recapitulation.[8]

Some further motivations seem to underlie the excision of mm. 52–70. The first part of this passage is rather innocuous—a sequence with chain suspensions in the top voices accompanied in the lower voices by running scales with an ambitus of an octave—hardly high-profile material. Perhaps Haydn calculated that a sufficient echo of this passage is preserved in the running scales of mm. 150 ff to free him from the obligation to restate it in the tonic. In the same vein, the arpeggiations and chords of mm. 58 ff are so much like mm. 81 ff (also in the dominant) that its transposed repetition is not really necessary, but is satisfactorily covered by mm. 167 ff—which is in the tonic.[9]

Thus, when Haydn begins in m. 157 with a transposition of m. 71, the net effect of the excisions to that point is that the equivalent of fifty-two measures from the exposition (mm. 19–70) have been answered by only nineteen measures in the recapitulation (mm. 138–56). We should expect that at some point between m. 157 and the end of the movement Haydn will add something to the recapitulation in order to right the balance between the sections.

Haydn—as is so often the case—devises a surprising response. He has already passed up the first and most common location for an interpolation (shortly after the beginning of the reprise). And he has let another prominent possible location (the rewritten transition) pass by without comment.

---

[8] For example, in all of the following works only the first measure or so of the principal theme is restated at the beginning of the dominant confirmation section (as is the case in Symphony No. 99): Keyboard Sonatas Hob. XVI: 24/i (?1773), mm. 15 ff; Hob. XVI: 38/i (–31 Jan. 1780 [?c. 1770–5]), mm. 13 ff; Hob. XVI: 43/i (–26 July 1783), mm. 21 ff; Hob. XVI: 49/i (1789–[1 June] 1790), mm. 24 ff; String Quartet Op. 55 No. 1/i (–?22 Sept. 1788), mm. 30 ff. In all of these cases—as in Symphony No. 99—the partial restatement of the theme does not return in the recapitulation. Contrast this treatment with that of Symphony No. 85/i, where the principal theme is stated at length at the beginning of the dominant confirmation section, and therefore returns in the recapitulation, transposed to the tonic.

[9] Perhaps a simpler explanation for the cuts of mm. 37–70 is simply that each excision draws with it the next. Once the (partial) restatement of the opening theme has been cut, the passage that follows has no foundation—and so forth, up to the cadence.

(continued)

Instead of using these obvious locations, he interpolates material in a spot that is guaranteed to attract our attention. After the appropriately transposed restatement (in mm. 157–62) of the first of the two statements of the theme that was presented in the dominant in the exposition (mm. 71–6), he suddenly breaks away from the model of the exposition. He returns to the second statement of the theme only in m. 179, having inserted no fewer than sixteen measures (mm. 163–78) between two measures that were adjacent in the exposition (see Ex. 10.5).

His first act in this interpolation (mm. 163 ff) is to restate the secondary theme in a quasi-inversion and in the tonic minor. Both the choice of mode and the use of the inversion are responses to earlier events. After all, the dominant minor was touched upon in two different places in the exposition (mm. 47 and 63–4), but both passages were excised from the recapitulation. If so, the statement in the tonic minor in the interpolation might be seen to be motivated by a loose interpretation of the sonata principle, as the suggestions of dominant minor from the exposition are now returned to the tonic. Moreover, both the quasi-inversion of the theme and the minor dominant can be traced back to the development section, for toward the end of the development section, when Haydn had reached the dominant for the first time, he landed on the minor dominant, and at that point stated the quasi-inversion in the dominant minor (see Ex. 10.6).

So too, the next two passages in the interpolation have obvious roots in prior passages. Measures 167–72 are none other than the tutti passage that prepared the final cadential flourish of the exposition—here transposed to the tonic. The following passage, mm. 173–9, is highly similar to the retransition to the reprise. Because of this extensive interpolation, Haydn balances the exposition and the recapitulation, a process that is completed by the short coda.[10]

Looking back over the movement, two essential conclusions should be drawn. The first is that the movement does not satisfactorily resolve the harmonic problems posed by the introduction. Yes, suggestions of the issues raised in the introduction are made again and again, but there never has been a satisfactory response to the problematic progressions. This has important implications for the remainder of the symphony. The second conclusion might be stated as a kind of paradox: Although

---

[10] It should be noted that there are no repeat signs for the second half of the movement. Up until the London symphonies Haydn invariably employed repeat signs for both the exposition and the development and recapitulation. But in the London symphonies, most of the first movements (that of No. 96 is an exception) have repeats indicated only for the exposition. For a thorough discussion of this issue, see Michael Broyles, 'Organic Form and the Binary Repeat', *Musical Quarterly*, 66 (1980), 339–60. Broyles not only presents some statistics documenting the change in use of repeat signs, but also relates their abandonment to a fundamental change in compositional style (ibid. 356–7).

Ex. 10.6

Haydn's late recapitulations seem completely free, it is because they have to be.

The second movement, by its very key—G major, the mediant major—marks a dramatic break with the norms of key-assignment in symphonies. In multimovement compositions dating from about 1730–90 composers followed several virtually inviolable guidelines for the choice of key of the movements. (1) The first and last movements were assigned the same key, though not necessarily the same mode.[11] (2) If there was to be a slow inner movement, the use of a key other than the overall tonic was possible, but composers restricted themselves to a limited range of key-choices—for a composition in major, I, i, IV, V, and vi. For a composition in minor, the choice was even more limited—usually III or I. (3) The menuet (if there was one) was invariably in the overall tonic, but the trio could be cast in a different key, in which case the composer made use of the same range of related keys used in the slow movement.[12]

The use of closely related keys for the slow movement and the trio of a multimovement cycle is a consequence of some of the most basic properties of the tonal system. The conventional key-choices for the inner

---

[11] A string quartet, possibly by Roman Hoffstetter (previously ascribed to Haydn—as 'Op. 3 No. 4'), is in two movements, the first in B flat, the second in E flat.

[12] In works dating from before *c.*1790 only isolated examples of the use of remote keys for inner movements can be found. Some are cited in Newman, *The Sonata in the Classic Era*, 137–8, 305, 373, 419, 574.

movement provided far more than tonal variety; they fostered an intricate network of relationships.

The basic tonal framework was provided by the common tonality of the outer movements. As a result, a middle movement in a different key can be understood to push away from the overall tonic, creating harmonic instability on the highest level of structure. This instability is resolved only by the return to the tonic in the final movement(s). By means of its departure from and return to the tonic, the middle movement imitates, on the largest scale, the fundamental pattern of tonal progressions.

In addition, conventional key-choices create powerful relationships between the collections of the movements. In a composition in a major key, the use of the subdominant, dominant, or relative minor for the slow movement or trio demands the change of but one element from the referential collection. Aside from the ease of transition this affords, the near-identity of the collections permits references to be made to a closely related key merely by citing the one pitch-class that differentiates the collections.

When closely related keys are used, harmonic cross-references fall out as byproducts of the system. Normally, the principal key of the inner movement will be the secondary key of the outer movements or vice versa.

In sum, the conventional key-plans of the late eighteenth-century multimovement cycle offered the composer a useful arsenal of compositional techniques that had the potential to permit the disparate movements to be organized into a tonally integrated whole. Even without special effort, the normative key-plan endowed a multimovement work with a simple standard of tonal coherence.

Until the 1790s deviations from these norms were quite rare. Rather, with extraordinary consistency, composers chose closely related keys for the slow movement and the trio.[13] Haydn was no exception. Throughout

---

[13] Quantz, referring to the middle movement of the concerto (and writing more than forty years before Symphony No. 99), has the following to say: 'If the Allegro is written in a major tonality, for example, in C major, the Adagio may be set, at one's discretion, in C minor, E minor, A minor, F major, G major, or G minor. If, however, the first Allegro is written in a minor key, for example, C minor, the Adagio may be set in E flat major, F minor, G minor, or A flat minor. These sequences of keys are the most natural ones. The ear will never be offended by them, and the relationships are acceptable for all keys, whatever their names. Anybody who wishes to surprise his listeners in a rude and disagreeable manner is free to choose other keys; but since they may be pleasing only to him, he should at least proceed with great circumspection.' *On Playing the Flute*, 313. Riepel was a good deal more adventuresome in his list of potential keys. For a brief discussion, see Ritzel, *Die Entwicklung*, 60–1. Nearly fifty years later, theorists could no longer prescribe as narrow a range of keys as that suggested by Quantz. 'In pieces of *three* and *more* movements, the first and last should be set in the same *key*, to preserve the impression of one and the same piece, but they may be different in *mode*, the same as in those of *two* movements. And the one or more movements between the first and last, may be set in any variety of related keys and modes; which a judicious fancy can suggest.' Augustus

TABLE 10.3. *Haydn's Remote-Key Multimovement Compositions*

Work	Keys of movements*			
String quartets				
Op. 74 No. 1	C	G	C/A	C
Op. 74 No. 2	F	B flat	F/D flat	F
Op. 74 No. 3	G m	E	G/G m	G m
Op. 76 No. 5	D	F sharp	D/D m	D
Op. 76 No. 6	E flat	B	E flat	E flat
Op. 77 No. 1	G	E flat	G/E flat	G
Op. 77 No. 2	F	F/D flat	D	F
Piano trios				
Hob. XV: 14	A flat	E	A flat	
Hob. XV: 19	G m–G	E flat	G m	
Hob. XV: 20	B flat	G	B flat	
Hob. XV: 22	E flat	G	E flat	
Hob. XV: 23	D m	B flat	D	
Hob. XV: 25	G	E	G	
Hob. XV: 27	C	A	C	
Hob. XV: 29	E flat	B	E flat	
Hob. XV: 30	E flat	C	E flat	
Symphonies				
No. 99	E flat	G	E flat/C	E flat
No. 103	E flat	C m–C	E flat	E flat
No. 104	D	G	D/B flat	D
Keyboard sonata				
Hob. XVI: 52	E flat	E	E flat	

*The keys of a menuet and trio are shown in the form C/A. A dash (as in G m–G) indicates a change of mode within a movement.

Kollmann, *An Essay on Practical Musical Composition* (London, 1799; repr. New York, 1973), 6. A few pages later, Kollmann, citing Haydn's late trios (Hob. XV: 27 and 29), gives an indication of just what kind of variety he is talking about, and in so doing, reveals what kinds of progressions he found problematic: 'I must mention four cases of abrupt changes of the key from one movement to another, which are found in *Haydn's* Sonatas Op. 75. The first is in Sonata I, where the first movement is in C major and the second in A major. This change is allowable, according to the rules of abrupt modulation by omission, in my Essay on Harmony, Chap. X, § 13; for C is the key, and the triad of A the leading chord to a related key; but A is retained, and made a substituted key. The second case is in the same Sonata, where the second movement ends in A major, and the third one begins in C major, which as it is too great a skip in harmony, ought not to be imitated by young composers. The third and fourth case is in Sonata III, where the first movement is in E flat major, the second in B (or C flat) major, and the third is in E flat major again. Both these changes of the key are very good, according to the rules mentioned just now.' Ibid. 10. It is interesting that Kollman could tolerate the move from C major to A major but not the reverse.

the bulk of his career he restricted his key-choice to the most closely related keys.

However, in the late 1780s, Haydn made a startling change in his compositional approach: in his late multimovement compositions, the use of remote keys for the slow movement or the trio became a common occurrence, not an exception (see Table 10.3).

Although composers may not have been consciously aware of all of the compositional properties of the conventional key-plan, those who challenged convention by using a remote key for the slow movement, or for the trio, must have been aware of the problems posed by such key-plans, for none of the relationships described above hold for remote keys: the collections involve multiple alterations, inhibiting common identity; the primary or secondary harmonic region of one movement does not coincide with that of another; the tonic of one movement does not function as one of the principal harmonic chords of another. It might seem as if the use of a remote key could be a willful, even perverse, flouting of convention, without compositional purpose.

Nothing could be further from the case in Haydn's late compositions. The use of a remote key for a middle movement in these works is not an arbitrary decision, made to defy convention, but—as we will see in detail—a precisely calculated compositional decision, rooted deep within the formal logic of the work.[14]

The exposition of the second movement is quite compact.[15] The principal theme is stated twice in the tonic region, the first statement (mm. 1–6) ending on the dominant, the second (mm. 7–12) on the tonic. After a quick transition (mm. 13–15), the new key is announced with an additional statement of the principal theme (mm. 16 ff). After a modest extension, a closing theme (mm. 27 ff) prepares the cadence that marks off the end of the exposition.[16]

The development section is—at first—unremarkable. But the recapitulation arrives just slightly too early, and it is prepared, not by a dominant chord, but by its V/vi (see Ex. 10.7).

When the second movement began, we had no real basis upon which we could construct a framework for its harmonic relationship with the first movement. Tonal theory regards E flat major and G major as remotely related keys, with strongly contrasting collections. In any event, within the first movement—with two exceptions—G major played

[14] I discuss the issue of Haydn's remote-key, multimovement cycles in my 'Remote Keys and Multi-movement Unity'. A bibliography of the relevant literature appears in n. 8.

[15] Bard, *Untersuchungen*, 203–14, suggests that, in addition to its sonata form characteristics, this movement has some suggestions of rondo, perhaps because of the restatements of the theme in the secondary key. To me, it seems unwise to extend the term 'rondo' to include movements of this sort.

[16] Marx suggests that the theme in mm. 27 ff is related to the principal line in the introduction to the first movement: 'Über thematische Beziehungen', 4 and 12.

Ex. 10.7

absolutely no role. Similarly, E flat major plays no role whatsoever in the exposition and development sections of the second movement. As a result, we have two incompatible and contrasting harmonic blocks, with no hints given as to how the harmonic tension created by their opposition might be resolved. Thus the use of the mediant major as the key of the second movement should be seen as an unresolved harmonic-formal problem, a powerful violation of intermovemental norms. We can be certain that, in contrast with movements in closely related keys, the collections will be incompatible, the tonic of one movement will not have diatonic function in the other, the primary key of one will not be the harmonic goal of the other, and so forth. Therefore, the further we proceed into the second movement without a resolution of this crisis, the more severe the crisis becomes.

This brings us back to Ex. 10.7 and the preparation for the reprise. With this harmonic progression Haydn makes some obvious references back to the first movement. The progression (V/vi–I) is (transposed) virtually the same one (minus the intervening dominant chord in the wind-band) that bound the introduction to the Vivace assai in the first movement.

Furthermore, the neighbor-figure in the uppermost voices in mm. 51–3 (A♯–B) is the enharmonic equivalent of the profoundly significant, and inadequately resolved, neighbor-figure from the introduction to the first movement (mm. 9–11, B♭–C♭ (=B)). The harmonies that are so roughly juxtaposed here in mm. 53–4 (B major and G major) were central to the disruptive harmonic progression that followed the frozen neighbor in the introduction.

And most obvious, of course, the key of the movement itself is a forceful expansion of the harmonic problem of the introduction. In particular, the choice of G major reminds us of the never-resolved half-cadence on G, one measure before the end of the introduction.

Reference does not imply resolution. Haydn has referred to the introduction and its central harmonic problem, reminded us of it, but he has scarcely resolved it. By utilizing the same surprising harmonic progression and by recycling the same chords in a new context, he has revived the problem in the second movement, but nothing is settled. Up to the end of the development section, the second movement—by virtue of its remote key—remains a disturbing, incompatible, disruptive harmonic presence.

The recapitulation does nothing to lessen that harmonic tension.[17] Rather, it responds to the premises of the exposition, apparently oblivious of the harmonic challenge the Adagio poses to the first movement. The

---

[17] But Haydn has a lovely touch in m. 57. He has varied the second oboe's part (cf. m. 4), producing a B–B♭ succession not present in the exposition.

two statements of the principal theme in the tonic (mm. 1–6 and 7–12) and the third statement in the dominant (mm. 16 ff) are reduced here to two statements (mm. 54–9 and 60 ff), with the latter a conflation of the second and third thematic statements from the exposition (mm. 60 ff are a transposition to the tonic of mm. 16 ff, but orchestrated for strings alone—like mm. 7–12). In m. 71, the closing theme returns, restated in the tonic as per the sonata principle.

However, the appropriately conclusive cadence does not occur any-where near m. 78. Instead, Haydn appends a lengthy coda—the move-ment does not end for twenty more measures, a span of music longer than the development section. Perhaps the coda functions as a response to the unsatisfactory harmonic progression at the end of the development section and the foreshortened development section, as its effect is to prolong the tonic and strengthen it. However, there is a slight emphasis on G minor, which is not otherwise explained (but see below).

In spite of several references to events of the first movement (and in particular the introduction), the second movement remains a difficult, unresolved, unanswered, harmonic challenge. If it is to be a coherent part of the symphony as a whole, further responses are necessary.

At one time the menuet was a pleasant, unpretentious movement—so much so that it was thought by some to be inappropriate for inclusion in a serious symphony. The third movement of Symphony No. 99 is hardly a pleasant respite between weightier events. Rather, it makes a central contribution to the resolution of the harmonic–formal crisis posed by the first two movements.[18]

At first, the Menuet seems to ignore the second movement and its harmonic challenge. The A section defines the tonic (mm. 1–8), moves to the dominant (mm. 9–18), and then stands on the newly tonicized dominant for the concluding nine measures of the section (mm. 18–26). With the exception of a hint of C minor in mm. 9–10, nothing in the A section would remind us that the second movement had been cast in a remote key, nor would recall the introduction and its progressions.

In the B section, Haydn returns to touch upon some of the most prominent harmonic issues of the introduction to the first movement. He begins with an arpeggiation of the dominant chord, extending it first to a seventh chord, and then to a minor ninth—C♭, a clear reminder of the introduction with its disruptive C♭. The C♭ resolves down to B♭ in a far more explicit and far less problematic manner than in the introduction (in m. 30 and again in m. 32).

---

[18] For an extended analysis of this Menuet, with particular attention to the challenges its structure poses to normal expectations (and the relationship of that to wit and humor), see Wheelock, 'Wit, Humor', 200–7.

Even more significant, though, are the harmonic emphases at the end of the B section. Here, Haydn tonicizes G minor (mm. 36–42)—perhaps a reference to the second movement, and in particular its coda.

This reference is made even more explicit by the way in which Haydn closes the B section and begins the reprise. In mm. 42–3 he arpeggiates through the G minor triad, which is followed, not by the dominant chord, but rather, in mm. 44–5, by an arpeggiation of the theme in E flat, marking the beginning of the reprise (see Ex. 10.8).

Haydn has slipped into the reprise and E flat major directly from G minor. He has carefully, and purposely, omitted the dominant, replacing it with a chord whose function can be properly understood only in the context of the multimovement plan. In so doing, he has touched upon the most prominent issues of the composition—the grand tonal plan, with its opposition of E flat and G.

In Haydn's works of the 1790s, as has already been indicated, the trio in the menuet was, like the slow movement, sometimes assigned a remote key. In the present instance the choice of key is C major. This compositional decision is the capstone of the whole architectonic structure of this multimovement work.

The Trio is introduced by a transition of octave Gs in the oboes. This common tone acts as a pivot to C major and a blissfully ingenuous rounded binary follows. The purposeful simplicity of the Trio highlights the harmonic crisis. How can this Trio, so unapologetically in C major, possibly relate to the overall tonic, E flat?

The transitional octave Gs (mm. 69–70) recall the second movement and its tonicization of G, and so too, the function of G as the dominant of C is a direct reference to the introduction. Still further, the choice of C major, and not C minor, reminds us of the turn to C major at the beginning of the development section in the first movement. Haydn has gone out of his way to recall virtually all of the problematic features of the first two movements, but he has not yet placed them into a coherent tonal framework to relate them to E flat, the overall tonic.

The sense of harmonic crisis reaches its zenith at the end of the second section of the Trio. After moving to G at the double bar, Haydn dutifully returns to the local tonic and at m. 100 comes to a perfect authentic cadence in C major. It would seem as if the Trio has concluded—in a remote key—without resolving the large-scale harmonic and formal issues.

Instead of concluding the Trio at this point, Haydn adds an extraordinary lead-back to the Menuet. In this added section, the various pieces of the multimovement puzzle begin to fall into place.

The passage begins with dominant-substitutes applied to and proceeding to a G major triad. This immediately recalls the tonality of the second movement—and, of course, the extended emphasis on G in the

Ex. 10.8

introduction of the first movement. When, in the measures that follow, G is transformed back into the dominant of C, the connections between the second movement and this movement are made even more explicit (see Ex. 10.9).

Having transformed G into the dominant of C, Haydn prolongs this harmony, arpeggiating upwards through the elements of the chord and adding, as he goes, the minor ninth to the sonority. In m. 116 the bass drops out, leaving only the fifth, seventh, and ninth of the dominant ninth chord: D, F, A♭.

As every undergraduate harmony student knows, this trichord is part of both the dominant ninth in C and vii in E flat. Haydn exploits these common tones to make a sudden switch back to E flat, and the reprise of the Menuet.

We should recognize this harmonic progression: it is a version of the very same progression that concluded the introduction of the first movement, with its move from the dominant of C directly to the dominant of E flat. In returning to that idea, Haydn has demonstrated how the entire composition up to this point is, in many important respects, a derivation of, a commentary on, and an expansion of the extraordinary harmonic progression of the introduction to the first movement.[19]

Taken as a whole, the Menuet and Trio has brought into the confines of a single movement explicit references to all of the problematic harmonic, tonal, formal, and voice-leading problems raised by the previous movements. But it has done much more than simply recall these events. It has responded to them and resolved them. By repeating problematic ideas raised by other movements in the context of a single movement in E flat, Haydn has made the Menuet and Trio function as the structural and architectonic climax of the work.

Haydn is not done. Specific and significant details of the finale (a movement with a mixture of rondo and sonata form characteristics) play an important role in the response to the problematic events of the first three movements.

The connections between the movements are given some support by motivic relationships. Most notably, an idea from the first couplet (violin 1, mm. 27–9) is rather similar to the quasi-inversion of the secondary theme from the first movement that appeared in the interpolation in the recapitulation (mm. 126 ff.)

---

[19] Similar lead-backs (with important formal implications) occur in Symphony No. 104 (1795) and the String Quartet Op. 74 No. 2 (1793). For a brief discussion of the latter work, see Landon, *Chronicle and Works*, iii. 479.

Ex. 10.9

Far more significant, and far more wide-ranging in their impact, are the harmonic details. Some important features of the finale's structure are determined by, and related to, the grand tonal plan which was sparked by the extraordinary progressions in the introduction to the first movement.[20]

In the second couplet (mm. 120 ff)—the development section—after touching in passing on several keys, Haydn settles down on two key-areas that have played central roles in the large-scale harmonic structure of this work, giving them extended emphasis: first C minor, prolonging this in mm. 137–42, and then G minor, giving this key extensive attention, including a powerful cadence in m. 160. Immediately after this strong cadence, the cellos and basses drop out, and after moving quickly through a sequence of descending fifths, Haydn arrives on the dominant of E flat (see Ex. 10.10).

Once again, an essential point of the formal structure has been fashioned to elaborate upon the formative harmonic progressions of the preceding movements. By moving from G at the cadence in m. 160 more or less directly to the dominant of E flat, Haydn has recalled not only the last two measures of the introduction of the first movement, but the preparation for return to the Menuet from the Trio.

After dwelling on the dominant, marking the end of the development section, Haydn has prepared the return of tonic and the restatement of the refrain theme. In mm. 169 ff, although the tonic does return, and although Haydn does state part of the refrain theme, it is never presented in its completed form.

[20] An interesting continuity draft has survived for the finale of this symphony. It has been given extensive attention: see Nowak, 'Die Skizzen' (which includes a facsimile), and Schafer, ' "A Wisely Ordered *Phantasie*" ', 122–34, 220–38. Schafer takes issue with Nowak's hypothesis that the sketches preserve a rejected early draft of the finale. She suggests that there were three principal stages (possibly with variants and substages) in Haydn's compositional process and that these can be documented by the surviving sketch material: *phantasieren* (at the keyboard, with the results only indirectly visible in sketches), *componieren* (working-out of a continuity draft, mostly for a single line); *setzen* (setting the completed continuity draft into full score). The sketch for the finale of Symphony No. 99 conforms to the *componieren* stage. Some of Schafer's observations and conclusions about Haydn's process of composition support the theories advanced in this book, in particular her observation that in the sketches for the slow movement of the String Quartet Op. 20 No. 3, most of the recapitulation is absent—with the exception of 'the passage connecting the second theme and the closing section, a passage that is rather different from the corresponding one in the exposition', and that this minimal material is found on the same sketch page as the exposition (ibid. 152). This would support the theory that Haydn used the exposition as he planned out the recapitulation, responding to the premises of the exposition by working out the details of the passages that he felt needed to be altered—leaving the rest unaltered. Also, Schafer calls attention to Haydn's tendency to organize sketches with important events (*hervorstechende Stellen*) entered in strategic locations on the page. If this is correct, then perhaps the placement of the crucial reharmonization of the theme of the finale of Symphony No. 99 is no accident. This passage is placed in the upper left-hand corner of its page. For a brief discussion of these sketches and the musical 'idea', see Jürgen Neubacher, ' "Idee" und "Ausführung". Zum Kompositionsprozeß bei Joseph Haydn', *Archiv für Musikwissenschaft*, 41 (1984), 198–9.

Ex. 10.10

What follows is one of Haydn's boldest touches. After a thunderous cadence in E flat, the refrain theme starts up again, but everything about it is wrong (see Ex. 10.11).

Instead of presenting it in its original harmonization, Haydn has taken the principal theme and recast it as if it were in C minor. Under the sixteenth-note run from D to Ab, instead of the dominant seventh chord of E flat, he has placed the elements of the diminished seventh chord on Bᵇ, suggesting C minor.

Immediately afterward, he moves directly back to the dominant of E flat, exaggerating the chord with a dramatic slowing of the tempo. Only then does he return to recapitulate the principal ideas of the movement.

At yet another critical point in the form, Haydn has turned back to the extraordinary harmonic progression of the introduction. As elsewhere in this movement, he has done more than simply remind us of that problematic progression. Rather, he has finally, and totally, brought all of the formerly disruptive elements into the context of E flat major.

In summary, we can see that many of the most significant details of this symphony are the result, not of a series of unrelated compositional decisions, but of the harmonic structure of the opening measures of the composition: the introduction is related in the most thoroughgoing manner, not just to the first movement, but to all the movements; the four movements are related to one another, not through motivic identity, but through their common exploration of the compositional possibilities of a problematic harmonic progression; the keys chosen for the individual movements are dictated not by custom, but determined by the context; the forms of the individual movements can be properly understood only in the context of the multimovement totality; the recapitulations are totally rewritten from the necessity of responding to the premises of the remainder of the movement; the harmonic emphases within the development sections are chosen to reflect upon central formal issues; codas are added, not as arbitrary addenda, but to address issues not covered in the main body of the movement, or to create problems that must be resolved elsewhere.

Although Symphony No. 99 is more or less unique among the symphonies in its use of a remote-key slow movement (and trio), that should not be taken to mean that its treatment of form is completely unique. Rather, as we have seen, increasingly in Haydn's late symphonies—and in each in its own way—the opening premises of the composition have consequences for all of the movements.

11

Analytical and Historical Contexts

EACH of the preceding nine chapters has consisted of an analysis of a single symphony by Joseph Haydn. Perhaps each of these analyses is illuminating in its own right, even if taken in isolation. However, in presenting analyses of all of the movements (and the multimovemental organization) of nine chronologically ordered symphonies by a single composer, the implicit assumption has been that there is something essential to be gained by studying these compositions in their entirety, as a group, and in chronological order.

The inclusion of a number of works for discussion in this book was motivated by far more than the desire to document the many different formal types and procedures found in Haydn's symphonies. And the choice of works spanning Haydn's career was not merely a pretext to demonstrate the obvious point that enormous changes in style took place in Haydn's symphonies between the late 1750s and early 1790s. Rather, many of the specific observations made in the course of this book were possible only because the analyses were presented in a context wider than that of the individual work (and of the individual movement). It is therefore appropriate at this point to discuss some of the issues this raises.

Analysis and the Composer's Viewpoint

My analyses of Haydn's treatment of form within and between movements are founded on the notion that five basic principles, outlined in Chapter 1, constituted fundamental components of his formal thought. In light of these principles, I have attempted to explain specific details of individual compositions by reconstructing what may have been the composer's rationale for some of his compositional decisions. (It might therefore be termed a 'compositional theory'.) This suggests that the principles would have been invoked by Haydn as the justification for specific decisions that he made during the process of composition. It may not have been the case that Haydn invoked them consciously or that he formulated them with precisely the words that I have used. But, from an examination of his instrumental works, I have concluded that something very much like these five principles must have guided Haydn's hand as he composed.

Whether or not my reconstruction of Haydn's formal thought is accepted or amended (in whole or in part) by others, some readers might well ask whether there is justification for attempting to reconstruct a composer's thought in the first place. Even beyond the highly speculative (some might say presumptuous) nature of the enterprise, could it not be argued that attempting to look at a composition from the composer's viewpoint merely reconstructs the details of the composer's procedures, and that the knowledge of such procedures has no bearing for today's listener, performer, analyst, or composer?

As the preceding chapters make clear, it is my firm belief that the reconstruction of the composer's compositional thought provides us with a particularly useful guide for analysis. Not only does an analytical method aid us to hear things that would otherwise be missed, but it also helps to attenuate the distortions of historical distance and to place what we hear into a meaningful context. Though I do not wish to suggest that reconstructing the composer's thought is the only valid approach to analysis—or that there is a single 'thought' that can be retrieved—I do feel that analytical methods that are rooted in the composer's thoughts afford us some of the best opportunities for a rich and meaningful hearing of the composition.[1]

Reconstructing a composer's thought is a means of bringing the listener into the process of composition. If successful, it illuminates the implications of the material so thoroughly that the listener can begin to anticipate what can or cannot follow from the composer's premises. If we learn to hear the potential of the evolving argument in the way that the composer planned it, then we will understand the consequences that should result, and will anticipate what has to come, what cannot come, what must receive additional attention, what can be regarded as satisfactorily addressed, and so forth. We then approach the work not as passive listeners but as active (re)constructors of the musical logic. When we make Haydn's logic our own, when we begin to be able to predict what must happen (or must not happen) in response to the material as it unfolds, then we are understanding Haydn's music on its own terms. Ultimately, then, the compositional theory presented here is, at its root, designed as a program for informed listening.

But, as the previous analyses have implied, a composer's 'logic' is not independent of the historical background in which the composition was written. Context is essential. Musical 'logic'—to explain one facet of the

---

[1] In this book, I have concentrated entirely upon reconstructing Haydn's formal thought. Of course, Haydn's compositional thought has more dimensions than just the formal, and my attention to that dimension must not be taken to imply a rejection of the importance of the others.

purposely ambiguous subtitle of this book—is not a universal truth, but is dependent on style and historical context.

Other Genres, Other Composers

Can the proposed reconstruction of Haydn's formal thought have applicability beyond the symphonies of Haydn? Would it be useful for other composers of the late eighteenth century? Were Haydn's five compositional principles a universal feature of late eighteenth-century formal thought? Or, even more modestly, can they be applied to Haydn's other genres, his other types of instrumental compositions?

To take the latter issue first, it seems that the five principles are general aesthetic notions, the specific implementation or interpretation of which depended on a variety of other factors, including genre. This means that different genres have slightly different normative expectations, which, in turn, necessarily affect the way the listener is expected to respond.

For instance, we saw that there were certain normative lengths for the development section in a symphonic movement. When, as in Symphony No. 49/i, the development section was shorter than the expected length, this occasioned challenges to the listener's expectations, with significant formal consequences. However, the norms were different in other genres, and thus the expectations appropriate for symphonies were somewhat different from those for sonatas.

The range of acceptable sizes of the development section is but one of many subtle differences between the symphonic and sonata genres. There are other differences as well, ranging from the amount of repetition that was considered acceptable (non-redundant) to the length of phrases, and so forth. There were also distinctions between types of movements—between quick first movements, slow internal movements, menuets, and finales.

In view of this, we must conclude that we cannot examine every type of composition and every type of movement with precisely the same standards. This implies that our analytical observations will be more reliable the more carefully they are grounded in the expectations and norms of a specific movement type, in a specific genre.

What about the other composers of Haydn's time? Are the principles that have been suggested for Haydn's symphonies valid for their works?

The more I look, the more I am convinced that some version of these principles does indeed seem to be an essential component of many composers' approach to form in the late eighteenth century, at least within the Viennese and south German orbit. The specific interpretation of the principles may differ from Haydn's, but the principles themselves appear to have been common property of late eighteenth-century musical thought and aesthetics.

Mozart seems to have had slightly different interpretations of the unity, redundancy, and variation principles. He seems to have been willing to permit the introduction of new material later in the movement, appears to have tolerated more literal repetitions than Haydn, and apparently felt somewhat less compelled to vary his repetitions. For example, in the first movement of the Keyboard Sonata K. 330, he continues to introduce new thematic ideas throughout the development section. This would clearly have been in opposition to Haydn's interpretation of the unity principle, in which the introduction of new material was considered inappropriate shortly after the internal double bar.

These are, however, essentially minor differences in style, emphasis, and interpretation. Generally speaking, Haydn's principles seem to be valid for Mozart's treatment of form. If we look at Mozart's compositions the way we have looked at Haydn's, we can often understand the rationale for specific compositional choices.

In the Symphony in D Major K. 504 ('Prague'), Mozart transposes much of the dominant key-region of the exposition back to the tonic in the recapitulation—but not all. He excises some of the material for a reason that is familiar from our experience with Haydn's 'monothematic' sonata forms: because the opening theme of the Allegro (mm. 37 ff) returns transposed up a fifth at the beginning of the dominant section (mm. 71 ff), it is excised from the recapitulation—the redundancy principle.

However, there is a critical difference between the two statements of the theme in the exposition: in the dominant-key statement, the second violin plays an E♯, making the supporting sonority in m. 72 into an augmented triad (A, C♯, E♯), instead of a simple triad as in the corresponding place in m. 38. Although Mozart omits the retransposition of mm. 71 ff back to the tonic because of the redundancy principle, he clearly felt that the augmented triad sonority was an important idea that—according to the corollary of the unity principle—ought to return at some point. He does this by altering the opening theme at the beginning of the recapitulation—its accompaniment includes the augmented triad.

This is not to claim that Haydn influenced Mozart here. Rather, it seems that Mozart responded as Haydn would have done in similar circumstances: because they shared an approximately common set of compositional principles.

At the same time, one of the most obvious differences in the formal structure of their compositions might well be explained by their common use of these basic principles of form. Just as much as Haydn's recapitulations (particularly those dating from after 1780 or so) are often thorough rewritings of the exposition, Mozart's recapitulations tend to be appropriately modified repetitions of the expositions.

In the first movement of Mozart's Symphony in E flat K. 543, the recapitulation follows very closely the model of the exposition, rewriting the transition to stay in the tonic, transposing the dominant region to the tonic, and interpolating a short passage before the final cadence to strengthen the close. It would be hard to imagine Haydn around 1790 writing a sonata form first movement with this degree of correspondence between the exposition and recapitulation.

But these differences might best be traced to different premises, not to entirely different principles of form. Unlike Haydn in his late period, Mozart introduces a constant stream of different musical ideas throughout the exposition. As none of the themes in the tonic region recurs in the dominant region, the sonata and unity principles dictate the reappearance of all of this material in the recapitulation. By the same token, the lack of repetition in the exposition means that there will be no necessity for the invocation of either the redundancy or variation principle in the recapitulation. Different premises filtered through the same compositional principles yield different results.

The present view of Haydn's formal thought also seems to have at least some applicability to the music of Beethoven. Beethoven's early published compositions, from the period of his arrival in Vienna to study with Haydn and shortly thereafter, seem to be composed in a manner like that of Haydn's music of the same time or earlier. Notwithstanding Beethoven's claim that he learned nothing from Haydn, some of these works seem closely related to his teacher's approach to form both within the movements and between them.

Because Beethoven did not complete his first symphony until well after he finished studying with Haydn, I will take as my example one of Beethoven's early piano sonatas—Op. 2 No. 3 in C major. Given the 'symphonic' character of this sonata (four movements of remarkably broad scope), and Beethoven's tendency to diminish the differences between symphonic and sonata genres, the work serves well as a point of comparison.

Beethoven's Op. 2 No. 3 was not only dedicated to Haydn, it also works out many of Haydn's favorite compositional problems. In the first movement, the grand arpeggios at mm. 13 ff return in slightly varied form in the dominant section (mm. 61 ff). Ergo, in the recapitulation, this material is excised as per the redundancy principle. After the development section is already under way, Beethoven introduces some new material (mm. 97 ff). We might simply dismiss this as typical passage-work designed to show off the talents of the aspiring virtuoso. However, nothing quite like this has occurred in the exposition, and the introduction of the material therefore seems to be a destabilizing event that will need to be addressed (corollary of the normative principle). The recapitulation intensifies our puzzlement, for it makes no reference to the passage-work introduced in mm. 97 ff. Moments away from what we might have expected to be the end of the recapitulation, Beethoven veers off into a sudden deceptive cadence, launching into a surprising turn to the flat side (mm. 218 ff). Here too he makes use of a similar (though slower) passage, comprised of wide-ranging arpeggios, a clear reference and response to the unexplained passage in the development section. The extended coda may not really be justifiable (except as a chance to show off virtuosity) unless we connect it with this.

Furthermore, as Haydn was wont to do in the 1790s, Beethoven casts the second movement in a remote key: the mediant major. Like Haydn, he treats this as a violation of norms that must be resolved, and in so doing relates the movements to one another. By moving to the parallel minor (E minor) for the B section, Beethoven diminishes the sharp differences in collections between C major and E major. The shift to E minor permits him to establish G major as its secondary key—as in the first movement. Finally, he has even less subtle means of drawing the first two movements together. In m. 52, the variant of the A section comes to a close on the dominant (= m. 10). Presumably this could lead to a repetition of the B section, as at mm. 11 ff. Instead, Beethoven makes a surprising deceptive cadence, which initiates a dramatic restatement of the beginning of the A theme in C major. A chip off the old block indeed.

A caution is in order. With each passing year, Beethoven's approach to form changed more and more from that of his early music.[2] Therefore, I am far less confident that Haydn's five principles of form offer an effective means of explaining Beethoven's later music. Certainly these principles of form seem, if not irrelevant, then surely far less central, with respect to the late string quartets and piano sonatas.

What of Haydn's many other contemporaries, particularly those whose professional activities were concentrated in Austria or southern Germany—Vanhal, Ordonez, Gassmann, von Dittersdorf, Pleyel, Michael Haydn, and so on? Are the five principles of form valid for their music as well? From my admittedly limited survey, the answer frequently appears to be yes, again with the caution that each composer seems to have slightly different interpretations of the principles, with different thresholds for what is considered redundancy, what needs variation, what must be transposed, and so forth.

But frequently, in the symphonies and other works of his contemporaries, events occur that—when viewed from the perspective of Haydn's norms and Haydn's procedures—seem inscrutable, or unmotivated, or unnecessary. This is undoubtedly a reflection of the fact that slightly different expectations and norms are appropriate for other composers.

[2] The evolution of Beethoven's 'middle' and 'late' periods has been the subject of much scholarly attention. For a recent discussion, see Broyles, *The Emergence and Evolution*.

Therefore, proper scholarly caution should take over at this point, as anecdotal evidence is merely that. Although I can report that the five principles appear to have some degree of applicability for music in the late eighteenth century, so many specific deviations occur that no conclusions should be drawn without extensive further study.

The Analysis of Complete Works

It is a fair generalization to state that, over most of the past century, the overwhelming tendency in the analytical literature relating to late eighteenth-century music has been to analyze separate, individual movements, and not all of the movements of a multimovement work considered as a whole. There have been individual exceptions to this, but the overall tendency has been clear.

We might well ask—with some surprise—why this is the case. There is a remarkable disparity between the activities of composers on the one hand and the interests of theorists on the other. Virtually all of the symphonies, string quartets, string trios, keyboard sonatas, keyboard trios, and so forth written in this period were multimovement compositions that were conceived as a unit, not assembled from unrelated parts. It is stunning to compare the extraordinarily consistent behavior of composers with the virtual lack of meaningful interest in that behavior in the theoretical and analytical literature. Why have so many writers been content to analyze individual movements of works without making reference to the other movements?

Clearly, this must stem from the belief that nothing of significance is lost by examining movements individually, or that nothing particularly useful is to be gained by examining them together. I believe that there are at least three reasons why this has been the case: the interests of eighteenth-century musical theory, the character of nineteenth-century cyclical organization, and the predominant theory of tonal music in the twentieth century.

Although there have been some who have questioned the value of eighteenth-century theoretical treatises as tools for the analysis of music from the period, there have been many others, particularly in recent years, who have argued eloquently and persuasively that it is a serious mistake to underestimate the usefulness of eighteenth-century theories (those of Koch in particular) as analytical tools. In many ways the interests of the eighteenth-century writers have served as a kind of agenda for modern writers. Given that issues of multimovement organization are scarcely treated by the contemporaneous theorists with the thoroughness with which they discussed phrase, cadence, period, section, and movement, it should not surprise us that their approach is reflected in modern scholarship. It would have been quite a different story if eighteenth-century theory had devoted much attention to the topic of multimovement organization. This might beg the question as to why it did not do so, but for our purposes, it is sufficient to note the historical fact that discussions of these issues play a relatively minor role in the late eighteenth-century theoretical literature.[3]

The effect of nineteenth-century multimovemental organization on our perception of similar phenomena in the eighteenth century has been equally influential. No one would deny that cyclical organization is an important, if irregular, component of nineteenth-century compositional theory, practice, and aesthetics. But the very obviousness of the cyclical relationships in works by Beethoven and later composers has had the effect of blinding us to relationships that existed in works composed before that point. Late eighteenth-century music—with isolated and limited exceptions—lacks the kind of explicit thematic connections or transformations that characterize relationships between movements in some nineteenth-century multimovement cycles. Therefore it has been easy to draw the conclusion that it has no meaningful intermovemental relationships, or that, if such connections do exist, they are rudimentary, incipient, or immature.[4]

Finally, this century's most influential theories of tonal music—those of Heinrich Schenker—have not been conducive to debate over intermovemental relationships in the music of the eighteenth century. For one thing, Schenker scarcely addressed this problem at all, a fact amply reflected in his graphic analyses. Given the extraordinary influence his theories have had on modern theoretical thought, it is scarcely surprising that his approach has done much to deter further consideration of this issue.

Thus eighteenth- and twentieth-century theories have combined to discourage consideration of the topic of intermovemental relationships in eighteenth-century music. At the same time, our knowledge of cyclic features in nineteenth-century music has served to lead us on a false path, making it difficult for us to see the relationships that do exist in music composed before that time.

To be sure, for quite some time, many authors have asserted that there are numerous instances of intermovemental relationships in Haydn's music—primarily motivic or thematic. Some of the relationships these authors have identified are persuasive, but many others seem rather forced. By comparison with the explicit thematic interrelationships that occur in some nineteenth-century works, the connections claimed for

---

[3] For an excellent survey of 18th-cent. musical theory, see Joel Lester, *Compositional Theory in the Eighteenth Century* (Cambridge, Mass., 1992).

[4] And this is only a small part of the way in which 19th-cent. notions about music led to the decline of appreciation and understanding of Haydn's music. For a survey of this topic, see Ludwig Finscher, 'Joseph Haydn—Ein unbekannter Komponist?', *Neue Zeitschrift für Musik*, 143/10 (1982), 12–18.

Haydn's works are often convincing only to those who believe in rarefied, subcutaneous, thematic relationships.

However, a new picture should be emerging of intermovemental relationships in Haydn's works—one in which they are not primarily dependent on motivic or thematic relationships. In two articles, published in 1988 and 1990, I suggested some specific (and largely non-thematic) ways in which Haydn's works can be understood as integrated, multimovemental cycles, supporting my argument with analyses of a number of works (including Symphony No. 99).[5] These studies have been followed (and dwarfed) by James Webster's recent exhaustive examination of the problem (1991).[6] In this important study, Webster has presented a comprehensive discussion of the problem of cyclic integration and through-composition in Haydn's works, and supported his argument with numerous analyses. On the basis of Webster's achievement, it seems clear that the argument should not be whether cyclic integration exists in Haydn's works, but which works have this feature. In that spirit, I hope that the analyses in this book will contribute to the recognition that there are significant intermovemental relationships in many of Haydn's symphonies, relationships that are rarely based upon explicit thematic recurrence. Clearly, it would be an error of the first magnitude to assume that any movement by Haydn, composed at any period in his career, is completely separate and unrelated to the other movements of the cycle in which it is found. This is not to say that significant intermovemental relationships are to be found in every one of his instrumental compositions, or that all the movements will necessarily be related, but I am convinced that the phenomenon is so widespread that one is obliged to consider the possibility in every composition one examines. At the same time, we must not overstate the case and see connections in every composition. We must confront the reality that although connections may be obvious in some works, they are either totally absent or completely obscured in others. Why that is so, why some works have strong intermovemental relationships, and others none, is a topic that needs further study.

Historical Understanding and Analysis

For some, the assertion that analysis ought to be dependent on a knowledge of historical context might seem self-evident, scarcely worth mentioning, let alone questioning. Even though I believe this position to be persuasive, there are certain aspects of the problem that may not be so immediately obvious, and thus warrant some discussion. As important

---

[5] 'Haydn's Altered Reprise' and 'Remote Keys and Multi-Movement Unity'.
[6] *Haydn's 'Farewell'*.

aspects of the analytical approach employed in the analyses in this book were determined by the answer to this question, it is fitting that the book should close with a consideration of this topic.[7]

To put what might otherwise be a somewhat abstract argument on to some concrete foundations, let me take a specific example from the analysis presented in Chapter 10. In the discussion of Symphony No. 99, I pointed out that the second movement was cast in a remote key. Central to my argument for understanding the intermovemental structure of that symphony was the assertion that the assignment of a remote key to the slow movement is a significant contravention of intermovemental norms, and as such creates a formal crisis that cannot be resolved without further information.

If our goal is the reconstruction of the composer's thought, there should be nothing particularly objectionable or problematic about these assertions. For Haydn, and surely for his contemporaries, the choice of a remote key for a middle movement must have been a striking event, one that could not possibly be ignored, and one that would eventually have to be reconciled with the home key. We cannot know whether events were contraventions of norms unless we know what the norms were.

But what possible relevance could this have for a modern listener? When we get down to the nitty-gritty of actually listening to a composition, do not historical considerations become irrelevant? Our understanding of music has been irrevocably altered by the music that has followed Haydn. Having heard Beethoven, Chopin, Wagner, Stravinsky, Schoenberg, Babbitt, Boulez, is it not impossible for us to be genuinely shocked or surprised or nonplussed by the contravention of norms in the music of Haydn? And if we cannot be truly surprised by contraventions of norms that are no longer norms, then would it not be artificial to attempt to approach a work with the presumption that we need to resolve something that we cannot really hear as a problem?

Again, to put this argument on to concrete foundations, let us compare the key-plan of Haydn's Symphony No. 99 with that of Schoenberg's early String Quartet in D (1897). The four movements of

---

[7] Perhaps the starkest illustration of the gulf between the advocates of historically informed analysis and those who believe in the benefits of analysis based on pure theory can be seen in the bitter exchange between Allen Forte and Richard Taruskin in *Music Analysis*, 5 (1986), 313–37. This was prompted by Forte's remarks about Taruskin in 'Pitch-Class Set Analysis Today', *Music Analysis*, 4 (1985), 36. It should be clear from the preceding ten chapters that I find Taruskin's arguments persuasive. My analytical approach is very much in line with Taruskin's dictum: 'unless a measure of understanding is reached as to what the composer thought he was about, analysis cannot be said to have taken place at all' (*Music Analysis*, 5 (1986), 318). For an interesting discussion of the pitfalls in the 'historicist' and 'presentist' positions, see Thomas Christensen, 'Music Theory and its Histories', in Christopher Hatch and David W. Bernstein (eds.), *Music Theory and the Exploration of the Past* (Chicago and London, 1993), 9–39.

Schoenberg's quartet have the following key-centers: D, F sharp, B flat, D—the division of the octave into a cycle of interval-class 4. Compared with Schoenberg's key-plan, Haydn's seems positively tame. How is it therefore possible for a listener in the late twentieth century (nearly a century after Schoenberg's quartet, no less) to make the assertion that the second movement of Haydn's Symphony No. 99, by its contravention of the norms of key-choices, creates a profound instability that must be resolved by subsequent events in the symphony?

Moreover, even if we accept the notion that the remote key of the Adagio of Symphony No. 99 could be surprising or shocking for a listener today, that could be the case only the first time the work was heard—and then only if the listener was aware that no symphony of Haydn's prior to this work made use of a similar remote-key relationship. On the second and all subsequent hearings there would be no possibility of being surprised by Haydn's key-choice—except through entirely artificial means (i.e. pretending to forget).

The issue of 'rehearing' does not shake my belief in the validity of historically based analysis—quite the contrary. I believe the justification for historical consciousness in analysis can best be illustrated by drawing an analogy with our response to other, less subtle, musical surprises or contraventions of norms: the *Paukenschlag* in the second movement of Haydn's Symphony No. 94, the departure of the musicians in the last movement of 'Farewell' Symphony, or the breathtakingly long GP (mm. 167–72) in the middle of the recapitulation in the finale of Symphony No. 90. However shocking any of these events may have been on first hearing (and—in the case of the 'Farewell'—first seeing), they cannot possibly surprise us again. Does this mean they have exhausted their usefulness within these works of art?

It could, if the surprises were not essential premises of the structure of the works in question. The point of interest is not the surprise itself, but how Haydn treats the surprise as a compositional premise. This is one of the reasons why these works survive repeated listening. What is interesting is how Haydn works out the implications of that surprise, what response he makes to that surprise, what other features of the work contribute to the formation or resolution of that surprise. Clearly, we can still understand the responses, long after the literal effect of surprise is but a distant memory.

In today's context we can scarcely be shocked by the contravention of the norms of symphonic writing from two centuries ago. What is rewarding—even more on the hundredth hearing than on the first—is not the contravention of norms itself, but how Haydn responds to the premises, how he works out the problems created by the contraventions of norms, how he supports the surprise in other dimensions. But we must remember that we could scarcely even be aware of those premises without a knowledge of the historical context—and if we were unaware, we could not possibly understand how Haydn responded.

There is yet another reason, also related to the problem of rehearing, why I believe that the historical context ought to be a component of our analytical thought. This argument is the exact inverse of the argument used to support the contention that rehearing invalidates the historical basis of analysis.

If it is artificial for us to pretend, on second and subsequent hearings, that we do not know what surprises are coming, then it is even more artificial to pretend that we can erase from our thinking our historical consciousness. If we have learned anything from the intellectual battles of the past half-century, surely it is that the way in which we 'hear' music is not absolute, not independent of environment and cultural factors, not entirely free from the influences of what has followed. If this is so, then it would be a foolish prejudice to dismiss as invalid that knowledge we have gained of the historical context.

Of course, we cannot free ourselves from the present. We must inevitably listen to eighteenth-century music with ears that have been influenced by the intervening centuries of music. But surely that is hardly an optimal or desirable condition, not a reality to which we must resign ourselves. Rather, if we can reconstruct the composer's thought and recover the listeners' expectations, then we may come closer to hearing the works as the composer intended. To my mind, that is a worthwhile goal.

Bibliography

Alston, Charlotte L., 'Recapitulation Procedures in the Mature Symphonies of Haydn and Mozart', Ph.D. diss. (Univ. of Iowa, 1972).

Andrews, Harold L., 'The Submediant in Haydn's Development Sections', in Larsen, Serwer, and Webster (eds.), *Haydn Studies*, 465–71.

Bard, Raimund, *Untersuchungen zur motivischen Arbeit in Haydns sinfonischem Spätwerk* (Kassel, 1982).

—— ' "Tendenzen" zur zyklischen Gestaltung in Haydns Londoner Sinfonien', in Christoph-Hellmut Mahling and Sigrid Wiesmann (eds.), *Gesellschaft für Musikforschung: Bericht über den internationalen musikwissenschaftlichen Kongress, Bayreuth 1981* (Kassel, 1984), 379–83.

Barford, Philip T., 'The Sonata-Principle: A Study of Musical Thought in the Eighteenth Century', *Music Review*, 13 (1952), 255–63.

Barrett-Ayres, Reginald, *Joseph Haydn and the String Quartet* (New York, 1974).

Benary, Peter, 'Die langsamen Einleitungen in Joseph Haydns Londoner Sinfonien', in Anke Bingmann, Klaus Hortschansky, and Winfried Kirsch (eds.), *Studien zur Instrumentalmusik: Lothar Hoffmann-Erbrecht zum 60. Geburtstag* (Tutzing, 1988), 239–51.

Bonds, Mark Evan, 'Haydn's False Recapitulations and the Perception of Sonata Form in the Eighteenth Century', Ph.D. diss. (Harvard Univ., 1988).

—— *Wordless Rhetoric: Musical Form and the Metaphor of the Oration* (Cambridge, Mass., 1991).

Börner, Wolfgang, ' "Was eine Sache nicht im ersten Moment enthüllt": Die Pariser Sinfonien von Joseph Haydn', *Musik und Gesellschaft*, 32 (1982), 135–40.

Brown, A. Peter, 'The Structure of the Exposition in Haydn's Keyboard Sonatas', *Music Review*, 36 (1975), 102–29.

—— 'Critical Years for Haydn's Instrumental Music: 1787–90', *Musical Quarterly*, 62 (1976), 374–94.

—— 'The Symphonies of Carlo d'Ordonez: A Contribution to the History of Viennese Instrumental Music during the Second Half of the Eighteenth Century', *Haydn Yearbook*, 12 (1981), 5–121.

—— *Joseph Haydn's Keyboard Music: Sources and Style* (Bloomington, Ind., 1986).

Broyles, Michael, 'Organic Form and the Binary Repeat', *Musical Quarterly*, 66 (1980), 339–60.

—— 'The Two Instrumental Styles of Classicism', *Journal of the American Musicological Society*, 36 (1983), 210–42.

—— *Beethoven: The Emergence and Evolution of Beethoven's Heroic Style* (New York, 1987).

Burnham, Scott, 'The Role of Sonata Form in A. B. Marx's Theory of Form', *Journal of Music Theory*, 33 (1989), 247–71.

Busch, Ulrich, ' "Ein brandneues Menuett": Das Menuett beim späten Haydn in Symphonie und Quartett', *Musica*, 36 (1982), 148–51.

Butcher, Norma P., 'A Comparative-Analytical Study of Sonata-Allegro Form in the First Movements of the London Symphonies of Franz Joseph Haydn', Ph.D. diss. (Univ. of Southern California, 1971).

Caplin, William, 'The "Expanded Cadential Progression": A Category for the Analysis of Classical Form', *Journal of Musicological Research*, 7 (1987), 215–57.

Christensen, Thomas, 'Music Theory and its Histories', in Christopher Hatch and David W. Bernstein (eds.), *Music Theory and the Exploration of the Past* (Chicago and London, 1993), 9–39.

Churgin, Bathia, 'Francesco Galeazzi's Description (1796) of Sonata Form', *Journal of the American Musicological Society*, 21 (1968), 181–99.

—— 'The Italian Symphonic Background to Haydn's Early Symphonies and Opera Overtures', in Larsen, Serwer, and Webster (eds.), *Haydn Studies*, 329–36.

—— 'The Recapitulation in Sonata-Form Movements of Sammartini and Early Haydn Symphonies', in Eva Badura-Skoda (ed.), *Joseph Haydn: Proceedings of the International Joseph Haydn Congress* (Munich, 1986), 135–40.

Cole, Malcolm S., 'The Development of the Instrumental Rondo Finale from 1750 to 1800', Ph.D. diss. (Princeton Univ., 1964).

—— 'The Rondo Finale: Evidence for the Mozart–Haydn Exchange?', *Mozart Jahrbuch* (1968–70), 242–56.

—— 'The Vogue of the Instrumental Rondo in the Late Eighteenth Century', *Journal of the American Musicological Society*, 22 (1969), 425–55.

—— 'Rondos, Proper and Improper', *Music and Letters*, 51 (1970), 388–99.

—— 'Czerny's Illustrated Description of the Rondo or Finale', *Music Review*, 36 (1975), 5–16.

—— 'Haydn's Symphonic Rondo Finales: Their Structural and Stylistic Evolution', *Haydn Yearbook*, 13 (1982), 113–42.

Cone, Edward T., 'The Uses of Convention: Stravinsky and his Models', *Musical Quarterly*, 48 (1962), 287–99.

—— *Musical Form and Musical Performance* (New York, 1968).

—— 'Schubert's Promissory Note', *19th Century Music*, 5 (1981–2), 233–41.

—— 'Schubert's Unfinished Business', *19th Century Music*, 7 (1983–4), 222–32.

Danckwardt, Marianne, *Die langsame Einleitung: Ihre Herkunft und ihr Bau bei Haydn und Mozart* (Tutzing, 1977).

Davis, Shelley, 'H. C. Koch, the Classic Concerto, and the Sonata-Form Retransition', *Journal of Musicology*, 2 (1983), 45–61.

Dunsby, Jonathan, 'The Formal Repeat', *Journal of the Royal Musical Association*, 112 (1987), 196–207.

Engel, Hans, 'Haydn, Mozart und die Klassik', *Mozart-Jahrbuch* (1959), 46–79.

Feder, Georg, 'Zur Datierung Haydnscher Werke', in Joseph Schmidt-Görg (ed.), *Anthony van Hoboken: Festschrift zum 75. Geburtstag* (Mainz, 1962), 50–4.

—— 'Haydns Paukenschlag und andere Überraschungen', *Österreichische Musikzeitschrift*, 21 (1966), 5–8.

Feder, Georg, 'Similarities in the Works of Haydn', in H. C. Robbins Landon and Roger Chapman (eds.), *Studies in Eighteenth-Century Music: A Tribute to Karl Geiringer on his Seventieth Birthday* (New York, 1970), 186–97.

—— 'Bemerkungen zu Haydns Skizzen', *Beethoven Jahrbuch*, 9 (1973–7), 69–86.

—— 'Joseph Haydns Skizzen und Entwürfe', *Fontes artis musicae*, 26 (1979), 172–88.

—— Worklist, 'Haydn, Joseph', in Stanley Sadie (ed.), *The New Grove Dictionary of Music and Musicians* (London, 1980), repr. in *The New Grove Haydn* (New York, 1983).

Fillion, Michelle, 'Sonata-Exposition Procedures in Haydn's Keyboard Sonatas', in Larsen, Serwer, and Webster (eds.), *Haydn Studies*, 475–81.

—— 'The Accompanied Keyboard Divertimenti of Haydn and his Viennese Contemporaries (*c*.1750–1780)', 2 vols., Ph.D. diss. (Cornell Univ., 1982).

Finscher, Ludwig, 'Zum Begriff der Klassik in der Musik', *Deutsches Jahrbuch der Musikwissenschaft für 1966*, 11 (1967), 9–34; repr. in Ellen Rosand (ed.), *The Garland Library of the History of Western Music*, vii: *Classic Music* (New York, 1985), 21–46.

—— *Studien zur Geschichte des Streichquartetts*, i: *Die Entstehung des klassischen Streichquartetts* (Kassel, 1974).

—— 'Joseph Haydn—Ein unbekannter Komponist?', *Neue Zeitschrift für Musik*, 143/10 (1982), 12–18.

Fisher, Stephen C., 'Sonata Procedures in Haydn's Symphonic Rondo Finales of the 1770s', in Larsen, Serwer, and Webster (eds.), *Haydn Studies*, 481–7.

—— 'Haydn's Overtures and their Adaptations as Concert Orchestral Works', Ph.D. diss. (Univ. of Pennsylvania, 1985).

—— 'Further Thoughts on Haydn's Symphonic Rondo Finales', *Haydn Yearbook*, 17 (1992), 85–107.

Forschner, Hermann, *Instrumentalmusik Joseph Haydns aus der Sicht Heinrich Christoph Kochs* (Munich, 1984).

Forte, Allen, 'Pitch-Class Set Analysis Today', *Music Analysis*, 4 (1985), 29–58.

—— Letter to the Editor in reply to Richard Taruskin, *Music Analysis*, 5 (1986), 321–37.

Geiringer, Karl, *Haydn: A Creative Life in Music*, 3rd edn., rev. and enlarged (Berkeley, Calif., 1982).

Gerlach, Sonja, 'Die chronologische Ordnung von Haydns Sinfonien zwischen 1774 und 1782', *Haydn-Studien*, 2 (1969–70), 34–66.

—— 'Haydns "chronologische" Sinfonienliste für Breitkopf & Härtel', *Haydn-Studien*, 6 (1986–92), 116–29.

Grave, Margaret G., 'First-Movement Form as a Measure of Dittersdorf's Symphonic Development', Ph.D. diss. (2 vols., New York Univ., 1977).

Gresham, Carolyn D., 'Stylistic Features of Haydn's Symphonies from 1768 to 1772', in Larsen, Serwer, and Webster (eds.), *Haydn Studies*, 431–4.

Grim, William E., *Haydn's Sturm und Drang Symphonies: Form and Meaning* (Lewiston, NY, 1990).

Gwilt, Richard, 'Sonata-Allegro Revisited', *In Theory Only*, 7/5–6 (1984), 3–33.

Haimo, Ethan T., 'Haydn's Altered Reprise', *Journal of Music Theory*, 33 (1988), 335–51.

—— 'Remote Keys and Multi-movement Unity: Haydn in the 1790s', *Musical Quarterly*, 74 (1990), 242–68.

Harutunian, John M., 'Haydn and Mozart: A Study of their Mature Sonata-Style Procedures', Ph.D. diss. (UCLA, 1981).

Hauschild, Peter, 'Liedthema und Entwicklung in den Expositionen von Haydns "Londoner" Sinfonien', in Eva Badura-Skoda (ed.), *Joseph Haydn: Proceedings of the International Joseph Haydn Congress, Wien, 1982* (Munich, 1986), 175–83.

Hill, George R., 'The Concert Symphonies of Florian Leopold Gassmann', Ph.D. diss. (New York Univ., 1975).

Hoboken, Anthony van, *Thematisch-bibliographisches Werkverzeichnis* (3 vols., Mainz, 1957–78).

Höll, Uwe, *Studien zum Sonatensatz in den Klaviersonaten Joseph Haydns* (Tutzing, 1984).

Hopkins, Robert G., 'When a Coda is More than a Coda: Reflections on Beethoven', in Eugene Narmour and Ruth A. Solie (eds.), *Explorations in Music, the Arts and Ideas: Essays in Honor of Leonard B. Meyer* (Stuyvesant, NJ, 1988), 393–410.

Hunter, Mary K., 'Haydn's Aria Forms', Ph.D. diss. (Cornell Univ., 1982).

—— 'Haydn's Sonata-Form Arias', *Current Musicology*, 37–8 (1984), 19–32.

Kamien, Roger, 'The Opening Sonata-Allegro Movements in a Randomly Selected Sample of Solo Keyboard Sonatas Published in the Years 1742–1774 (Inclusive)', Ph.D. diss. (2 vols., Princeton Univ., 1964).

Keller, Hans, 'K. 503: The Unity of Contrasting Themes and Movements', *Music Review*, 17 (1956), 48–58 and 120–9.

Kerman, Joseph, 'Notes on Beethoven's Codas', in Alan Tyson (ed.), *Beethoven Studies*, 3rd edn. (Cambridge, 1982), 141–60.

—— *Contemplating Music* (Cambridge, Mass., 1985).

Kirkendale, Warren, *Fugue and Fugato in Rococo and Classical Chamber Music*, rev. edn. (Durham, NC, 1979).

Klinkhammer, Rudolf, *Die langsame Einleitung in der Instrumentalmusik der Klassik und Romantik: Ein Sonderproblem in der Entwicklung der Sonatenform* (Regensburg, 1971).

Koch, Heinrich Christoph, *Introductory Essay on Composition*, trans. Nancy Kovaleff Baker (New Haven, Conn., and London, 1983).

Kolk, Joel, ' "Sturm und Drang" and Haydn's Opera', in Larsen, Serwer, and Webster (eds.), *Haydn Studies*, 440–5.

Kollmann, Augustus, *An Essay on Practical Musical Composition* (London, 1799; repr. New York, 1973).

Krabbe, Niels, 'A Critical Review of Fritz Tutenberg's Theory of First-Movement Form in the Early Classical Symphony', in Larsen, Serwer, and Webster (eds.), *Haydn Studies*, 487–93.

Landon, H. C. Robbins, *The Symphonies of Joseph Haydn* (London, 1955; New York, 1956).

—— 'La Crise romantique dans la musique autrichienne vers 1770', in André Verchaly (ed.), *Les Influences étrangères dans l'œuvre de W. A. Mozart* (Paris, 1956).

—— *Haydn: Chronicle and Works* (5 vols., Bloomington, Ind., and London, 1976–80).

—— (ed.), *Joseph Haydn: Kritische Ausgabe sämtlicher Symphonien / Critical Edition of the Complete Symphonies*, 2nd rev. edn. (12 vols., Vienna, 1981).

Larsen, Jens Peter, 'Zu Haydns künstlerischer Entwicklung', in *Festschrift Wilhelm Fischer zum 70. Geburtstag überreicht im Mozartjahr 1956* (Innsbruck, 1956),

123–9; trans. as 'On Haydn's Artistic Development', in Larsen, *Handel, Haydn*, 109–15.

Larsen, Jens Peter, 'Probleme der chronologischen Ordnung von Haydns Sinfonien', in Walter Gerstenberg, Jan LaRue, and Wolfgang Rehm (eds.), *Festschrift Otto Erich Deutsch zum 80. Geburtstag* (Kassel, 1963), 90–104.

—— 'Sonatenform-Probleme', in Anna Amalie Abert and Wilhelm Pfannkuch (eds.), *Festschrift Friedrich Blume zum 70. Geburtstag* (Kassel, 1963), 221–30; trans. as 'Sonata Form Problems', in Larsen, *Handel, Haydn*, 269–79.

—— 'Some Observations on the Development and Characteristics of Viennese Classical Instrumental Music', *Studia musicologica, Academiae scientarium Hungaricae*, 9 (1967), 115–39; repr. in Larsen, *Handel, Haydn*, 227–49; also repr. in Rosand (ed.), *History of Western Music*, vii. 47–71.

—— 'Zur Entstehung der österreichischen Symphonietradition (ca. 1750–1775)', *Haydn Yearbook*, 10 (1978), 72–80; trans. as 'Concerning the Development of the Austrian Symphonic Tradition (*circa* 1750–1775)', in Larsen, *Handel, Haydn*, 315–25.

—— 'Haydn's Early Symphonies: The Problem of Dating', in Alan Atlas (ed.), *Music in the Classic Period: Essays in Honor of Barry S. Brook* (Stuyvesant, NJ, 1985), 117–31; repr. in Larsen, *Handel, Haydn*, 159–70.

—— 'Joseph Haydn, eine Herausforderung an uns', in Eva Badura-Skoda (ed.), *Proceedings of the International Joseph Haydn Congress, Wien, 1982* (Munich, 1986), 9–20; trans. as 'The Challenge of Joseph Haydn', in Larsen, *Handel, Haydn*, 95–108.

—— *Handel, Haydn, and the Viennese Classical Style*, translations by Ulrich Krämer (Ann Arbor, Mich., 1988).

—— Serwer, Howard, and Webster, James (eds.), *Haydn Studies: Proceedings of the International Haydn Conference, Washington D.C., 1975* (New York, 1981).

LaRue, Jan, 'Bifocal Tonality: An Explanation for Ambiguous Baroque Cadences', in *Essays on Music in Honor of Archibald Thompson Davison by his Associates* (Cambridge, Mass., 1957), 173–84.

—— 'Significant and Coincidental Resemblance between Classical Themes', *Journal of the American Musicological Society*, 14 (1961), 224–34.

—— *Guidelines for Style Analysis* (New York, 1970).

Lester, Joel, *Compositional Theory in the Eighteenth Century* (Cambridge, Mass., 1992).

Levy, Janet M., 'Covert and Casual Values in Recent Writings about Music', *Journal of Musicology*, 5 (1987), 3–27.

Longyear, Rey M., 'Binary Variants of Early Classic Sonata Form', *Journal of Music Theory*, 13 (1969), 162–85.

—— 'The Minor Mode in Eighteenth-Century Sonata Form', *Journal of Music Theory*, 15 (1971), 182–229.

Marco, Guy, A., 'A Musical Task in the "Surprise" Symphony', *Journal of the American Musicological Society*, 11 (1958), 41–4.

Marx, Adolph Bernard, *Die Lehre von der musikalischen Komposition, praktisch-theoretisch*, 4 vols. (Leipzig, 1837–47).

Marx, Karl, 'Über die zyklische Sonatenform: Zu dem Aufsatz von Günther von Noé', *Neue Zeitschrift für Musik*, 125 (1964), 142–6.

—— 'Über thematische Beziehungen in Haydns Londoner Symphonien', *Haydn-Studien*, 4 (1976), 1–20.

Menk, Gail E., 'The Symphonic Introductions of Joseph Haydn', Ph.D. diss. (Univ. of Iowa, 1960).

Meyer, Leonard B., *Explaining Music: Essays and Explorations* (Berkeley, Calif., 1973).

—— *Style and Music: History, Theory, and Ideology* (Philadelphia, 1989).

Monk, Dennis C., 'Style Change in the Slow Movement of the Viennese Symphony: 1740–1770', Ph.D. diss. (2 vols., UCLA, 1971).

Neubacher, Jürgen, ' "Idee" und "Ausführung". Zum Kompositionsprozeß bei Joseph Haydn', *Archiv für Musikwissenschaft*, 41 (1984), 187–207.

—— *Finis coronat opus: Untersuchungen zur Technik der Schlußgestaltung in der Instrumentalmusik Joseph Haydns, dargestellt am Beispiel der Streichquartette* (Tutzing, 1986).

Newman, William S., 'The Recognition of Sonata Form by Theorists of the 18th and 19th Centuries', *Papers of the American Musicological Society* (1941), 21–9.

—— *The Sonata in the Classic Era*, 3rd edn. (New York, 1983).

Nicolosi, Robert J., 'Formal Aspects of the Minuet and "Tempo di Minuetto" Finale in Instrumental Music of the Eighteenth Century', Ph.D. diss. (Washington Univ., 1971).

Nowak, Leopold, 'Die Skizzen zum Finale der Es-dur-Symphonie GA 99 von Joseph Haydn', *Haydn-Studien*, 2 (1969–70), 137–66.

Quantz, Johann Joachim, *Versuch einer Anweisung die Flöte zu spielen* (Berlin, 1752), trans. Edward R. Reilly as *On Playing the Flute* (London, 1966).

Ratner, Leonard G., 'Harmonic Aspects of Classic Form', *Journal of the American Musicological Society*, 2 (1949), 159–68; repr. in Rosand (ed.), *History of Western Music*, vii. 101–10.

—— 'Eighteenth-Century Theories of Musical Period Structure', *Musical Quarterly*, 42 (1956), 439–54; repr. in Rosand (ed.), *History of Western Music*, vii. 85–100.

—— *Classic Music: Expression, Form, and Style* (New York, 1980).

—— 'Theories of Form: Some Changing Perspectives', in Larsen, Serwer, and Webster (eds.), *Haydn Studies*, 347–51.

Reti, Rudolph, 'The Role of Duothematicism in the Evolution of Sonata Form', *Music Review*, 17 (1956), 110–19.

Ritzel, Fred, *Die Entwicklung der 'Sonatenform' im musiktheoretischen Schrifttum des 18. und 19. Jahrhunderts*, 2nd edn. (Wiesbaden, 1969).

Rosen, Charles, *The Classical Style* (New York, 1971).

—— 'Influence: Plagiarism and Inspiration', *19th Century Music*, 4 (1979–80), 87–100.

—— *Sonata Forms*, rev. edn. (New York, 1988).

Rothstein, William, *Phrase Rhythm in Tonal Music* (New York, 1989).

Rummenhöller, Peter, *Die musikalische Vorklassik* (Kassel, 1983).

Russell, Tilden A., 'Minuet, Scherzando, and Scherzo: The Dance Movement in Transition, 1781–1825', Ph.D. diss. (Univ. of North Carolina at Chapel Hill, 1983).

Schafer, Hollace Ann, ' "A Wisely Ordered *Phantasie*": Joseph Haydn's Creative Process from the Sketches and Drafts for Instrumental Music', Ph.D. diss. (Brandeis Univ., 1987).

Schenker, Heinrich, 'Organic Structure in Sonata Form', trans. Orin Grossman, *Journal of Music Theory*, 12 (1968), 164–83; repr. in Maury Yeston (ed.), *Readings in Schenker Analysis and Other Approaches* (New Haven, Conn., 1977), 38–53; also repr. in Rosand (ed.), *History of Western Music*, vii. 112–31.

Schmalzriedt, Siegfried, 'Charakter und Drama: Zur historischen Analyse von Haydnschen und Beethovenschen Sonatensätzen', *Archiv für Musikwissenschaft*, 42 (1985), 37–66.

Schroeder, David P., *Haydn and the Enlightenment: The Late Symphonies and their Audience* (Oxford, 1990).

Schwarting, Heino, 'Ungewöhnliche Repriseneintritte in Haydns späterer Instrumentalmusik', *Archiv für Musikwissenschaft*, 17 (1960), 168–82.

Seidel, Wilhelm, 'Haydns Streichquartett in B-dur op. 71 Nr. 1 (Hob. III: 69)—Analytische Bemerkungen aus der Sicht Heinrich Christoph Kochs', in Georg Feder, Heinrich Hüschen, and Ulrich Tank (eds.), *Joseph Haydn: Tradition und Rezeption* (Regensburg, 1985), 3–13.

—— 'Schnell–Langsam–Schnell: Zur "klassischen" Theorie des instrumentalen Zyklus', *Musiktheorie*, 1 (1986), 205–16.

Shamgar, Beth, 'On Locating the Retransition in Classic Sonata Form', *Music Review*, 24 (1981), 130–43.

—— 'Rhythmic Interplay in the Retransitions of Haydn's Piano Sonatas', *Journal of Musicology*, 3 (1984), 55–68.

Sisman, Elaine, R., 'Haydn's Variations', Ph.D. diss. (Princeton Univ., 1978).

—— 'Haydn's Hybrid Variations', in Larsen, Serwer, and Webster (eds.), *Haydn Studies*, 509–15.

—— 'Small and Expanded Forms: Koch's Model and Haydn's Music', *Musical Quarterly*, 68 (1982), 444–75.

—— 'Haydn's Theater Symphonies', *Journal of the American Musicological Society*, 43 (1990), 292–352.

—— *Haydn and the Classical Variation* (Cambridge, Mass., 1993).

Solie, Ruth, 'The Living Work: Organicism and Musical Analysis', *19th Century Music*, 4 (1980–1), 147–56.

Somfai, László, 'Vom Barock zur Klassik: Umgestaltung der Proportionen und Gleichgewichts in zyklischen Werken Joseph Haydns', in Gerda Mraz (ed.), *Joseph Haydn und seine Zeit, Jahrbuch für österreichische Kulturgeschichte*, 2 (Eisenstadt, 1972), 64–72 and tables after p. 160.

—— ' "Ich war nie ein Geschwindschreiber . . .": Joseph Haydns Skizzen zum langsamen Satz des Streichquartetts Hoboken III: 33', in Nils Schiørring, Henrik Glahn, and Carsten Hatting (eds.), *Festkrift Jens Peter Larsen* (Copenhagen, 1972), 275–84.

—— 'An Introduction to the Study of Haydn's String Quartet Autographs (with Special Attention to Opus 77/G)', in Christoph Wolff (ed.), *The String Quartets of Haydn, Mozart, and Beethoven: Studies of the Autograph Manuscripts* (Cambridge, Mass., 1980), 5–51.

Sponheuer, Bernd, 'Haydns Arbeit am Finalproblem', *Archiv für Musikwissenschaft*, 34 (1977), 199–224.

Steinbeck, Wolfram, *Das Menuett in der Instrumentalmusik Joseph Haydns* (Munich, 1973).

—— 'Mozart's "Scherzi": Zur Beziehung zwischen Haydns Streichquartetten op. 33 und Mozarts Haydn-Quartetten', *Archiv für Musikwissenschaft*, 41 (1984), 208–31.

Steinberg, Lester S., 'Sonata Form in the Keyboard Trios of Joseph Haydn', Ph.D. diss. (New York Univ., 1976).

Stevens, Jane R., 'Theme, Harmony, and Texture in Classic–Romantic Descriptions of Concerto First-Movement Form', *Journal of the American Musicological Society*, 27 (1974), 25–60; repr. in Rosand (ed.), *History of Western Music*, vii. 133–68.

Taruskin, Richard, Letter to the Editor, *Music Analysis*, 5 (1986), 313–20.

Temperley, Nicholas, 'Testing the Significance of Thematic Relationships', *Music Review*, 22 (1961), 177–80.

Tobel, Rudolf von, *Die Formenwelt der klassischen Instrumentalmusik* (Berne, 1935).

Todd, R. Larry, 'Joseph Haydn and the *Sturm und Drang*: A Revaluation', *Music Review*, 41 (1980), 172–96.

Tovey, Donald Francis, *Essays in Musical Analysis* (London, 1935–9; repr. London, 1981).

Tutenberg, Fritz, *Die Sinfonik Johann Christian Bachs* (Wolfenbüttel and Berlin, 1928).

Vinton, John, 'The Development Section in Early Viennese Symphonies: A Re-valuation', *Music Review*, 24 (1963), 13–22.

Wagner, Günther, 'Anmerkungen zur Formtheorie Heinrich Christoph Kochs', *Archiv für Musikwissenschaft*, 41 (1984), 86–112.

Webster, James, 'Freedom of Form in Haydn's Early String Quartets', in Larsen, Serwer, and Webster (eds.), *Haydn Studies*, 522–30.

—— 'Prospects for Haydn Biography after Landon', *Musical Quarterly*, 68 (1982), 476–95.

—— 'Binary Variants of Sonata Form in Early Haydn Instrumental Music', in Eva Badura-Skoda (ed.), *Joseph Haydn: Proceedings of the International Joseph Haydn Congress, Wien, 1982* (Munich, 1986), 127–35.

—— 'The D-major Interlude in the First Movement of Haydn's "Farewell" Symphony", in Eugene Wolf and Edward Roesner (eds.), *Studies in Musical Sources and Style: Essays in Honor of Jan LaRue* (Madison, Wis., 1990), 339–80.

—— *Haydn's 'Farewell' Symphony and the Idea of Classical Style: Through-Composition and Cyclic Integration in his Instrumental Music* (Cambridge, 1991).

Wheelock, Gretchen A., 'Wit, Humor, and the Instrumental Music of Joseph Haydn', Ph.D. diss. (Yale Univ. 1979).

—— *Haydn's Ingenious Jesting with Art: Contexts of Musical Wit and Humor* (New York, 1992).

Wiesel, Meir, 'The Presence and Evaluation of Thematic Relationships and Thematic Unity', *Israel Studies in Musicology*, 1 (1978), 77–91.

Winter, Robert S., 'The Bifocal Close and the Evolution of the Viennese Classical Style', *Journal of the American Musicological Society*, 42 (1989), 275–337.

Wolf, Eugene, K., 'The Recapitulations in Haydn's London Symphonies', *Musical Quarterly*, 52 (1966), 71–89.

—— 'On the Origins of the Mannheim Symphonic Style', in John Walter Hill (ed.), *Studies in Musicology in Honor of Otto E. Albrecht: A Collection of Essays by his Colleagues and Former Students at the University of Pennsylvania* (Kassel, 1980), 197–239; repr. in Rosand (ed.), *History of Western Music*, vii. 231–73.

—— *The Symphonies of Johann Stamitz: A Study in the Formation of the Classic Style* (Utrecht and Antwerp, 1981).

Wyzewa, Théodore de, 'A propos du centenaire de la mort de Joseph Haydn', *Revue des deux mondes*, 79 (1909), 935–46.

Zaslaw, Neal, 'Mozart, Haydn, and the *Sinfonia da Chiesa*', *Journal of Musicology*, 1 (1982), 95–124.

—— *Mozart's Symphonies: Context, Performance Practice, Reception* (Oxford, 1989).

Index of Haydn's Compositions

General Index

aria 4, 14 n., 54 n., 71

Babbitt, Milton 277
Beethoven, Ludwig van 2 n., 92, 272–3, 277
  Piano Sonata in C major, Op. 2 No. 3
    272–3
  Piano Sonata in E flat, Op. 7 236 n.
bifocal close 32–4, 52, 62, 84, 86 n.
Bilson, Malcolm viii
binary form 53, 54 n., 59, 61, 89, 122, 123
  rounded binary 4, 7, 53–4, 54 n., 55 n.,
    56 n., 89, 140, 161, 202, 222, 259
  simple (ordinary) binary 4, 53–4, 56 n., 62 n.
binary sonata form, see binary variants
binary variants 11, 26, 43, 61–4, 67–8, 100, 155
Boulez, Pierre 277
Brioschi, Antonio 76 n.
Brown, Howard Mayer ix

cadenza 222, 225–9
canonic devices 89 n.
Chopin, Fryderyk 277
Classic era 3
Classical style 3
coda 51, 52, 56 n., 92–6, 118, 137, 139, 142,
    144, 149, 155, 156 n., 159, 160, 195, 201,
    202, 220–1, 234, 243 n., 244, 251, 258, 267,
    273
concerto 4, 14 n., 42, 43, 50 n., 54 n., 64 n., 71,
    222
Cone, Edward 3, 8 n.
Crousaz, Jean Pierre de 7 n.

Dahlhaus, Carl vii
disjunct recapitulation 30 n., 101 n.
Dittersdorf, Carl Ditters von 273

Esterházy, Prince Nikolaus 56 n.
expanded binary form, see binary variants
expectations, see listeners' expectations

false recapitulation 11, 31, 34, 106–13, 117 n.
false reprise, see false recapitulation
Forkel, Johann vii
French ouverture 180 n.

fugato 222
fugue 4, 229, 232

Galeazzi, Francesco 1 n., 14 n., 180 n.
Gassmann, Floriann 14 n., 43 n., 273
Griesinger, Georg August 12

Hanover Band viii
Haydn, Michael 273
Hoffstetter, Roman 252 n.
hybrid variations, see variations

immediate reprise 30 n., 105
incomplete recapitulation, see binary variants
inter-opus norms 8, 20, 24, 32, 66, 76 n., 83,
    92, 144, 169, 191
intermovemental relationships, see
    multimovement relationships
intra-opus norms 8, 22 n., 38, 66, 81, 83, 92,
    99, 144, 169
introduction:
  same-tempo, quasi-introduction 49–51, 74,
    79, 83, 155–6
  slow introduction 43, 49, 50–1, 73–5, 128–9,
    145, 148 n., 178–82, 188 n., 192, 202 n.,
    208–10, 214, 221, 229, 231, 232, 234,
    235–40, 241–3, 244, 251, 255 n., 257, 258,
    259, 261, 267

Jommelli, Niccolò 13 n.

Koch, Heinrich Christoph 1 n., 5 n., 13 n., 25,
    26, 54 n., 55 n., 58 n., 274
Kollmann, Augustus Frederic Christopher
    1 n., 253–4 n.
listeners' expectations 1, 8, 31–2, 73–4, 106–13,
    270, 279

Mannheim crescendo 13 n.
Marx, Adolph Bernhard 2
menuet and trio 5, 7, 24, 35, 42, 53–61, 87,
    88–96, 100, 117–18, 137–8, 145, 162–9, 170,
    195–201, 232–4, 258–61, 263
menuetto, see menuet
minuet, see menuet